CITIES OF SPAIN

Catedral de Toledo

CITIES OF
SPAIN

DAVID GILMOUR

IVAN R. DEE
Chicago

Library of Congress Cataloging-in-Publication Data:
Gilmour, David, 1952–
     Cities of Spain / David Gilmour.
          p.   cm.
     Includes bibliographical references (p. 199) and index.
     ISBN 0-929587-92-8
     1. Spain—History, Local. 2. Cities and towns—Spain—History.
     3. Spain—Description and travel—1981–   I. Title.
     DP66.G5   1992
     307.76'0946—dc20   91-38560

Photographs courtesy of the Tourist Office of Spain

*To those Spanish friends whose kindness
and hospitality made the research for
this book so enjoyable*

Contents

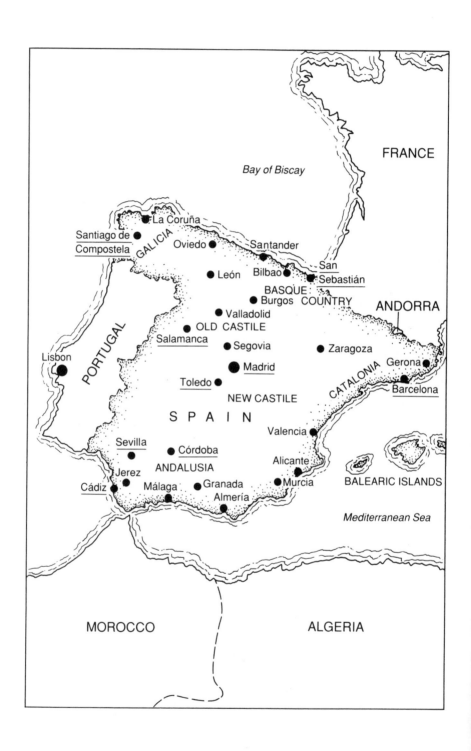

Introduction

'The history of Iberia', wrote the French historian Pierre Vilar, 'has been a ceaseless struggle between the will to unite, located generally in the centre, and the no less vital tendency – rooted in geography – to dispersion.' These competing traditions have produced one of Spain's innumerable paradoxes: despite repeated and sometimes successful attempts to create a centralized system of government, the regions retain a stronger sense of identity and a greater desire for autonomy than other parts of western Europe. Yet local aspirations have not prevented them from contributing to the national history. All Spain's cities, including those which have often claimed to be unSpanish, have played national as well as regional roles in their country's development.

Spain is not like France or England where the capital dominates so much of the story. Nor does it resemble Italy where major cities, belonging until the nineteenth century to different countries, could ignore each other for most of their history. None of Spain's cities has either been independent or has dominated the rest of the country. They have co-existed instead in a state of fluctuating interdependence, their roles and positions changing according to circumstances. This was partly because Madrid did not become the capital until 1561 and failed subsequently to become an important industrial city. But it was also a consequence of the country's history and its geography, of the complexity of its cultural traditions, and of the manner in which it became a nation.

All the cities in this book except San Sebastián have enjoyed supremacy in certain fields at various stages in their country's

1

history. Since the fall of Rome at least four of them – Toledo, Córdoba, Seville and Madrid – have at different times managed to establish a political and cultural primacy. Cádiz dominated the Spanish economy in the eighteenth century but gave way to Barcelona in the nineteenth. Santiago de Compostela was once Christendom's leading place of pilgrimage while Salamanca housed one of the great universities of medieval Europe. Even San Sebastián achieved pre-eminence of a kind at the end of the nineteenth century by becoming Spain's most elegant resort and the summer home of its royal family.

The focus of Spanish history shifts from city to city over the centuries, illuminating different aspects of the country's character. In some cases, such as Seville and Barcelona, the light returns after periods of eclipse; in others, such as Salamanca and Córdoba, it shines brightly over their ascent and then disappears for ever. In this book I have tried to describe certain features of Spain's history through the development of its leading cities, concentrating on the particular contributions that all have made to their country's past. I have not attempted to write a comprehensive history either of Spain or of the cities themselves; the book is a personal view, focusing on the characteristics of each place which seemed to me most interesting.

The selection of the cities, too, has been a personal one: I have chosen only those that I know well and like. The former ambassador to London, José Joaquín Puig de la Bellacasa, good-humouredly berated me for omitting his native city, Bilbao, which has of course played a much more influential role in both Basque and Spanish history than San Sebastián; yet in a book that flits over a period of 1,400 years I was reluctant to include, after Barcelona, a second great industrial centre of the nineteenth century. Perhaps I should have written about Valencia, which is now the third largest city in the country. I would certainly have liked to choose Segovia, one of the most attractive of Spanish towns, but I felt the book should not contain a third Castilian city arrested by Spain's seventeenth-century decadence.

Granada, which contains some of the most beautiful gardens and buildings in Spain, is a more controversial omission. Yet Córdoba is more representative of Moorish civilization in Spain and is today a better preserved city. A hundred years ago the writer Angel Ganivet complained of Granada's 'street-widening epidemic', and a generation later the poet Juan Ramón Jiménez criticized the 'appalling, boastful, aggressive buildings thrown up on Granadine plain and hill by a pride bloated with money...'. The process accelerated during the dictatorship of General Franco and modern Granada is now an ugly place, sprawling interminably over its fertile plain. The traveller can still delight in the wonders of the Alhambra, the tranquillity of the Generalife and the white lanes of the Albaicín, but it is no longer possible to enjoy the city as a whole.

British writers on Spanish cities have traditionally been divided between those who insist that the Spaniards are 'the true heirs' of Rome, the 'greatest builders since the Romans', and those who have seemed overfond of examining the deficiencies of the country and the defects of the native character. I hope I have not fallen into either group. I do not happen to agree with Sacheverell Sitwell's insistence that 'lovers of architecture must prefer Spain to Italy', but the country undoubtedly has some of the most beautiful and interesting cities in Europe. In two chapters I have been critical of the Spaniards' treatment of their historic buildings, particularly during the dictatorship when the greed and philistinism of Franco's regime allowed speculators to demolish large chunks of their architectural heritage. But the vandalism of the 1960s was hardly unique to Spain. If the standard of conservation in Spanish cities is lower than in Tuscany or the Italian north, it is higher than in Sicily or southern Italy. Seville and Córdoba are better preserved than Naples and Palermo, and in the smaller towns the green and white notices of the Andalusian government announcing a *monumento en restauración* proclaim the strong local interest in the conservation of the past.

The first of numerous debts accumulated during the writing of this book has been to my publishers John Murray and especially to my efficient and enthusiastic editor, Ariane Goodman, who suggested the subject. It would be difficult to claim that the 'ground' research for the book was anything but enjoyable. To wander around a city with Spanish friends, pausing from time to time to chat in a café or browse in a bookshop, approximates pretty closely to the ideal holiday. Frequent visits have led to many friendships and the realization that Spain has become a second country for me. Although my appearance, unmistakably and regrettably northern as it is, prevents me from acquiring what Richard Cobb has called 'a second identity' in a Latin country, I nevertheless feel at home in Spain and feel too, as I cross the border, that I have somehow acquired a different personality.

As with my earlier book on the country's politics, I have incurred a long list of Spanish debts which I cannot properly acknowledge here. For their limitless help and hospitality, however, I must particularly thank Isabel de Azcárate, Alfonso de Otazu, Ignacio de Medina and his wife María Gloria. I am also grateful to Luis Jessen, Beatriz Borrero, Mercedes Milá, Federico Correa, Eduardo Garrigues, Antonio Burgos, Rafael Atienza and several members of the Villavecchia family in Madrid and Barcelona who have all helped in various and important ways. So have Juan Pablo Fusi and the staff at the Biblioteca Nacional in Madrid, and Sir Brinsley Ford who kindly gave me permission to reproduce three drawings by his great-grandfather Richard Ford.

Above all, I must acknowledge my debt to the many historians and other scholars whose works I have used during my research. I would normally have done this through source references but the publishers and I agreed that a text of this nature should not be overburdened by footnotes. I have therefore compiled a list of the books I have found useful for the bibliography.

Finally I should thank my wife and children for their tolerance of my long absences in Spain and their forbearance during the months of writing.

Edinburgh
August 1991

ONE

Toledo

No city occupies a place in the Spanish psyche like Toledo. For centuries Spain's writers have exalted the town as the repository of Spanish values, a city embodying the country's history and civilization. Toledo, according to them, contains both the soul and the essence of Spain. A traveller limited to one day in the country, advised the art historian Cossío, should unhesitatingly direct himself to Toledo. For Cervantes, this 'craggy sorrow' was the 'glory of Spain and light of its cities', but his colleagues have usually preferred more extravagant praise. 'As the heart in the body', wrote Lope de Vega, 'is the core and fount of life, so is Toledo heart of Spain.' For Gregorio Marañón, the distinguished doctor and man of letters, even this was an understatement. Was there a name in all the languages of mankind, he mused in an essay in 1935, which resounded with so many beautiful, profound and transcendental echoes as the name of Toledo?

Toledo is an emblem of Spanish greatness, less a great city in itself than a place of historical dreams and ancient aspirations. Few other cities can have symbolized so many different sides and stages of a nation's history. It was, or claimed to be, the imperial city, the seat of the Spanish Church, the city of the three religions, the political capital and residence of the court. Later the symbolism changed. Aided by the paintings of El Greco, Toledo became the city that epitomized the soul of Spain, the nobility and asceticism of its Christian spirit. Later still it became a symbol of the country's fall, the Spain of the imperial defeats, the inward-looking nation that turned its back on Europe. The city of convents and deserted streets, horrifying to the Enlightenment yet delightful to the Romantics, embodied the failure and bankruptcy of Castile. A native poet, Félix Urabayen, even added the sun and the earth to the city's symbols: Toledo's sunsets, he claimed, dressed the land in the red and gold of the Spanish flag.

Toledans have always been inclined to believe in their town's mythology, accepting its medieval title 'the imperial city' although at that time there was no empire, and claiming it was once the Spanish capital although before Madrid the country never had a capital. There has also been a tendency to exaggerate Toledo's cultural influence. Writing in 1935, Marañón described the city as 'the sum of six civilizations superimposed, immortal crossroads of all cultures, illustrious bridge between the Orient and the West, refuge of all religions, the Rome of Spain.' Yet eulogies such as this are not merely the products of contemporary nostalgia and sentimentalism. From the Middle Ages, Toledo's priests and historians consciously embellished their city's past, likening it to Jerusalem and allotting it the second place in Christendom after Rome. Deciding that comparisons between Toledo and the papal city should be made as obvious as possible, one Jesuit priest claimed that the four hummocks on Toledo's rock were in fact seven hills. These hills might not have such celebrated names as their Roman counterparts, he conceded, but they contained equally impressive monuments.

As with many cities, the mythology acquired fantastic dimensions when applied to Toledo's foundation. In common with Seville and other towns, Hercules was advanced as a potential founder, although he was challenged by a number of rivals. Toledans of the sixteenth century debated the claims of various Greeks, an oriental king called Rocas, a son of the king of a Peloponnesian city and a Roman consul called Tolemon who bequeathed the city two syllables of his name. The most imaginative theory concerned a Greek king called Pynrrus, ruling for unexplained reasons in Spain, who went to help Nebuchadnezzar fight the Jews in Babylon. Realizing after capturing them how learned the Jews were, he brought many with him back to Spain and allowed them to found Toledo. Legends about the ancient Jewish population of the city continued to be told until the nineteenth century. It was widely believed that Jews were living in Toledo in the time of Christ and had written a letter of protest against the Crucifixion.

Foreigners have usually accepted the Toledans' assessment of their city's importance: 'a petrified scroll of Spain's history' is the typical description of an English visitor a hundred years ago. Richard Ford, the great nineteenth-century traveller whose criticisms of Spain were usually caustic, accepted much of Toledan mythology. 'Like Rome, it stands on seven hills,' he wrote. 'Imperial Toledo, the navel of the Peninsula', was a 'priestly capital', a 'Levite theocratic city', a 'Durham of a once golden hierarchy' that would soon 'decay and become a Thebes'. To others the city has appeared variously as Spain's Kyoto, 'Spain's Alexandria', 'the Pompeii of Spain' and the 'Spanish Lhasa ... a gigantic spiritual fortress'. Even Gerald Brenan, who knew the country as well as any foreigner, was tempted by hyperbole when he went to Toledo. 'Like Fez,' he remarked, 'it reeks of the Middle Ages: like Lhasa, of monks.'

Travellers visiting Toledo for the first time may be surprised by such comparisons. If they journey from the north they will see a view similar to that painted by El Greco (drawn on one occasion with accuracy and on another with a confusing rearrangement of buildings). If they approach from the south and look at the city from across the Tagus, they will see a skyline even less changed since the sixteenth century: from the east the dominating spires of the Alcázar (once the 'Spanish Sandhurst'); the low bulk of the cathedral, curiously sunken in the middle of the horizon yet powerful and impressive in spite of it; a few *mudéjar* towers scattered around the solemn Baroque façade of the Jesuit church; and finally, lower down the rock on the western end, the beautiful convent of St John, built – but not used – as the burial place of Ferdinand and Isabella, 'the Catholic Kings'. It is a fine view, competing with Santiago as the most beautiful urban landscape in Spain, and one to be grateful for in an age of desecrated skylines. But it is not Lhasa.

Toledo's site demonstrates the strength and the limitations of the city. It is a rock placed in a loop of the river, defended on three sides by water and on the fourth by a cliff. Augustus Hare exaggerated when he described the town as 'girdled in from the living world by the indescribable solitude of its utterly desolate hills', but he was right about its isolation. Toledo is a natural stronghold and has been used as such from the Roman era to the

7

Spanish Civil War. Under the Visigoths it also became the *urbs regia* or royal city, the principal centre of government. A succession of talented bishops, strong supporters of the Visigothic monarchy, were able subsequently to achieve the primacy for their see and establish Toledo as the predominant religious and intellectual centre of seventh-century Spain. Since then the military and the Church have dominated the city. Toledo's position thus made it a great medieval city while at the same time preventing it from becoming a great modern metropolis. With barely enough room on the rock for the religious orders, the noblemen and the military establishment, it could never have become a major commercial or industrial city; there was simply not enough room to expand.

Little remains of Visigothic Toledo beyond a few fragments incorporated into later churches. And there is little physical trace of the Moorish centuries except for an exquisite mosque and some other remains, yet the Moorish influence is still palpable. From the time of the Arab conquest Toledo was an important Moorish city, but its frequent rebellions against Córdoba decimated its population and provoked Islamic writers to refer to it as that 'accursed town, repudiated by Allah'. After the fall of the Cordoban caliphate, Muslim Toledo enjoyed a brief period of prosperity and cultural achievement before its Christian reconquest in 1085.

The conquest and reconquest of Toledo preserved far more than they destroyed. During the three and a half centuries of Muslim rule the city retained its archbishop and the primacy of Spain. Its Christian inhabitants, known as *mozárabes*, estimated at about 3,000 (or a fifth of the population), lived not in distinct quarters but among the Muslims; they had six parishes of their own and were allowed to build new churches. Even after the Christian Reconquest, when the Latin rite had been imposed on the rest of Spain, Toledo's *mozárabes* were allowed to keep their own Visigothic rite. Some families still practise it.

The physical similarities, above all the continuity of architectural style and urban development, between Muslim Toledo and the medieval Christian city are striking. Although substantial numbers of Muslims and Jews remained after 1085, the majority fled southwards, leaving their buildings to be exploited by their

8

conquerors. The Christians built few new churches, preferring to adapt the mosques for their own uses, transforming minarets into towers. Several buildings thus underwent a second metamorphosis: built as Visigothic basilicas, they survived for centuries as mosques before re-emerging as parish churches. Similarly, the Moorish souks were simply taken over and used for the same purposes as before: indeed, the main commercial zone today, between the cathedral and the Plaza de Zocodover, occupies much the same area as the souks a thousand years ago. In many cases the same trade was carried on as before, Christian dyers, weavers and sandal-makers, for example, moving into the souks of their Muslim counterparts. They even adopted various Moorish customs such as the closed souk at night (the Moors did not sleep 'above the shop') and the post of the *almotacén*, or inspector of goods.

Anyone who wanders around Toledo outside the commercial area will be surprised by how easy it is to get lost in the winding streets that often seem to lead nowhere. The explanation can be found in the layout of the Moorish city which was preserved by the conquerors and which still exists for the most part today. Over the centuries the Arab buildings have disappeared, but many of the characteristics of the Moorish town have survived. The lack of open spaces, especially of public squares and wide streets, was typical of Islamic cities. The streets were seldom planned and were regarded not as entities in themselves but simply as ways of getting from one place to another. There were no restrictions against corbels, overhanging roofs or other projections so long as people could walk freely underneath them. In Toledo this 'concept' of the street survived for many centuries after the Reconquest, the Christians persisting in building houses spanning tortuous blind alleys. Even a Moroccan ambassador of the seventeenth century, presumably accustomed to this sort of thing, found Toledo's streets too narrow.

For 400 years after the Reconquest, Toledans continued to build in the Moorish *mudéjar* style, using the same materials as their predecessors. The massive Gothic cathedral, built on the site of the main mosque and requiring the removal of the barbers' and rabbit-breeders' souks, is the one major exception, and that after all was a symbol of national rather than municipal pride; it was not until the end of the fifteenth century that another stone church in a European style was erected in Toledo. In the meantime the traditional pale bricks and mortar were used to build in a fashion largely of Cordoban origins which acquired characteristics of its own. The mosque subsequently known as 'Christ of the Light', which still exists, is a fine example of the caliphate style transformed by bricks and skilful masonry into Toledan *mudéjar*. Elements of Romanesque are also present in the style, although curiously they become less prominent than Moorish features in the later medieval churches. Horseshoe and lobed arches were increasingly used and the architecture of the present Puerta del Sol, completed in the fourteenth century, appears so Arab that it was long believed to date from before the Reconquest. In spite of the many later buildings, especially of the Renaissance period, *mudéjar* remains the most characteristic and authentic style of Toledo; as late as 1920 the town's railway station was adorned with a *mudéjar* tower.

Toledo's districts or *barrios* have many things in common – the shortage of trees and gardens, the small irregular squares, the narrow streets where no two houses are the same – but each has preserved a distinctive personality. It is in the *barrios populares*, the artisan and working-class areas that stretch southwards from the cathedral to the river, which today best conserve the feel of medieval Toledo. There the streets are often so narrow that the overhanging roofs nearly touch; some of them are so steep that in places they have been turned into steps. There you feel in fact that the town has no real streets, only houses that have turned their backs on the twisting lanes. The façades are smooth and undecorated and, as in Córdoba, family life revolves around the patio with its well and its pots of plants. Outside, the streets are silent and deserted at midday; only from time to time can you hear the laboured tread of old women, carrying their shopping up the arduous slopes.

After the Reconquest, Toledo regained its pre-eminent position in Castile, its conquerors emphasizing the city's pre-Islamic role when it was the centre of the Visigothic kingdom. As the Christian headquarters for many subsequent campaigns against the Moors, its strategic role was enhanced, and in religious and cultural matters it had no rivals among the cities of central Spain.

10

While retaining its reputation for rebelliousness, particularly during the revolt of the *comuneros* in the 1520s, Toledo also became the principal residence of the court. Following the town's capture by the Castilian king, Alfonso VI, in 1085, it acquired its inappropriate title 'the imperial city'. Ruler of about a third of the peninsula, Alfonso nevertheless called himself *imperator totius Hispaniae* and Emperor of Toledo. Although the practice died out in the following century, Alfonso VII dividing his 'empire' between his two sons who thus became kings of Castile and Leon, the city liked to retain its imperial association. Peter I, who was supported by Toledo in the civil wars of the fourteenth century, called it 'capital of the empire'. Six hundred years later, when the city's Francoist authorities wished to honour the murdered politician Calvo Sotelo, 'first martyr of the National Crusade', they signed their commemorative plaque 'the Imperial City 1940'.

One of the titles Alfonso VI most enjoyed using was 'King of the Three Religions'. It was certainly a more accurate designation than 'Emperor of all Spain'. Under him Toledo was a cosmopolitan city, its population comprised of different religions and ethnic groups which conserved their traditions and a certain autonomy in legal and administrative matters. The principal communities were granted their own *fueros* or privileges and allowed to retain their own magistrates, a *cadí* for the Moors, an *alguacil* for the Jews and a mayor for the Mozarabic Christians. The new arrivals also had their own officers, a mayor for the Castilians and a bailiff and judge for the Franks, a powerful group which included Alfonso's queen and his two sons-in-law. The ethnic diversity and generally tolerant atmosphere promoted a cultural flowering in Toledo, and in the twelfth and thirteenth centuries the city became renowned for its so-called School of Translators. Gerard of Cremona and other scholars went to Toledo in search of classical texts lost since the fall of Rome and surviving in Arabic translations. In Toledo Gerard learnt Arabic in order to translate the *Almagest*, the encyclopaedia of astronomy written by Ptolemy in Alexandria in the second century. He remained there until his death in 1187, translating an enormous number of books into Latin, including works of Aristotle and Euclid. In the following century the patron of the translators was Alfonso X, known as 'the learned' for his knowledge and encouragement of scholarship, although in view of his long and futile attempt to make himself Holy Roman Emperor he perhaps deserved a different epithet.

Toledo's Jews, subjected to dramatic shifts of fortune during more than a thousand years in the city, enjoyed one of their most prosperous periods after the Reconquest. Their previous experience of Christian rule had been much less fortunate. Throughout the Visigothic period civil laws and religious decrees from the Councils of Toledo had imposed a series of drastic restrictions on Jewish society. In the sixth century Jews were forbidden to have Christian wives, to hold public office or to build new synagogues. A more systematic assault on the Jewish religion was carried out in the following century, King Reccesuinth's law code of 654 prohibiting Jews from celebrating the Passover, performing their own weddings or even obeying their own dietary laws, although this was not comprehensively enforced. In 694 an article in the last Council of Toledo charges the Jews with political subversion, a recurrent and familiar accusation in Spanish history. Until the end of his life General Franco used to blame opposition to his rule on a mysterious phenomenon he termed the 'Judeo-masonic conspiracy'.

Visigothic persecution helps explain the traditional belief that Jews aided the Moorish army to capture Toledo in 715. On Palm Sunday, it is related, they opened the gates to the Moors while the Christians were walking in procession to the basilica of Santa Leocadia. The move, if true, certainly improved Jewish prospects. Muslim toleration was extensive and laws governing Jewish behaviour were far less oppressive than before: prayers had to be said not too loudly, certain clothes had to be worn, and the height of houses and synagogues was restricted. Later the Jews, like all other subjects of the Emir Hisham I, were required to learn Arabic, a demand which enabled them to play a crucial role in the city's cultural life both before and after the Reconquest. Although they lived in their own district, the Judería, they were more closely integrated in the life of Toledo than they had been under the Visigoths. Their architecture was Moorish and remained so after the Christian takeover. The two synagogues that survive (of the nine which existed in the thirteenth century) are Moorish in design with inlaid domes and horseshoe arches. The columns remind one of the Cordoban mosque in miniature; although built long after the Reconquest, only the Hebrew inscriptions suggest the buildings are not Muslim.

After a good start, conditions for the Jews in medieval Toledo deteriorated. The kings and sometimes the higher clergy practised a policy of toleration, and it is recorded that in 1212 Toledan knights defended the Judería against an attack by Castilian forces campaigning against the Moors. But among the poorer classes resentment against the Jews increased, exacerbated apparently by the presence of so many pawnbrokers and moneylenders in the community. Persecution became endemic from the end of the fourteenth century, directed not only against practising Jews but also against the *conversos*, those who had converted to Christianity. Pogroms might be incited by the appearance of a *converso* tax-gatherer, the news of violence in another city or the preaching of a fanatic priest, reminding his congregation of the Jews' responsibility for the crucifixion of Christ. In 1405 a mob was assembled to storm a Toledan synagogue and transform it into the church of Santa María la Blanca. The establishment of the Inquisition in 1478, set up to unmask insincere *conversos*, marked the end of official toleration and presaged the expulsion of the Jews from the peninsula. Fourteen years later about 150,000 of them were driven from Spain, taking their house keys with them. For centuries, it is said, Toledo's Jews exiled in Smyrna and other cities retained the keys of their old homes.

The sixteenth century encompassed the period of Toledo's greatest prosperity, the doubling of its population during the middle quarters to 60,000, and its most impressive building programme. It also saw the substitution of Moorish influence in architecture by Italian Renaissance styles. The Emperor Charles V rebuilt the Alcázar as a royal palace with a staircase sufficiently grand, he remarked, to make him *feel* like an emperor. The principal new buildings were hospitals, churches, the town hall and palaces of the nobility. Two great hospitals, the Santa Cruz and the Tavera, survive under different uses today, their spacious patios with classical arcades testifying to the eclipse of the *mudéjar* style. Much of this building was carried out by a line of outstanding prelates, the cardinal-archbishops Mendoza, Cisneros, Tavera and Siliceo. This tradition was broken, however, when their successor Carranza was incarcerated by the Inquisition, leaving the primate's seat empty for seventeen years.

The sixteenth century also saw some attempt at town planning in Toledo. Now that Spain really did have an empire, its citizens found it embarrassing that the imperial city should be so very unimposing. There was a reaction against the medieval legacy and the playwright Tirso de Molina complained that the Moors had 'spoilt part of the beauty of our Toledo by their miserly buildings and narrow streets leading nowhere': what did he imagine Toledo to have looked like under the Visigoths? Urban improvements were begun by the Catholic Kings, who ordered the streets to be paved with stone instead of brick, and were carried on throughout the century in accordance with a series of regulations. Among other things, these banned the building of corbels and other projections, stated that the eaves of a house must not overhang more than a third of the road's width, and decreed that rooms connecting houses across a street must be high enough 'to allow an armed knight to pass by unimpeded'.

The city authorities also decided to rectify Toledo's lack of squares and open spaces. After much wrangling, three main squares were planned and subsequently laid out: the Plaza Mayor, which was designed as the commercial centre, the Plaza del Ayuntamiento, across which the town hall and the cathedral face each other, and the Plaza de Zocodover, used as a market as well as a site for bullfights, public festivities and executions. Yet compared with the great squares built in other Spanish cities, they are an unimpressive lot and the Plaza Mayor is particularly ill-named. Toledo suffered both for its past as an Islamic city and for its position on a hill where steep gradients and shortage of space made expansive urban planning impossible. It was very much easier to arrange a *plaza mayor* in flatter cities built by Christians after the Reconquest.

In spite of its municipal shortcomings, Toledo remained one of Spain's most celebrated cities during the country's 'golden century'. You had to go to Toledo, it was said, to find the best sword blades, the finest silk, the most exquisite tiles. Various sayings proclaimed that the city produced 'the best women, swords and quince' in all Spain. Sixteenth-century Toledo also became famous for the excellence of its inns, a reputation it has subsequently failed to maintain, and for its marzipan, which the local

14

poet Urabayen found unique and indigestible. According to the Italian philosopher and historian Benedetto Croce, it also gained a more dubious fame: while Bologna, he noted, was the seat of law and Salerno the seat of medicine, Toledo was known as the centre for occult sciences.

Certain countries possess a particular city where it is claimed, not necessarily correctly, that the national language is most purely spoken. Nobody goes to Siena without learning that its population apparently speaks the best Italian, and generations of English children have been sent to Tours in the mistaken belief that there they will learn the best French. Once the claim is made, it is no doubt difficult to refute it: how can anyone decide what is the purest form of a language? Toledo acquired a similar status in the sixteenth century and has held it ever since. 'Here', announced Richard Ford in the 1840s, 'the glorious Castellano is spoken in all its purity of grammar and pronounciation, which is slow and guttural. To speak *en proprio Toledano*, has since the time of Cervantes been equivalent to "the best Spanish".' A century later, Marañón could assert that 'the speech of those Toledans uncorrupted by the unfortunate proximity of Madrid still sounds today like water running over stones'.

Although Cervantes is frequently cited in support of Toledo's claim to speak the best Castilian, it is doubtful that he himself would have endorsed it. At any rate, in the second part of *Don Quixote* he suggests that good Castilian is the product of education and leisure rather than the property of a particular city. After acknowledging Toledo's reputation, Sancho Panza points out that 'there may be Toledans who aren't so slick at this business of speaking pretty'. His listener, a student, agrees with him: 'Men bred in the tanneries and in Zocodover cannot speak as well as those who spend most of their day strolling in the cloisters of the cathedral; and yet they are all Toledans. You will find the pure, correct, elegant and clear language among educated people at Court, even though they may have been born in Majadahonda.'

From this age also comes the idea that Toledan gentlemen were particularly gallant and intelligent. In one of Lope de Vega's plays a character says he wants to love like a Toledan and die like a Cordoban. Centuries later, the qualities of the men were applauded by Ford who compared them to their houses, 'solid and

15

trustworthy old Castilians, sober and *muy hombres de bien'*. The city's women have received even greater praise. Not only were they extremely beautiful, but apparently very chaste and honest as well. A character in Cervantes's story 'The Illustrious Serving-Maid' declares that of 'all the cities of Spain, Toledo has the reputation of being that in which the women surpass all others, whether in beauty or conduct'. Lazarillo de Tormes, the eponymous narrator of the picaresque tale, suggests their conduct was not universally upright in the sixteenth century: the town had no shortage of prostitutes, he reported, who spent the day by the river knowing they would earn a free lunch by its banks for their services; later Lazarillo married a priest's mistress who had had several illegitimate children. But the hungry *pícaro* seldom saw any but the bleakest sides of life, and his was a minority view. By contrast, the writer Gracián claimed that Toledo's ladies were so cultivated they could 'say more in a single word than an Athenian in a whole book'. Was there any quality, one wonders, which they might have lacked? Marañón, who found it difficult to make any criticism of his city, recognized their pale and melancholy beauty but conceded that they might possess a minor defect. Was there not perhaps something, he mused, just a little bitter in their hearts?

In 1561 Philip II removed his court from Toledo and established Madrid as Spain's capital city. Different explanations have been given for the transfer. The king preferred the hunting around Madrid, he did not like *mudéjar* architecture, he wanted to live far away from the primate (who presumably was not expected to live for ever in the prisons of the Inquisition*), his young queen Elizabeth de Valois felt ill in Toledo and hated the city: it could not have been more unlike her beloved Amboise. But the principal reason was surely that Toledo, despite its title, was thoroughly unsuited to be the capital of a real empire. The cramped medieval town of narrow streets and fluctuating gradients could not possibly have housed the court and bureaucracy needed to

---

* In fact he nearly did. Arrested in 1559, Archbishop Carranza was transferred from a Spanish prison to a Roman one in 1567, but he was not acquitted until 1576. He died eighteen days after his release.

govern the vast expanse of territories in America, Italy and the Low Countries.

Later generations of Toledans blamed all their city's subsequent problems on the decision to transfer the court. The imperial city, they believed, had been ruined by a single ill-judged and unjustifiable political move. The fact that the city enjoyed at least two generations of prosperity after 1561, that its most ambitious building projects also took place afterwards, that Toledo's later decline was partly a reflection of national decline in the first half of the seventeenth century, were beside the point. Sudden decadence inspired by the king was a myth accepted by the Toledan people and one in which they believed passionately. In 1583 the town hall asked Philip to return with his court, and for many years it was asserted that the 'restoration' of the capital would be the solution to all ills. The modern journal *Toletum* indicates that the matter is not yet dead. A few years after Franco's death it carried an article arguing that if Toledo could not be the political capital it should at least be Spain's cultural capital, the place where 'the search for Spain's contemporary soul must begin'. A subsequent issue was more obdurate. The city must return to what it had been 'so many times in the past', Spanish capital and 'heart of the Spanish spirit'. For historical, political, economic and cultural reasons, declared the writer in 1982, Toledo should once again be 'capital of Spain, seat of the Crown and residence of the Royal Family'.

The image of declining Toledo, impoverished and enwrapped in the mysticism of St Teresa of Avila, is still very much associated with the allegedly mystical El Greco, painting in a state of apparent ecstasy his strange distorted visions. The French writer Barrès, in whom it was said breathed the soul of France, considered that the soul of Spain breathed through El Greco. The Cretan, he claimed, had 'captured the secret of Toledo', and the association of the city with the painter's work later flourished to such an extent that they were almost conflated. James Morris wrote with perhaps some poetic truth that Toledo even looked like an El Greco character, 'towering, handsome, humourless, sad, a little bloodless'. The Greek writer Kazantzakis made a more tasteless and disagreeable identification. On first visiting Toledo before the Civil War, he had been 'disappointed'; instead of a

17

barren rock inhabited by slender, taciturn people, he had found a jolly provincial city full of merchants, photographers and priests. However, when he returned with Franco's army after the relief of the Alcázar, he was elated to discover that 'Toledo had become a canvas of El Greco, full of fiery palpitating forms . . .'. Destruction and death had 'delivered' the city 'from its self-assured prudence and mediocrity', turning it into 'a lofty, ghostly, pale vision – a martyr wounded on behalf of an idea'. 'Perfected . . . by the explosions and the bombs, [Toledo] was so like El Greco's vision that as I wandered below its fierce and battle-scarred, unyielding walls, I seemed to be floating inside some work of El Greco.' 'The essence of Toledo', he was relieved to say, 'has remained. Only the superfluous parts have been turned into ashes.' Yet 'the exalted meaning of Toledo' had been revealed not only by its ruins; the soldiers too had reverted to El Greco's soldiers. A Francoist diplomat told Kazantzakis that he had only understood El Greco's paintings after seeing the emaciated survivors of the siege of the Alcázar in 1936: 'I realized from what deep regions of his mind, and what painful yearning, El Greco had brought his heroes forth into the light.' Kazantzakis himself made the comparison with the troops of Franco's relief force. 'Weren't these El Greco's soldiers in the "Espolio" and the "St Maurice"? The people painted by the old Cretan had come to life, flooding over the streets of Toledo, raising that same ecstatic cry, "Long live Christ the King!"'*

A less whimsical and more attractive view of El Greco's art was put forward by Cossío, who wrote the first major study of the painter, and by Marañón. They believed that El Greco was a second-rate painter during his years in Italy who was able to 'fulfil' himself only in Spain, absorbing the Spanish spirit in Toledo and transforming its eternal values into great art. He portrayed 'the essence of Spain and the Spanish race' like no other painter, wrote Cossío. To Marañón his work 'represents the soul of Spain' at the end of the sixteenth century.

El Greco's secular works did of course depict the Spain, or at any rate the Spaniards, of his time, as his portraits of Toledan

---

* The soldiers in the *Espolio* (*The Disrobing of Christ*) were Romans who were unlikely to be raising this particular cry just before the crucifixion.

society show. His patrons presumably wanted themselves to be portrayed accurately and not transformed into the elongated figures of his religious scenes. And so we see them as they were, the scholars, doctors, jurists of Toledo, the powerful, unsmiling cardinals, the unknown hidalgos, proud and lean-headed gentlemen in black. In *The Burial of the Count of Orgaz*, the masterpiece in the church of Santo Tomé, we see a crowd of mourners witnessing a miracle of the fourteenth century. Yet they are all portraits of El Greco's contemporaries painted in sixteenth-century costume, pale, pessimistic men in black suits and white ruffs. They have heavy-lidded eyes, pointed beards and elegant moustaches, and they tell us a lot about Spanish society in that period. Yet El Greco's view of his adoptive compatriots was far from comprehensive. He declined, for example, to paint fat people, whether because, as Marañón held, he despised mortal flesh or for some other reason. And although Lazarillo de Tormes describes a Toledo swarming with hungry people, it must have contained some fat inhabitants.

Portraying a society is one thing; portraying its soul, and attempting to explain this portrait through an examination of the painter's own soul, is very different. Various writers have built theories around El Greco's 'Arab blood', his 'oriental soul' and his conversion of Toledo into Gethsemane, Marañón's being the clearest and most eloquent. Toledo's oriental character, he believed, its Arab traditions and biblical landscape, appealed to the 'oriental roots of the painter's Greek soul' in a way that Venice and Rome, his previous homes, could never match. Toledo and Judaea were almost identical, possessing the same scenery of rocks and olives, the same smells, the same sounds. If you closed your eyes on a Toledan hillside, he wrote, you would hear the bleating of the same sheep, breathe the scents of the same herbs, perhaps even feel the breath of the same Judases. And when you awoke, you could not be sure that the dust rising between the olive trees was not the dust of crowds following the footsteps of the prophets.

El Greco went to Toledo, wrote Marañón, 'with his Orient inside his soul, in search of another Orient'. There his genius blossomed, nurtured in a city of churches built upon the ruins of ancient synagogues. And there he became a mystic, a little unbalanced perhaps, an artist according to one historian who 'alternated between reason and delirium'. Distinguished art historians of recent generations have drawn parallels between El Greco and the Spanish mystics, claiming that he shared their craving for union with God and making comparisons between his work and the writings of St Teresa and St John of the Cross. It is a case of looking for evidence to fit a theory. Cossío and Marañón did the same when they claimed that the models of El Greco's apostles were the inmates of Toledo's lunatic asylum: in fact the expressions in the portraits indicate men who may have been spiritual and even tormented but who were not insane. An even less tenable theory was advanced by Hemingway. In a dreadful passage in his book on bullfighting, he calls El Greco, against all evidence, *Rey de los Maricones*, 'King of the Queers'. The saints, asserted the obnoxious American writer, were clearly portraits of the painter's homosexual friends.

El Greco's pictures may look as if they were painted by a mystic, but modern historical research suggests that there was nothing unusually mystical about him. Instead of being a semi-delirious ecstatic in Spain's Judaea, yearning for union with the Deity, El Greco appears to have been very much an intellectual Renaissance figure, a humanist who wrote about art and architecture: his library contained the poetry of Petrarch and Ariosto, the major Greek authors, Plutarch's *Lives*, architectural treatises of Vitruvius, Palladio and others. Such evidence does not deny the strong religious motivation behind his work, his devotion to the New Testament, or the Byzantine and even oriental inspiration of his painting. But it does suggest he was not a deranged Van Gogh figure, immortalizing his visions for himself. El Greco was successful in Spain primarily because a good number of friends and patrons admired his pictures and wanted to buy them. It is true that he became a great painter in Toledo (though difficult to assert that he would not have become one elsewhere), that he liked the city and might have been reminded of Crete by its 'oriental' landscape. But Toledo's main gifts were the clients it produced and the freedom it gave him to develop his art unchallenged by rivals and untroubled by financial anxieties.

The existence of a group of patrons learned and wealthy enough to buy El Greco's pictures rather spoils the traditional view of Toledo rapidly declining some decades earlier when Madrid became the capital. It perhaps also dents the image of the city's mystical character, which may have been subsequently exaggerated in an effort to explain the taste for El Greco's paintings. St Teresa visited Toledo several times, had a number of followers in the city and founded there an enclosed convent of Carmelite nuns, a community which occupied various buildings in the city before ending up in the beautiful Casa de la Cerda, an old palace in the long Calle Real that slopes westwards to the Cambrón gate. But she also had many opponents and her influence was limited. As one would expect of the city of the primate, religion in Toledo at the end of the sixteenth century followed the doctrines of the Counter-Reformation. El Greco himself kept a copy of the proceedings of the Council of Trent in his library.

Toledo also remained in the mainstream of the nation's cultural life, its leading citizens – many of them educated at the city's university – displaying unusual interest in subjects such as astronomy and mathematics. After the Academy of Mathematics was founded in 1582, recalled a visitor, 'it became fashionable to talk mathematics, to read mathematics and to write mathematics'. Intellectual vitality was matched by a surprising economic resilience. Toledo was affected by harvest failures in the late sixteenth century, a depression in its textile industry and the emigration of several of its noble families as well as numerous artisans to Madrid. But it does not seem to have suffered more drastically than other cities of Castile. A good deal of new building took place during this period, especially in the 1570s under the control of the *corregidor* Gutiérrez Tello, and again in the decade after El Greco's death in 1614. Some of this was probably undertaken in an attempt to attract the court back to Toledo. The municipality exhorted its citizens to build elegant new houses and lectured them on the importance of having 'grand and sumptuous buildings' in their city. The town's authorities set a distinguished example. Among the best buildings of the period is the town hall, designed by the architect of the Escorial but lacking the austerity and forbidding dimensions of the great monastic palace.

The city, however, continued to mourn its lost pre-eminence and exaggerated its troubles after 1561. Letters to the king

21

described a city of poverty and misery, without shops or markets, a place of ruined houses and nuns dying of hunger in their convents. Outsiders who had heard of these woes were puzzled when they saw the situation for themselves. González de Cellorigo, an official of the Inquisition, visited Toledo in 1619 expecting to arrive in a desert. Yet he found a city with crowded streets and buildings in good condition. 'Although it enjoyed greater prosperity in the past,' he reported, 'Toledo is less affected than anywhere else by the common decline from which these kingdoms are suffering.'

A few years later the grumbles appeared more justified. During the second quarter of the seventeenth century the city went downhill so rapidly that by 1640 it had lost more than half its population. The silk industry, Toledo's largest employer, went into terminal decline, although it was not finished off until the nineteenth century. Three-quarters of its looms disappeared in a single generation, many of the weavers becoming casualties of epidemics in the 1680s. The picture in the eighteenth century is even bleaker. While certain minor sectors of the economy, such as the production of hats and guitar strings, seem to have prospered, the overall impression is one of misery and decay. Officials wrote of starving schoolmasters and silk weavers begging in the streets; hospitals were so impoverished they were unable to operate. The city was in a dismal state, 'half the streets', reported an English traveller, 'choked up with heaps of ruined houses of brick'. Henry Swinburne's description of Toledo as 'exceedingly ill built, poor and ugly' would not have been disputed by the town's authorities. It was, they admitted, dirty and badly planned. A commission recommended measures which included closing the blind alleys, 'useless' places where people 'deposited filth and committed grave offences against God'.

Attempts were actually being made both to improve the town and to revitalize its industries. Weapons had once rivalled silk as Toledo's main product, a fact which the tourist is reminded of by the displays of miniature blades in every souvenir shop. Toledan swords had had an international reputation in the sixteenth century when Catherine of Aragon had given one as a present to her unworthy English husband. Decaying to the point of disappearance, the industry was resurrected by the establishment of a new weapons factory using Biscayan steel in 1761. Moved from the town to an orchard beside the Tagus in 1780, it produced blades of good quality even if they did not achieve the renown of their predecessors. According to an English vicar travelling at the end of the eighteenth century, the steel was 'excellent, and so perfectly tempered, that in thrusting at a target the swords will bend like whalebone, and yet cut through a helmet without turning their edge'.

Little construction took place in Toledo in the eighteenth century until the final quarter when Cardinal Lorenzana, reviving the tradition of builder-prelates, made the last important contribution to the city's architecture. Among other works, he restored the Alcázar and the archbishop's palace, erected a hospital for lunatics, and built a new university over former property of the Inquisition. This imposing neo-classical building served its intended function until 1845 when it was suppressed on the strange pretext that it was too close to Madrid; however, after a spell as a teaching college, it was again awarded university status in 1969. Perhaps the most interesting of Lorenzana's projects was the restoration of the Alcázar which for a brief period enjoyed neither a royal nor a military existence. The vicar who had admired the well-tempered swords was also impressed by the Alcázar's conversion to a 'general workhouse for the poor. All the magnificent apartments,' he wrote, were 'now occupied with spinning wheels and looms, and instead of princes, they are filled with beggars'.

Lorenzana's ability to undertake such enterprises in the gloomy economic climate of the time testifies to the power and wealth of the Toledan see. There was nothing new about this: as far back as the fifteenth century an observer had noted that the archbishop was 'more like a pope than a prelate'. But in the past he had at least had wealthy rivals, the monarch, the nobles, the traders and small industrialists. Now the Church was supreme. By the middle of the eighteenth century about a quarter of Toledo's population were ecclesiastics, nearly 5,000 people, excluding those merely employed by or dependent on the Church. There was understandably some resentment of the religious monopoly of power. 'This is a town', complained the director of the weapons factory, 'in which the clergy corrupt everything and where they can despotically commit the worst iniquities in contempt of all jurisdiction because they recognize none . . .'.

By the middle of the seventeenth century, Toledo justified its later description as a 'convent-city'. But the transformation had begun much earlier. For reasons of space, royal decrees had tried to limit the growth in size and number of convents since the Middle Ages. No doubt these slowed down the process, but they were unable to halt it. As early as the thirteenth and fourteenth centuries, convents and monasteries were eating up adjacent houses and even devouring cemeteries and neighbouring streets in the rush to expand. Alfonso X, 'the learned', failed to set an example of restraint. Born in Toledo on St Clement's Day, the king subsequently rewarded St Clement's monastery with large donations. The effect of these can still be seen in the Calle San Clemente where Alfonso's monastery is over a hundred yards long and takes up the entire side of the street. The whole of the opposite side is taken up by the monastery of St Peter the Martyr, an even larger institution which at the end of the street turns a corner and carries on for an even longer way down the Calle San Pedro Martír.

The most frequent victims of this monastic expansionism were the homes of the aristocracy. There was no convent in the city, noted one historian, that had not been built on the ruins of a private residence. The takeovers began in the Middle Ages – as a result there are no *mudéjar* palaces left in Toledo – but the most radical changes took place in the sixteenth and seventeenth centuries. In spite of still more stringent restrictions on new religious buildings, the number of convents and monasteries grew from twenty-five to forty-one in the century before 1632. Sometimes the religious orders destroyed the existing buildings and erected their own, sometimes they merely moved into the old palaces. The Casa de la Cerda, inhabited for a long time by the nuns of St Teresa's order, still exists much as it was built in the sixteenth century. But now it stands gaunt and desolate, over-looking the valley and its own abandoned garden, the cracked stonework and broken windows providing an appropriate image for the forlorn city in its decline.

Religious life was disrupted and partly destroyed by Spain's 'dissolution of the monasteries' in the 1830s. In Toledo the

decrees were applied much more rigorously to the communities
of monks and friars than to the female orders. All the monasteries
were suppressed and their buildings put up for sale. The nuns, by
contrast, lost only two of their convents, although the surviving
foundations were relieved of much of their wealth. Seventeen of
the forty-one religious houses thus disappeared, their buildings
converted for other uses or knocked down and built over. In
Spain's 'liberal' age* there was little respect for historical nostalgia, and these properties were treated without regard for religious
sentiment. They became warehouses, military buildings, prisons
and public offices: after serving for many years as a barracks, the
site of the Trinitarian monastery is now a car park. The monastery
of the 'discalced' or shoeless Augustinians became successively a
storehouse, a theatre and a hotel before ending up today as the
Institute of Social Security. Their 'calced' or shod brothers fared
even worse, their buildings being razed to make way for the
municipal slaughterhouse. None, however, went through so
many metamorphoses as the monastery of St Peter the Martyr.
Serving in turn as a provincial museum, a barracks, a maternity
hospital, a home for beggars and old people, a school and an
orphanage, it was being restored in 1991 as the future seat of the
autonomous government of New Castile.

In spite of so much havoc and upheaval, Toledo retains the
atmosphere of the convent-city, especially in those northern
streets within the triangle encompassed by the two Dominican
convents and the monastery of St Peter. Those ancient enclosed
institutions still impose their presence on the district, vast, almost
uninhabited buildings extending their spirit over much of the
city. In the time of El Greco there were sixty nuns in the convent
of Santo Domingo el Antiguo, the most ancient in Toledo,
founded shortly after the Reconquest; in 1989 there were only
eleven, all of them elderly. The convent of St Clement covers
about two acres of the town, but only fourteen nuns live in it. Yet
the district remains dominated by these immense, poorly preserved monuments of stone and dusty brick facing each other

---

* The inverted commas are necessary because, although many politicians of the nineteenth
century called themselves liberals and practised a certain amount of economic liberalism,
no government of this period could be described as politically liberal.

across narrow streets; interspersed among them, the parish churches and derelict houses of tiny squares seem like an earlier tribe threatened with extermination but reprieved when the religious orders were checked from further expansion.

Like Santiago, Toledo is a city for noctambulists, although in Santiago it is difficult to get lost because all roads lead ultimately to the cathedral. In Toledo you can walk along street after street without hearing a voice or seeing a person. You can walk between the high convent walls, ill-lit by glassless, rusting lanterns, and see nothing but shadows. Even in daylight the streets around Santo Domingo el Real would be silent were it not for the cooing and flapping of doves. You look up at the convents with their peeling plaster and broken shutters, and nothing, except the rare intrusion of an air-conditioning vent stuck incongruously into a high window, disturbs the impression that you are wandering in a forgotten past. You stare at the ivy-sprawled walls and try to imagine what goes on in the enclosed worlds behind them. What is life really like in the cloisters of Santo Domingo el Real, that enormous convent of three courtyards whose original inhabitants, the Dominican nuns, restricted now to the smallest of the patios, are forced to share their buildings with brother Dominicans and the Knight Commanders of Santiago?

By the middle of the nineteenth century, Toledo's population had been reduced to 13,000, less than a quarter of its 1570 figure. Native and foreign writers alike agreed that it was a fossil inhabited by indolent and useless people. The rich and the talented, wrote the Italian novelist De Amicis, had departed, and the town was 'now worse than poor', it was dead. According to Alexandre Dumas, it was dying 'and, though too proud to admit it, dying of starvation'. 'Dark, ruinous, alone and forgotten,' Zorrilla wrote in a savage poem, nothing remained of Toledo but its 'gigantic name', a cathedral and some ruins, and 'an imbecile population vegetating' among them. Observers agreed that the Toledans made no attempt to halt the decay of their city. In one of Félix Urabayen's plays a character angrily criticizes an outsider for wanting to promote change: 'Idiot! What does he know of such things? He thinks that modernity, force, machines are everything ... And the centuries, are they nothing? Or history? Or tradition? To change Toledo is a blasphemy which, if human

26

laws cannot prevent, divine Providence will assuredly punish.'

This conservatism still exists and is still criticized by outsiders. Spaniards from Madrid who are in some way involved with Toledo frequently complain about its population, arguing that the best Toledans have long gone and that the present inhabitants are the descendants of those who had neither the strength nor the initiative to leave. The people are always looking to the past, they say, mistrustful of change, suspicious of the suggestions of other Spaniards. A proposal to convert a disused church into a museum of modern art was rejected recently on the grounds that pictures of nude women could not be hung in a place where nuns had once worshipped.

In spite of their complaints, most of Toledo's critics loved the city and loved it for precisely those reasons for which they also excoriated it. They loved it for its pride and its nobility, for its unbending austerity, for its refusal to modernize. They loved it because its spectral desolation set it apart from the materialism of the time, reminding them of more selfless and heroic ages. Dumas may have called it 'the hungriest town in Spain', too proud to admit it was dying of starvation, but all the same he found it magnificent. 'If you ever go to Spain', he wrote, 'and visit Madrid, hire a carriage, find a coach, wait for a caravan if need be, but go to Toledo, Madame, go to Toledo.' The Spanish poets loved it and liked to roam at night through silent and abandoned streets. Urabayen loved the quietness of Toledan nights, the silence spread over every district except that of the taverns and brothels near the Bisagra gate. Gustavo Adolfo Bécquer, the Romantic poet, loved the town so much that he dedicated one of his most ardent verses to the basilica of Santa Leocadia and moved with his family to Toledo. He used to ramble around in the moonlight and is commemorated by a plaque by his favourite square, Santo Domingo el Real.

This ambivalence towards Toledo was typified by Galdós, the most famous novelist of nineteenth-century Spain. Its position, he wrote, was 'inaccessible, harsh, sombre, obscure and silent'; Toledo itself was 'uncomfortable, inhospitable and sad', a place of 'retreat and melancholy', a city 'of illustrious rubble' incapable of resurrection, destined to be nothing more than a home for archaeologists. Yet he loved Toledo and knew it as well as

27

anyone. He stayed there for long periods but even when living in Madrid he made a point of travelling to Toledo for certain religious festivals, for Holy Week and Corpus Christi and various saints' days. In the evenings after dinner he used to plan his walks for the following morning, showing off to his friends his knowledge of the city's topography. He liked to set himself childish tests, recalling suddenly all the streets which had happy names or sad ones, reciting lists of those named after kings or saints or garden plants. The next day he would set off from his house in the Calle Santa Isabel, staying faithfully to his planned itinerary, visiting the cathedral and clambering over its roofs, stopping off at such and such a convent to buy jam and cakes made by the nuns. When he lived in Santander he used to take his afternoon rest on a bench made from fragments of tiles he had personally collected in Toledo's Judería.

The only writer who loved Toledo without any reservations was Gregorio Marañón, who adopted the town and in 1921 bought one of its *cigarrales*, those lovely country villas surrounded by gardens and orchards which look at the city from hillsides to the west. Admittedly he said the Toledans had no sense of humour – looking for humour in Toledo was as unprofitable, he wrote, as searching for gold in the Tagus – but nobody would have disputed that; in Toledo, remarked Urabayen, a humorist was always considered a 'bad fellow'. And anyway, how could a sense of humour survive in a city whose tragedy, declared Marañón, was only comparable to the magnitude of its glory?

Marañón was an eminent doctor who taught and practised during the week in Madrid and came to Toledo on Saturdays to live for himself on Sundays. His son has described the routine of his days in the *cigarral*, rising early to be in his study, its walls lined with books and photographs of his closest friends, by eight o'clock. There he wrote his biographies or read his favourite books – the Bible, *Don Quixote*, the works of Quevedo and Galdós – disturbed only by a mid-morning glass of sherry before stopping at one o'clock to set off with friends and family to hear mass beside El Greco's masterpiece in Santo Tomé. Lunch at home almost invariably consisted of potato omelette, partridge, custard and Toledan marzipan, which Don Gregorio praised each Sunday as if he were tasting them for the first time. Afterwards, putting on his cloak and grasping his Navarrese stick, he went for a long walk in the city, sometimes visiting his favourite convents which he regarded as 'the essential and permanent part of the city's soul', before returning at sunset. He never tired of looking at the town's silhouette from his *cigarral*, the spires of the cathedral and the Alcázar rising beyond the cypresses and olive groves, and on the day of his death he was heard to murmur, 'Toledo, light of my life'.

In the 1920s the city became a place of pilgrimage for Luis Buñuel, the future film director, and his friends. They founded the 'Order of Toledo' in 1923, with Buñuel as grand master, the poets Lorca and Alberti among the knights or *caballeros*, and various lesser beings as squires or *escuderos*. Salvador Dalí started off as a *caballero* but was relegated, for some unremembered misdemeanour, to the ranks of the *escuderos*. The objects of the order were sybaritic and its rules undemanding. 'To advance to the rank of *caballero*,' explained Buñuel, 'one had to adore Toledo without reservation, drink for at least an entire night, and wander aimlessly through the streets of the city. Those who preferred to go to bed early became *escuderos* at best.' Little was required of each member except that he was expected 'to go to Toledo as often as possible and place himself in a state of receptivity for whatever unforgettable experiences might happen along'. Apart from wandering the labyrinthine streets, these experiences seem to have consisted mainly of eating and drinking in taverns, particularly in the Posada de la Sangre which luckily had changed little since Cervantes used its courtyard for the setting of 'The Illustrious Serving-Maid'. 'Donkeys still stood in the yard,' recalled Buñuel later, 'along with carriage drivers, dirty sheets and packs of students. Of course, there was no running water, but that was a matter of relatively minor importance, since the members of the Order were forbidden to wash during their sojourn in the Holy City.' The pranks of the group came to an end with the Civil War, Buñuel refusing to visit Toledo after the Posada de la Sangre had been destroyed during Franco's capture of the city. Belonging to the order subsequently proved hazardous to at least one member during the war. Anarchists searching his house in Madrid came across the membership document and, not seeing the joke, accused him of being an aristocrat and threatened his life.

Civil War damage followed the degradations of the nineteenth century, notably the destruction caused by the French occupation of the city in the Peninsular War and the vandalism which followed the sale of the monastic properties. Yet, as if in compensation, Toledo was spared the horrors imposed on so many other cities by Francoist town halls in the 1960s. The town was declared a national and historic monument in 1940 and various later measures regulated the height and volume of new buildings, the density of housing, and the materials that could be used. An English journalist, writing before the First World War, optimistically suggested that Toledo's 'position on abrupt rocks with no level spaces seems to promise an eternity of medievalism and individuality'. The city *could* have been ruined, like so many others, by the building boom of the 1960s, but Toledo, like Santiago – medieval symbols of the empire and the Church – was protected. Much of the new building is undistinguished but, because it preserves the dimensions and materials of the old, it is not obtrusive.

The Calle Cervantes is in an area to the north of the Alcázar completely destroyed in the Civil War. All the buildings there are new and not beautiful, yet they respect the proportions and contours of the street and they are made of brick, with iron grilles and wooden balconies and red tiles on the roofs. They do not disrupt, like concrete blocks, their medieval surroundings, and they do not disturb the city's unique skyline. Of course one should not expect less of a national monument, the most representative of Spanish cities, the place that symbolizes the glories and defeats of the nation's history like no other. But Franco's was a regime which appealed to history for its justification yet expunged it where profits could be made, and so we must be grateful for the preservation of Toledo.

TWO

Córdoba

The Spanish mainland has forty-seven provincial capitals. Many of them have multiplied their size and population several times during the course of this century; nearly all have expanded very considerably since the Middle Ages. Córdoba is the only one that is now smaller than it was a thousand years ago, although the intervening centuries have been almost equally harsh to Almería. The city has long been regarded as a symbol of irreversible decline, a thousand years of decadence between the glories of the caliphate and the misery encountered by Gerald Brenan on his travels in 1950. Even the lepers of Marrakesh, observed the English writer, seemed less wretched than the hungry children of Córdoba.

Yet the decline of the Christian city, captured 750 years ago from the Moors, has been slow, irregular and at times temporarily reversed. Córdoba's spectacular rise – and its even more spectacular fall – belong to Moorish history. It is less an image of the decline of Spain than a symbol of the decadence of Arab civilization. For Córdoba was once the greatest city of the Arab west, a rival to Cairo and Baghdad. Its mosque, ignored by Arab tourists who now prefer Marbella, is one of the most beautiful Islamic buildings of the world, a shrine more striking and original than Kairouan or Damascus. In the eighth century Córdoba became a sanctuary for the fallen Ummayad dynasty of Syria, its surviving prince hoping to recreate Damascus on the banks of the Guadalquivir: he even imported palm trees and wrote an ode to one of them, lamenting their mutual loneliness and exile so far from the Middle East. To the Arabs and Berber tribesmen from northern Africa, Córdoba was an oasis, its gardens and orchards places of

31

ease and meditation after the hardships of the desert. Moorish poets, who disliked both the sand and the sea, wrote of its flowers and fertility, of the beauty of the buildings, of the arches of the great bridge which reminded them of a caravan of camels crossing the river. To them Córdoba was 'the mother of towns; the abode of the good and godly, the homeland of wisdom, its beginning and its end; the heart of the land, the fount of science, the dome of Islam, the seat of the Imam; the home of right reasoning, the garden of the fruits of ideas, the sea of the pearls of talent'.

At the heart of the Moorish city, dominating the medina, was the great mosque, expanding over three centuries to the south and east as the population increased. The seventeen aisles, divided by tiers of arches spanning columns often taken from Roman and Carthaginian sites, still have a mesmerizing impact on the visitor entering from the Courtyard of the Orange Trees. They have been well described as 'a holy jungle' and 'a forest of palm trees', but it is more difficult to sum up the mosque's cumulative effect, its strange mixture of the sumptuous and the simple, the character of a building vast in extent yet small in scale. The visitor is aware of space and distant recesses but is not overawed by them. The mosque has little grandeur or solemnity: it may even have a certain fragility, like the Alhambra in Granada, a fragility implying impermanence, as if suggesting that the Moors knew they would not be there for ever. No Moorish building in Spain has the massiveness or self-confidence of the Roman aqueduct of Segovia.

Islamic Córdoba had very few public buildings beyond its mosques, the *alcázar* or royal palace, and the customs house. There were no special buildings for schools or law courts, no open spaces, no squares for tournaments or markets; in contrast to Spain's Christian cities, cemeteries were placed beyond the walls and military parades were held outside the city. The great mosque and its courtyard were thus not merely places of worship but the centres of teaching, of justice and of social life. The Courtyard of the Orange Trees has always been a meeting point and a place to stroll in. Even today, when Córdoba is full of open spaces, it is a good place to rest and talk, to sit among the hundred orange trees, the palms and cypresses, the solitary olive,

32

so old, so hollow, its trunk so frail and ruined that it seems miraculous it can still bear fruit. Islamic cities are among the noisiest in the world, but the traditional architecture is adept at dealing with the problem. In the courtyard of the great mosque at Córdoba you can hear water and the white doves and the murmur of subdued voices, but the sound of traffic is excluded.

The lack of public building was matched by an absence of urban planning. One of the principal streets zigzagged across the city from a gate in the eastern wall to a gate in the wall opposite, while the other wound down from the north, passing between the mosque and the *alcázar* and ending at the bridge. The twenty-one *arrabales*, the walled and largely autonomous quarters of the city, each had a principal lane slightly wider then the others, but most streets were narrow, twisting alleyways. Like Toledo, Córdoba preserves much of its Moorish layout, particularly in the western half of the old city, between the mosque and the principal square, the Plaza de las Tendillas. There you realize that the 'idea' of the street, a thoroughfare fronted by buildings, simply did not exist. Streets were merely gaps between houses serving as passages for their occupants.

From these alleys little could be seen of the houses except for their whitewashed walls of sun-dried clay bricks. There were no façades, no external decoration, no balconies or even windows; the only gap in the wall was the door. The *ajimez*, the wooden lattice balcony which women could look out from without being seen, came from Egypt in the thirteenth century after Córdoba and the rest of western Andalusia had been lost by the Moors. Christian society did not share the Islamic need for the *ajimez* but nevertheless adopted it, *mudéjar* craftsmen constructing *ajimeces* in much of southern Spain; there are some even today attached to convents in Toledo. Later the *ajimeces* evolved – retaining part of their original purpose, the protection of women – into the iron grilles familiar all over Andalusia through which young couples were supposed to do their courting. In a subsequent metamorphosis they became the glass and wooden miradors so fashionable in nineteenth-century Spain from Cádiz to La Coruña.

Córdoba's houses turned their backs on the street, their walls protecting the occupants from smells and noise and other intrusion. They also helped to preserve the privacy of the family and

33

its life around the patio. The Moors did not invent the patio, which is a Mediterranean tradition, but they regarded it as essential to their lives and extended its use through much of Spain. Every Moorish house in the peninsula which has been excavated contains at least one such courtyard. For more than six centuries after the Reconquest, houses in Córdoba and Seville were built with patios, and only in our century has the custom unfortunately been abandoned. Yet those existing from previous eras are preserved and embellished. Córdoba has an Association of Friends of the Cordoban Patios and holds an annual festival to award prizes for the most beautiful. They usually possess a well or a fountain and a citrus tree, climbing plants such as jasmine and plumbago, and green pots of geraniums nailed to the walls. They are enchanted places, oases of silence and tranquillity glimpsed from a busy street, a cooling contrast to the noise and animation traditionally associated with an Andalusian town.

The great wealth of Islamic Córdoba was based on an urban economy well supplied by minerals from the sierra and agricultural produce from the Guadalquivir valley. The fertility of the *campiña*, the Cordoban countryside, had long been praised by classical writers, Pliny extolling its artichokes, Martial recommending its fruit and olive oil and the excellence of its wool. The Moors improved and extended the Roman irrigation system and introduced various fruits including peaches, apricots, bitter oranges (subsequently known as Seville oranges) and pomegranates. The *campiña* also produced, in spite of the Prophet's prohibition, a good deal of wine, as well as cotton, saffron and, according to one Arab writer, 'the sweetest acorns in Spain'.

Commercial life began at the gates of the great mosque, the merchants and artisans spreading out from the centre according to their trade. In Córdoba and other Moorish cities sellers of spices and perfumes were allowed to establish their souk beside the mosque, but messy or evil-smelling businesses were kept away. Rabbit-sellers, dealers in olive oil, even people trying to sell truffles were banned from trading in the centre of the city. Merchants were required to set up their shop in the souks allotted to their particular trade, and street names still recall the blacksmiths, cobblers or parchment-makers who once worked in them. Beyond the souks were the artisans' workshops. Córdoba was famous for its luxury goods, particularly silk, ceramics and ivory carving, and its leather was so celebrated it was sent as a gift to Charlemagne. The city even gave its name to leather-workers in France (*cordonniers*) and England (cordwainers). The trade survives today, attempting to entice tourists, but the quality must surely have declined: the leather chests are so spattered with brass studs that they look like buccaneers' loot in a child's picture-book.

Everyone agrees that Córdoba in the tenth century was the greatest city to the west of Constantinople and that the caliphate was the most prosperous and powerful state in Europe. But there is little agreement about how large it actually was. For many years it was widely accepted that at its peak Córdoba had a population of one million, but that figure was subsequently reduced to half a million and more recently to 100,000. Considering the extent of the city, whose suburbs stretched for virtually five miles from the great mosque to the royal place of Medina az-Zahra, the last figure seems too small, and revisionist views put the population at about 250,000. The eulogies and exaggerations of Moorish historians also make it difficult to assess the number and size of the city's buildings. The streets were paved and had some form of public lighting, but there were neither several thousand mosques nor several thousand public baths. Medina az-Zahra, the 'Moorish Versailles' built by the Caliph Abd al-Rahman III* to house his family, court and bodyguard, was a magnificent palace and is now a magnificent ruin, but one cannot tell if the statistics of its construction are accurate. According to Moorish chroniclers, 10,000 men with 1,000 mules and 400 camels worked daily for 20 years to construct a palace with 4,000 columns and 15,000 doors.

There may also have been some exaggeration of the extent of the city's culture, yet Córdoba was undeniably the greatest centre of learning in Europe. Mathematicians, astronomers, botanists and doctors, many of whom had studied in Baghdad, were well in advance of their Christian counterparts. When King Sancho 'the fat' of Leon lost his throne in 957, he went to Córdoba to be cured

---

* Abd al-Rahman III made himself caliph in 929. His Ummayad predecessors were known as emirs.

of his corpulence; he also received sufficient help from the caliph to regain his throne. The most talented member of the court of Abd al-Rahman II was the musician Ziryab, who added a fifth string to the lute and claimed that angels gave him the melodies of his songs while he slept. Yet the capital of Moorish music was Seville. It was said that when a musician died in Córdoba his instruments were taken to its sister city to be sold, but when a scholar died in Seville his books were sold in Córdoba.

The capital of the caliphate was indeed a place of obsessive bibliophiles which claimed to have more books than any other city of the world. Among the most voracious collectors were the caliphs themselves: at the end of the tenth century al-Hakam II was said to have a library of 400,000 volumes. Calligraphy, 'the geometry of the spirit' according to the delightful definition of a Sufi mystic, was an important business in Córdoba. In one district alone 170 women worked as copiers of manuscripts. The fastest writers were said to be able to complete a Koran in two weeks, and it has been estimated that at least 60,000 books were pro-duced annually in the city.

Cordoban society was on the whole tolerant and easy-going. If a test of a civilized society is the treatment of its Jewish minority, then Córdoba scored very high indeed. According to Jewish historians, the city's Jews enjoyed eight consecutive generations without persecution, the longest period in any country in the history of the diaspora. Loyalty and service to the Ummayad state preserved the synagogues from the profanations and pogroms common at a later date in Christian Spain. Tolerance was also offered to the Mozarabic community but was sometimes thwarted by the intransigence of Christian zealots. The chief interests of Abd al-Rahman II were collecting books and concubines; the last thing he wanted to do was persecute Christians. But towards the end of his reign it became fashionable in Christian circles to aspire to martyrdom. In Córdoba in the middle of the ninth century this was quite a difficult aspiration to achieve because, apart from a tax and restrictions on dress, there was no discrimination against either Christians or Jews. Almost the only route to martyrdom was the public denunciation of Muhammad, which carried a mandatory death penalty. To the amazement of the Muslims, several dozen people between 850 and 859 decided to take it, standing up and blaspheming the prophet until they were arrested and taken before the *cadí*. If, as sometimes happened, the *cadí* was disposed to be lenient, the would-be martyr left him no option by repeating his charges, alleging that the Prophet was an impostor and a devil who had not ascended to Heaven but had been dragged off to Hell where his followers would join him. When the *cadí* refused to execute two young girls for this crime, a priest called Eulogius prevailed upon them to repeat their blasphemy until eventually they were beheaded. Eulogius himself, who was the chronicler of this aberration, was finally brought before a judge who tried to remonstrate with him. One word of repentance, said the man, would save him, but the aspiring saint refused to be cheated of his ambition. He repeated his list of insults and was executed the same afternoon.

Social life in Córdoba was generally indulgent, rejecting the austerity and puritanism of Muslim societies elsewhere. Wine was made and drunk in large quantities, even by the emirs and caliphs: al-Hakam I was said to be often too drunk to pray in the mosque, and judges were usually lenient in cases of drunken behaviour. The chief arbiter of Cordoban fashion seems to have been the musician Ziryab, who persuaded his fellow citizens to cut their hair short, clean their finger-nails and use a deodorant. He also encouraged them to play chess, eat asparagus and drink from glasses rather than heavy goblets of gold. Perhaps we owe the modern menu to Ziryab. Dishes should not be served at random, he declared, but in an orderly progression from soup and hors-d'oeuvres to fish, meat and pudding.

The Cordoban caliphate was immensely civilized and at the same time astonishingly cruel. To describe it in the words of the Greek writer Kazantzakis as 'the pleasant, gentle Arabic civilization of Spain with its human warmth' is to proclaim a barely credible ignorance. Cordoban society was undeniably more sophisticated than the Christian kingdoms of northern Spain, but it was also more brutal. Its history is bespattered with the cruelty of civil wars, massive reprisals, the crucifixion of prisoners, the severed heads of enemies piled high on the battlefield to form minarets before being taken home and displayed as trophies of war.

This cruelty was shared by emirs and caliphs. They may have

been poets and bibliophiles, sensitive to nature and experts on the Koran, but they were capable of brutality that was both savage and cold-blooded. It was not just the cruelty of delinquents, of Moorish equivalents of Nero and Elagabulus, of a solitary psychopath who used his opponents' heads as flowerpots: the men most likely to order an instant execution and enjoy watching the sentence carried out were the strongest and most intelligent rulers, the first and third Abd al-Rahmans. Abd al-Rahman III became emir at the age of 23 because his grandfather had killed his father and connived at the murder of his uncle. Brought up by his grandfather, and presumably living in some fear that he would share his father's fate, Abd al-Rahman might have been expected to disapprove of the custom. In fact he had his own son beheaded in the throne room in the presence of himself and his court officials. The nature of this bewildering civilization, a civilization which makes the Rome of the Borgias seem tame in comparison, is neatly illustrated by a remark of the Emir al-Hakam I. During an uprising which he was observing from the terrace of his palace, al-Hakam retired to his chamber to cover his head with oil and scent. On being asked how he could do this at such a desperate moment, he replied, 'Today I must prepare for death or victory, and if I die I want the head of al-Hakam to be distinguished from the heads of those who die with me.' Alas he did not die but lived to crucify 300 insurgents upside down and expel the population of the rebellious quarter to Africa.

There was one caliph whose wisdom was unstained by bloodletting. Al-Hakam II, whose father Abd al-Rahman III was the greatest of the Ummayad warriors, dutifully led his armies in defence of the state but took no pleasure in campaigning. 'Don't make wars unnecessarily,' he advised his son in a testimonial letter. 'Keep the peace, for your own well-being and that of your people. Never unsheathe your sword except against those who commit injustice. What pleasure is there in invading and destroying nations, in taking pillage and destruction to the ends of the earth? Don't let yourself be dazzled by vanity; let your justice always be like a tranquil lake.' Al-Hakam II was a poet and historian, patron of the university and the man who extended the great mosque towards the river and built the beautiful *mihrab*, decorated with mosaics and carved marble, in the south wall. His passions were calligraphy and book collecting, and he sent secret agents abroad not to assassinate his enemies but to search for rare volumes. His principal anxiety, justified as it turned out, was the fate of his library after his death. Al-Mansur, the powerful vizir who ruled during the reign of al-Hakam's feeble son Hisham, burnt the philosophical books to please the Muslim clergy of Córdoba; most of the other works were destroyed in the civil wars a few years later.

Córdoba experienced no gradual decline, no lingering sunset, no Ottoman limping into an alien age. Its downfall was sudden, devastating and self-inflicted. For most of Hisham's nominal reign the caliphate remained powerful, its armies strong enough to allow al-Mansur to batter the Christians of the north and to sack in turn Barcelona, León and Santiago de Compostela. But a few years later, at the beginning of the eleventh century, disputes between aspirants to the caliphate and antagonism between Cordobans and Berber soldiers led to civil war, a series of atrocities and a siege lasting two and a half years which resulted in the sack of Medina az-Zahra, the destruction of much of the city and the massacre of large numbers of citizens by the victorious Berbers. Córdoba was reduced to the size of the old city today, the outer quarters and suburbs razed, the gardens and orchards returning to a wilderness inhabited by wolves. Medina az-Zahra, the palatine city built by Abd al-Rahman III, was sacked by both sides and then burnt twice by the Berbers. After the Reconquest the ruins were used as a quarry by Christians, columns and stone slabs being removed to build the monastery of San Jerónimo in the hills behind. Over the centuries the palace became overgrown, hidden and forgotten so that no one knew what it had once been. An historian of the sixteenth century, who lived in the monastery overlooking the ruins, described the place as a Roman colony founded by Claudius Marcellus; not until the nineteenth century was it correctly identified as the site of Medina az-Zahra. Since then it has been excavated and the layout of palace and gardens – the mosque attached at an angle looking towards Mecca – can be appreciated. A few things such as the throne room have been restored, but of the rest there are only fragments: some delicate arches, the dense outlines of stone walls, a few exquisite examples of intricate decoration. The desolation remains. It needs only a bust of Abd al-Rahman and the inscription of Ozymandias to complete it.

Córdoba after the devastation recalls the worst days of imperial Rome. Eight caliphs struggled against each other for eighteen years before their office was finally abolished in 1031. Córdoba remained a Muslim city for another two centuries, but political power had gone, dispersed to Seville and the other petty kingdoms which emerged from the ruins of the caliphate. It would probably have fallen to the Christians soon after the loss of Toledo in 1085 if the Hispanic Muslims had not called in reinforcements from Berber tribes in north Africa. It was better to be a shepherd of camels, they argued, then a swineherd for the Christians. Two Berber groups, the Almoravids and later the Almohads, temporarily reunited the Moors and halted the Reconquest, but the Christian victory at Navas de Tolosa in 1212 opened the way for the seizure of western Andalusia. Córdoba fell in 1236 and its Muslim inhabitants left the city for ever.

A contemporary chronicler rejoiced that the city had been 'cleansed of all the filthiness of Muhammad', but one of the earliest effects of Christian rule was to make Córdoba a much dirtier place than it had been before. The Moors' sophisticated systems of water supply and sewage disposal fell into disrepair and the city became notoriously unhygienic. In other respects Córdoba changed little in the early centuries of Christian government. Mosques were transformed into churches and shops attached to the wall of the great mosque were removed, but the character of the place survived. In the sixteenth century attempts were made to change the city's urban structure by forbidding various oriental devices: in 1550, for example, the authorities ordered the demolition of *ajimeces* and projecting balconies. The Moors had been ignorant of architecture, claimed a historian of the time, and had destroyed the beauty of the city.

Churches and palaces were built in the sixteenth century and a number of streets widened, but the Moorish layout of the city remained largely unaffected. Small irregular squares emerged from gardens or demolished buildings, but only one square, the Plaza de la Corredera, was specifically planned; lined by arcades and three tiers of balconies, it was designed for bullfights and tournaments. Certain districts retained their functions from the

40

previous regime: the mosque became the cathedral, its surroundings the homes of clergy and officials, the artisans' quarter remained in the east of the city. The inns and brothels clustered around the Plaza del Potro ('Square of the Foal'), the haunt of soldiers, travellers, and writers such as Góngora, the great Cordoban poet who was also a priest and an addict of gambling, whoring and bullfighting. A plaque in the square announces with pride that 'the prince of Spanish geniuses, Miguel de Cervantes Saavedra, of Cordoban ancestry, mentions this site and district in the greatest novel of the world'.

The most drastic act carried out by the Christians was the construction of the new cathedral in the middle of the great mosque. The building had in fact become the cathedral immediately after the Reconquest but the architectural changes had been small, limited largely to the placing of chapels in the outer aisles. Three hundred years later, the cathedral chapter overcame the opposition of the city council and erected a tall cruciform church in the centre of the building; the Emperor Charles V, who had supported the scheme from afar, later repented and reproached the chapter for destroying 'what was unique in the world'. Destruction is too strong a description. From a distance outside, the cathedral seems like a brooding, dominating power, its towering bulk controlling the lower roofs of the mosque, but when you enter the building you are not at first aware of the intrusion beyond the forest of pillars and striped arches. Even when you reach the cathedral it does not seem quite real because it has no outside walls: it is like a gilded stage, ostentatious and a little vulgar and somehow artificial. Services on feast days are a curious sight. On the morning of the Immaculate Conception, half the populace seems to be waiting in the cathedral, a vast choir dressed in black ties is chanting, and distantly you can perceive the procession winding between the Muslim pillars, the bishop and his turquoise-cassocked priests preceded by four youths in jeans bearing the silver tabernacle of the Virgin.

The sixteenth century was Córdoba's only real period of growth between the tenth century and the twentieth. Its leather and its eau-de-toilette became European articles of fashion, highly esteemed in France. The population increased from about 28,000 inhabitants in 1530 to 48,000 in 1587, but epidemics subsequently reduced the number and at the end of the eighteenth century it was still smaller than it had been 200 years earlier. An observer travelling with Philip IV in 1624 described Córdoba as a city of 'noble inhabitants but poor and depopulated'. He was writing even before the mid-century plagues and the economic crisis which severely damaged the town's silk industry and its leather production. By the end of the seventeenth century almost the only healthy part of the economy was the trade in snow from the sierra which was prized as both a luxury and a remedy for certain illnesses.

National developments of the eighteenth and nineteenth centuries failed to stimulate the Cordoban economy. Newly exploited mines in the sierra were unable in the long run to compete with coal imports from England or the Asturias. Nor did the coming of the railway bring industry to the city. Paradoxically, it may even have encouraged investment in land by people who now had better opportunities to export agricultural produce. Part of the problem lay with the Cordoban ruling class, whose members were chiefly interested in enlarging their estates with disentailed church property. Cordoban society had always been very conservative, based on a nobility reluctant either to work or to share power with members of other classes. In their decline the hidalgo families became increasingly inward-looking, obsessed by the issue of *limpieza de sangre* ('clean' or non-Jewish blood) in which they could count on the support of a vicious local Inquisition. They had not the generosity nor the intellectual curiosity nor usually the mixed blood of the Sevillian nobility; they patronized no great painters and failed to support the foundation of a university. In the nineteenth century Richard Ford observed that they were always boasting they had the bluest blood since the Romans, while an earlier English traveller noticed how the leading families spent every evening together consuming chocolate and ice-cream. The short horizons, the lack of interest in the outside world, the expertise on local subjects to the detriment of most things beyond, is perhaps an Andalusian trait, possibly even a Spanish one; it was after all a Sevillian poet, Antonio Machado, who condemned Castile for despising what she did not know. But in Córdoba, say Spaniards from other cities, this attitude is taken beyond all limits. Its people, writes a Sevillian journalist, are

42

virtually illiterate, educating themselves not at school but in the bullring and the flamenco show.

In Córdoba, according to the Victorian traveller Augustus Hare, 'Spanish idleness reaches its climax'. As the inhabitants could 'live luxuriously on an orange, a piece of dried fish, and an air on the guitar,' they did not need to work. Hare's evidence may not be wholly reliable, because most of his judgements seem to have been anticipated a generation earlier by the French writer Théophile Gautier. Indeed the plagiarism is so extensive one wonders why Hare bothered to visit Córdoba at all. Just as Gautier met nobody in the streets 'but a few evil-looking beggars, pious women muffled in black veils, or majos', so Hare encountered 'only miserable beggars wrapped in their mantas . . . an occasional veiled lady gliding by to mass, or a majo . . . erect upon his tall mule'. While Gautier described Córdoba as 'a dead city' with 'a more African appearance than any other in Andalusia' and complained that the ubiquitous whitewash prevented him from distinguishing the age of the houses, Hare called it 'a city of the dead' with 'a more thoroughly African appearance than . . . any other town in Spain' and regretted the fact that 'every mark of antiquity is effaced by the coating of whitewash which clothes everything'.

Most nineteenth-century writers agreed with the Gautier/Hare standpoint, particularly the view that Córdoba was 'dead'. It was 'poor and servile' according to Ford, and 'dying of atrophy', but he did not blame this condition entirely on the inhabitants: 'the first blow was dealt by the barbarian Berbers, the last by the French [armies of Napoleon]'. George Borrow found it 'a mean, dark, gloomy place, full of narrow streets and alleys' – a remark that might have been made by almost any English traveller of the time about almost any Spanish town – in which 'the silence of death not only seemed to pervade the house, but the street in which it was situated'. Death also provided Edward Hutton with the imagery for his description at the beginning of this century. Córdoba was 'a dead city of the dead' impregnated by 'the empty odour of death', a place like 'some old dead city of Egypt, forgotten beside the Nile'. It was 'an image of desolation, tragic and lamentable. She is like a ruined sepulchre forgotten in the midst of the desert from which even the dead have stolen away.'

The city's houses were, as in Moorish times, better from inside than out, a fact which hurried travellers tramping along unpaved streets, allowed only rare glances at sunlit patios and cool interiors, may not have been able to appreciate. But their criticisms were substantially accurate, as the municipal authorities themselves recognized. Even today much of the old city retains a depressed and dilapidated air. In the area between the main square and the Avenida del Gran Capitán, among the boutiques and nightclubs and smart women in fur coats congregating outside the Gran Teatro, you could be in any city of the West. But in the rest of old Córdoba, in the silent squares and long white streets punctuated by ruined or demolished houses, you understand what the travellers meant, even if nowadays we are more tolerant of failures to modernize. You understand also the epithets of the poets, the 'silent Córdoba' of Manuel Machado, the 'remote and lonely' city of García Lorca. Down by the Guadalquivir you realize how Córdoba in its decadence has turned its back on the river. The bed is wide and shallow, dotted by abandoned water wheels and small islands of oleander and eucalyptus. No attempt has been made to exploit or embellish it. There is no promenade or even a pathway along its banks; nothing today impedes the surge of heavy lorries.

The Spanish journalist Azorín, visiting at the turn of the century, was one of the first people to appreciate the melancholy silence of Córdoba, the charm of its labyrinthine streets, the aroma of burning olive wood, the feelings of nostalgia and regret which the city inspired. There is a special charm in the dozens of small squares. Some unfortunately have become little more than picturesque car parks, but most have conserved their beauty and their essential simplicity. Perhaps the loveliest is the Plaza de Jerónimo Páez, at one time more accurately and more attractively called the Plaza de los Paraísos ('Square of Paradises'): bounded by two fine palaces and a line of ruined houses, it is crammed with cypresses, palms, a magnolia and orange trees. There is no vegetation, however, in the square of the Capuchins. It is a deserted and desolate place by day and by night, though there may be some animation if a bride comes in the evening to pose for her wedding photograph before the famous statue of *Christ of the Lanterns*. The martyred God nailed to a marble cross and surrounded by eight lanterns stands in the middle of a square austere and undecorated, lined by the stark white walls of a monastery. It is difficult to walk past without experiencing a sense of anguish.

Córdoba is still a melancholy place to explore at night, through uneven streets lit by black lanterns leaning out from whitewashed iron-grilled houses, streets which end in deserted squares dominated by a shuttered palace or the façade of an enormous church. These squares are usually presided over by the bust of an illustrious Cordoban, for the city is proud of its citizens, enthusiastically erecting statues or plaques in homage to this or that 'glory of Córdoba'. It is also quick to avenge external disparagement of its heroes. The city was outraged when the painter Julio Romero de Torres failed to gain the medal of honour from Madrid's National Exhibition of Fine Arts in 1910. On his return to Córdoba afterwards, the municipal band serenaded him, the Philharmonic Centre dedicated an evening of music to him and a huge banquet was held in his honour. Pupils of the School of Arts and Crafts even organized a strike to protest against the decision.

Greatest and most admired of the city's native sons is Seneca, the Roman Stoic philosopher and victim of Nero. It is rare to find a secular figure born 2,000 years ago who continues to have influence in the place of his birth. But Cordobans still identify with Seneca, referring to *senequista* behaviour and a *senequista* temperament. Beside the city's western wall stands a bust of Seneca and in the Salinas tavern nearby an inscription informs you that 'in the Almodóvar gate you will admire Seneca, and passing through it you will find in Pepote's bar another Seneca and a handful of good companions'. Indeed it has been suggested that there are two sides to the Cordoban character: the colourful Baroque spirit of the poet Góngora and his contemporaries contrasting with the quiet reflective nature of Seneca and the bullfighter Manolete.

It is always dangerous to talk about the 'look' of a people, especially at the end of the twentieth century when almost every city contains large numbers of immigrants. It would be reckless, for example, to proclaim a Catalan look in Barcelona when so much of its population comes from Murcia and Andalusia. Yet although the majority of Cordobans are indistinguishable from the inhabitants of Jaén or Málaga, the distinctive look of others, the pale, grave, unsmiling features of *senequista* citizens, crops up too often to be exceptional. You see these dignified, impassive expressions in the streets and restaurants, in the paintings of Julio Romero, in the tragic photographs of Manolete, killed at the age of 30 although looking far older, in the bullfighting museum. The Bar Mezquita, a small, wholly unpretentious place beside the great mosque, is run by a whole family of pallid, imperturbable faces, although in this case lack of expression may be encouraged by the job. Doña María has spent forty-three years preparing rations of her delicious speciality, sardines in vinegar, handing some four million saucers of them across her counter.

Like Seville and Salamanca, Córdoba is one of the traditional centres of bullfighting, producing some of the best bulls and the finest bullfighters. Andalusian matadors, like Andalusian flamenco dancers, have inherited a grace from their gypsy blood or Moorish ancestry which their counterparts in Castile cannot match. But Córdoba has brought its own dimension to the ritual. Not only have its greatest bullfighters – Lagartijo, Manolete, the picador Zurito – had typically sad Cordoban features, they have often fought in a restrained, peculiarly Cordoban style. José Bergamín, one of the most knowledgeable of bullfighting critics, even called it a *senequista* style. The show-off antics of El Cordobés, on the other hand, owed nothing whatever to the Cordoban tradition.

'Where is the artist', asked Azorín at the beginning of the century, 'who can portray the soul of this city? To do so he would have to express this profound harmony of things, this intimate interpenetration of shades, this serenity, this repose, this silence, this melancholy.' Cordobans think they found him shortly afterwards in the person of Julio Romero de Torres, the inevitable plaque on his house in the Plaza del Potro recording that he expressed the city's soul in his pictures. Perhaps it was true, in so far as a spirit or a soul can be expressed on canvas. Even outsiders like the Galician novelist Valle-Inclán endorsed the view, while one critic proclaimed that in Romero's portraits 'wanders the spirit of eternal Córdoba, the spirit of Seneca and the Talmud, the spirit of the Koran, of Góngora and of flamenco'.

In appearance and tastes Julio Romero was very Cordoban. He

had the usual rather dejected air and melancholy expression, and the usual passion for bullfighting and flamenco. He played the guitar, roamed the streets of his city singing flamenco songs with his friends, and once claimed he would rather have been the singer Juan Brava than Leonardo da Vinci. Córdoba and its people are present in most of his works but one enormous picture of seven distinct panels is dedicated to the spirit of the city portrayed through its most celebrated citizens. Unfortunately, Romero hated painting the male body, so the work, which he entitled *Poema de Córdoba*, consists of portraits of women with the heroes depicted as statues in the background. It is a striking composition, the women symbolizing the different sides of Córdoba: Baroque, Jewish, warlike, religious, bullfighting and Roman. Perhaps they owe something to the Pre-Raphaelites, but Romero's women could never have been painted by anyone else. With their large eyes and wistful faces, they represent the contradictory sides of every nature, perhaps more pronounced in Andalusia than elsewhere: voluptuousness and mysticism, love sacred and love profane, the simultaneous proclivity towards eroticism and religious fervour. There is even a sensuousness in Romero's *Virgin of the Lanterns* which forms part of a shrine affixed to the outside wall of the cathedral. But there is nothing profane about the message which accompanies it: 'If thou, sinner, wishes to convert thy sorrow into happiness, thou will not go by without praising Mary.'

In a speech in Buenos Aires made after Romero's death, Valle-Inclán declared that 'Córdoba, the city full of echoes, remote cadences of races and sacred civilizations, purifies and refines itself in the soul of this great artist . . . Stirring a long chain of atavistic resonance, the painter revives the bloom of Seneca's olive and the gold laurel crown on the imperial forehead of Trajan.' It is overblown, of course, as a comment on Romero or Córdoba. But as an unintended parody of the city's view of itself and its official artist, it is very accurate.

Rua del Villar, Santiago

THREE

Santiago de Compostela

Most cities owe their foundation to the advantages of their site. They are built on hills from which they can be defended or on coasts where they can harbour a fleet, they grow around military camps, they sprout in fertile country beside navigable rivers or in areas where minerals have been found. None of these circumstances, however, were considered for the foundation of Santiago de Compostela in the Celtic north-west corner of Spain. This magnificent town is a monument to credulity, erected because an ingenious churchman of the ninth century announced that a tomb discovered on the site contained the bones of an apostle who had never been within 2,000 miles of the place. Perhaps even the churchman would have been embarrassed by the success of his ploy. The city he launched with his announcement later became the second religious centre of Christendom and the primary goal of pilgrims for about 900 years. It was also the inspiration for some 130 towns in Latin America which are called Santiago.

According to legend, James the Great, the son of Zebedee, befriended some Iberian sailors in Palestine and travelled to Spain where he preached in Galicia, Zaragoza and various other places. To conform with evidence from the Acts of the Apostles, legend accepts that James returned to Palestine and was martyred there, but insists that subsequently his body was recovered by his disciples and shipped by them to Spain. The voyage, during which the sailors were inspired by 'the aroma of sanctity' of the saint's body, took only seven days, a feat, remarked Ford, 'which proves the miracle, since the modern Alexandria Steam Company can do nothing like it'. Various problems confronted the disciples on arrival at the Galician port of Iria Flavia. Imprisoned at first by a hostile queen, they later encountered a dragon which fortunately lay down on receiving the sign of the cross. A pair of wild bulls were similarly affected by the sign and became docile, allowing themselves to be harnessed to the cart carrying the saint's remains. The disciples then decided to let the bulls roam where they liked and to bury the body at the place where they halted.

About 800 years later, a hermit noticed a particularly bright star shining above the same spot and informed Theodemir, the bishop of nearby Iria. Theodemir hastened to the place and decided to investigate the floodlit field. Three graves were discovered there and for some reason – unfortunately the surviving documents dealing with the case come from two and a half centuries afterwards – one of them was pronounced to contain the remains of St James (Santiago). According to legend again, the place became known as 'the field of the star' (*campus stellae*), later corrupted to Compostela. According to modern historians, however, the site was a Christian burial place from the late Roman period and the name comes from a Latin verb 'to bury' (*componere*).

The Middle Ages were of course littered with incredible miracles attributed to various relics, phenomena which continue on a smaller scale today. But one can only be impressed by the sheer scale of the Santiago myth and the gullibility of the nations and epochs which accepted it. At the beginning of the eleventh century a French abbot claimed to have discovered the head of John the Baptist and invited several kings and bishops to view it. But the cult did not catch on, presumably because his contemporaries were suspicious. How had the head got to France, a monk from Angoulême inconveniently wanted to know; who had brought it, where had it come from, and above all how could one be sure it had belonged to John the Baptist? It is hard to understand why such scepticism was so entirely absent with regard to the tomb of St James.

Many legends contain a speck of truth, a distant seed which can be cultivated with exaggeration and fantasy. But with St James there is no speck at all. Almost a hundred years ago, a French scholar, Monsignor Duchesne, showed that there is no evidence from the six centuries after Christ's death which suggests the apostle ever came to Spain or that anyone believed he had done so. Recent historians have confirmed his findings. Indeed the paltry knowledge we have of the apostle's life after the Crucifixion suggests he lived and was buried in Palestine. It was not until the end of the seventh century that chroniclers were writing of St James preaching 'to the peoples of Spain and the western places, at the world's edge', although they denied that he was buried there. Not until after Theodemir's discovery, in fact, did any document suggest the apostle was interred in 'the uttermost region' of the Iberian peninsula.

Theodemir's discovery of the tomb, which took place between 813 and 842, did not make a great impact at the time. The Asturian kings, who controlled the north-western areas of Spain outside Moorish rule, merely helped him build a small church on 'the field of the star'. Some decades later their successor Alfonso III, who called himself 'the great', saw the political advantages of identifying the saint with his kingdom. He built a large basilica in the field, endowed it with generous grants of land and referred repeatedly to the apostle's assistance in the successes of his reign. From then on the saint was unstoppable, although there remained some confusion as to which St James was actually being venerated. While the Compostelan church maintained it was James the brother of John who had been buried in Galicia, the saint was frequently conflated with James the brother of Christ. In fact it was popularly believed in the region that the St James of Compostela was a twin brother of Jesus. The ecclesiastics of the shrine magnified the importance of the apostle, awarding him a role in the Transfiguration for which there is no evidence in the Gospels, but they did accept that Christ and their saint were not blood relations; not that it mattered, they argued, because it was 'more important to be the brother of the Lord in the spirit than in the flesh'.

In any case, neither of the saints of the New Testament had much in common with the St James who emerged as Spain's patron saint, Santiago Matamoros or St James 'the Moor-slayer'. Gibbon remarked on the 'stupendous metamorphosis' which transformed a Galilean fisherman into a crusading warrior, but few earlier commentators seem to have noticed the incongruity. A Spanish writer of the sixteenth century reflected that Christian saints had been allocated the duties of pagan gods, with the result that Mars had been superseded by St James and St George. But it was not an arbitrary allocation. In the twelfth century Spanish Christians saw the reconquest of the peninsula as more than an endemic struggle between natural enemies. It became what – in spite of later patriotic mythology – it had never been before, a national and religious crusade. Such a movement needed a warrior saint comparable to Muhammad, a saint who could be used as a war cry, a figure who could inspire a man like James Douglas, a Scottish soldier known to history as 'the Good Sir James' mainly because he fought the English, to crusade against the Spanish Moors and in his dying gesture throw the heart of Robert the Bruce at them. It was unfair to make the son of Zebedee 'patron and captain general' of Spain, but there have been even less suitable nominations. In the early nineteenth century the Cortes of Cádiz, the first liberal parliament of Spain, elevated St Teresa to the same position, while General Franco appointed Our Lady of the Fuencisla, the patron saint of Segovia, a field marshal for her role in the city's defence in 1936.

During the twelfth century St James was besieged by requests for assistance and showered with gratitude for the help he had been able to give. Alfonso VII attributed his capture of Coria and Baeza to a vision of the saint's hand grasping a sword beside him. In 1158 his son Ferdinand II called himself 'the standard-bearer' of the saint, and a few years later the military Order of Santiago was founded. Simultaneously, a certain amount of touching up was done to the apostle's past record. A Greek pilgrim, visiting Santiago at the time of the siege of Coimbra in 1064, apparently found it difficult to understand why people were invoking the military assistance of a saint who could not ride a horse and had never fought a battle. His perplexity was resolved by the appearance of St James himself in a dream. A description of the incident a few years later transformed the pilgrim into a bishop who orders his colleagues to call the apostle a fisherman rather than a horseman but repents on seeing St James appear on a white horse, wearing armour and promising to assist the king at Coimbra.

The most notorious non-event of St James's supernatural existence – the one upon which his Spanish glory ultimately rests

– is his appearance at the battle of Clavijo, an incident which some historians date between 822 and 859 although others doubt that it ever took place. Threatened with defeat by the Moors, runs the legend, the Asturian King Ramiro I besought the help of the apostle. The saint dutifully appeared, declaring that Christ had entrusted him with the defence of the true faith in Spain, and charged into battle on a white horse, slaying thousands of the infidel. As Ford lamented, the legend demonstrates a sad 'poverty of imagination', for it is plainly inspired by pagan myths, in particular the appearance of Castor and Pollux on white horses at the Roman victory of Lake Regillus. In gratitude for the victory at Clavijo, Ramiro I allegedly decreed that every part of Christian Spain must annually donate a certain amount of corn and wine, as well as a share in any booty captured from the Moors, to the church at Santiago. While it is not clear whether there was a battle of Clavijo and if so that Ramiro fought in it, what does appear certain is that the document recording his gratitude and his decree is a forgery crafted in the twelfth century by a canon of Santiago.

Bishop Theodemir seems to have been content to erect a small church over the tomb he had discovered, leaving it to a successor at the end of the ninth century, Bishop Sisnando, to begin building a town over what Americo Castro called this 'encampment of the spirit'. Working in conjunction with King Alfonso III, Sisnando erected a stone basilica and other buildings intended to welcome pilgrims and encourage the growth of a resident population. Threatened by Norman raids in the second half of the tenth century, another Bishop Sisnando fortified the growing town with a moat, a wall and towers. In the event, however, the decisive attack came a generation later from the south, a Moorish army under al-Mansur sacking the place and carrying off the church bells to be used as lamps in the mosque at Córdoba. Nothing remained undamaged, apparently, except the apostle's tomb: according to legend, al-Mansur found a very old priest guarding it and decided to leave him in peace.

The walls were rebuilt in the eleventh century and the town expanded both to the south and also to the north-east, along the road travelled by pilgrims at the end of their journey. Pilgrimages to Santiago became widely popular in the eleventh century when

Spain was referred to in northern Europe as 'Jakobsland'. But they had begun some time before. Pilgrims from the tenth century included a count and a bishop from France, and an Arabic poem praising al-Mansur's expedition in 997 refers to Santiago as a place of pilgrimage. The sheer volume of visitors in subsequent centuries was responsible for the town's expansion. Many pilgrims were poor and slept outside or in the cathedral where they smelt so bad that a huge censer, the *botafumeiro,* was installed and swung on ropes across the transept to fumigate the place. Others were wealthier and spent money on lodgings and footwear and even prostitutes, although at least one bishop tried to abolish this particular trade. Almost all would have wanted to take home a souvenir of their visit, a jet rosary or a piece of metalwork or at any rate a decorated scallop-shell, the emblem of St James.*

The pilgrimages encouraged the growth of the first middle class in northern Spain. Stalls, inns and artisans' workshops spread out along the new roads to the south of the town, particularly along the Rúa Villar and the Rúa Nova, streets which still exist today although since the seventeenth century the wooden houses have been replaced. This commercial community acquired the status of a Villa Burguensis or borough, later to become a municipality. But the *señorio* or lordship of the town remained in the hands of the bishop, a state of affairs which irritated the townspeople so much that they rebelled early in the twelfth century. The powerful Bishop Gelmírez was besieged together with Queen Urraca† in a belltower in the cathedral and only managed to escape after the intercession of an abbot.

The buildings which survive from that period, however, were

---

* Various legends connect St James and the shells. According to one, he used them for baptisms during his mission to the peninsula. Another claims that a drowning knight was saved off the Portuguese coast by the intercession of the apostle. As the boat returning the saint's body to Spain sailed by, the knight was rescued by a raft of shells and seaweed which brought him safely to the shore. Whatever else it may have achieved, the shell inspired a beautiful verse of Sir Walter Raleigh.

> Give me my scallop-shell of Quiet,
>   My Staff of Faith to walk upon,
> My scrip of Joy, immortal diet,
>   My bottle of salvation,
> My gown of Glory, Hope's true gage,
> And thus I'll take my pilgrimage.

the work not of the commercial class but of Gelmírez. Apart from the Romanesque cathedral, this indefatigable prelate built the bishop's palace, the cloister, a refectory for the canons, a hospital and several churches inside the city. He also put up a second ring of walls with seven gates which encompassed almost the whole of the old town as we know it, apart from the monastery of San Martín which was absorbed in the thirteenth century. By the early Middle Ages, therefore, the town's shape and size had been determined. For the next 600 years, until the middle of the nineteenth century, there was no expansion of Santiago's urban area.

The wealth and prestige gained from pilgrimages encouraged Santiago's pretensions as a great religious city. As its pre-eminence was threatened by competition from Toledo, reconquered by Christian forces in 1085, Bishop Gelmírez embarked on a programme designed to establish his see's independence of the primate and to build a position for Santiago from which it could challenge even Rome. Elected bishop in 1100, Gelmírez spent most of the next twenty years campaigning to raise the status of Compostela to an archbishopric. An early success was a papal bull permitting him to create cardinals who, like their Roman counterparts, were allowed to wear mitres on important feast days. The next stage was more difficult, requiring a good deal of canvassing, letter-writing and journeys to Rome and elsewhere to convince people he should be made an archbishop. It was unjust, he argued, that his church should be the only one in Christendom containing an apostle's tomb which lacked metropolitan status; surely, he continued, there was a case for transferring the archbishopric of Mérida, a city still in Muslim hands, to Santiago? This argument eventually prevailed. In 1120 Gelmírez was appointed not only archbishop but also papal legate for most of western Spain and Portugal.

The influence of Gelmírez on Santiago can still be seen in the churches and other buildings he constructed. The Romanesque

---

† Urraca was Queen of Castile and Leon. As the Christian Reconquest moved south, the titles of the monarchs changed. The kings of Asturias became kings of Asturias and Leon, then kings of Castile and Leon and finally kings of Castile. In the twelfth century the peninsula also had Christian kings of Navarre, Portugal and Aragon.

style came to Spain from France along the pilgrim route before spreading southwards to dominate the ecclesiastical architecture of such Castilian towns as Segovia. In Santiago Gelmírez built a number of delightful Romanesque churches, particularly Santa Susana standing on what is now the summit of the town's park, the Herradura. He also built much of the cathedral, although the east end dates from a generation earlier. The Portico de la Gloria, carved by Master Mateo after the death of Gelmírez, contains some of the finest Romanesque sculpture to be found anywhere.

The first great phase of building in Santiago was Romanesque; the second, separated by almost five centuries, was Baroque. Although the city contains several fine buildings from other epochs – notably the great Plateresque hospital and the eighteenth-century Rajoy Palace – Compostela is essentially a synthesis of the Romanesque and the Baroque. Surprisingly, against all the odds, it is a harmonious synthesis, both on the grand scale of the cathedral, where the vast twelfth-century church has an almost entirely Baroque casing, and at parish level where a simple Romanesque church can have a Baroque belltower without looking ridiculous.

As with the Romanesque, the Baroque works were erected by the Church, by a line of prelates who rivalled those of Toledo in their architectural enthusiasm. Santiago's nascent middle class failed to develop. Crippled by famine and disease during the later Middle Ages, the city and its surroundings remained under the control of the Church and the local nobility. Doubtless it was difficult for commercial enterprise to flourish in the shadow of such a powerful archbishopric, but perhaps there was also a failure of imagination, a failure to see that economic growth required more than the sale of scallop-shells and jet trinkets to pilgrims. In any case, by the early seventeenth century Santiago's commercial life had almost disappeared and a *rentier* society composed largely of clergy, lawyers and minor noblemen had taken its place.

In Compostela, as in Toledo at the end of the eighteenth century, the Church's building programme seemed immune to the economic tribulations of the period. Years of hunger and disease did not prevent the construction of great monasteries or the embellishment of the cathedral. 'My heart is pierced', wrote

Archbishop Monroy in 1710, 'by the sight of our city, the second and new Jerusalem, weighed down by the lamentations of Jeremiah; a population groaning for lack of bread, hungry and miserable, babies quivering on the shrivelled breasts of their mothers, little children asking for bread although no one can give it to them. It pains me greatly, I feel deep sympathy . . .'. There is no reason to doubt the archbishop's sentiments, although he does not seem to have let his sympathy interfere with his building ambitions. The great wealth of the Compostelan see was invested in architecture rather than famine relief.

The visitor to Santiago today naturally appreciates the single-mindedness of Monroy and his fellow prelates. The dome of the cathedral, the clock tower, the northern entrance (the Azabacher-ía) are all superb achievements of Baroque art, and the west side, the Obradoiro, with its soaring façade flanked by magnificent towers 230 feet high, is among the most wonderful things built in Spain. It dominates one of the great squares of Europe, the other sides consisting of a Romanesque college, a Plateresque hospital and an eighteenth-century palace which is now the town hall. In this enormous space, whose buildings might claim to represent the chief ingredients of civilization – religion, learning, medicine and justice – you feel you are, or should be, in the middle of a great city. And yet Santiago has never been a great city, and this square, so out of proportion with the rest of the town, has never really served as its centre. It has sometimes been compared with the marvellous squares of Venice and Nancy and other cities where the inhabitants have traditionally congregated in large open spaces, but the comparison can only be architectural. Santiago's plaza has no shops or cafés and very little movement. Apart from tourists and pilgrims and people who try to sell them things, it is often deserted, although at the far end by the town hall one sometimes sees the banners of demonstrating farmers and hears occasional speeches interspersed with folk music blared through a loudspeaker.

Santiago's aspirations to become a second Rome or a new Jerusalem were doomed. Both places it hoped to emulate had of course been major cities before acquiring a Christian connection, whereas the Galician town owed its existence to a single religious myth. So long as the myth persisted it could survive as a centre of pilgrimage, although its remoteness and lack of natural wealth ensured that it could never become a great city. The myth in fact lasted a surprisingly long time, long after the saint's role as 'Moor-slayer' had become redundant with the expulsion of the Moors. His influence, fortunately, could be directed against other non-believers. At Cuzco in Peru in 1535 thousands of Indians fled from a battlefield when he appeared on his white horse, and in Mexico during the same period the horse itself joined in the fighting by biting and kicking Aztecs. In 1639 and in 1663 St James is recorded as having returned to his original duties by helping outnumbered Spanish forces vanquish Moorish troops in Africa, but in 1688 he went east to release a Hungarian chaplain in the Duke of Bavaria's regiment from a Turkish prison. So numerous were the miracles performed by the apostle that a notary in Rocamadour was employed to register all those which could be attributed to him.

The pilgrimages, having enjoyed a good run for about 800 years, finally began to decline at the end of the seventeenth century. It seems that the pilgrims and the inhabitants of the town became increasingly disenchanted with each other: the Compostelans resented the idle vagrants who camped among them, while the pilgrims objected so vehemently to the thievery of their hosts that in 1681 Louis XIV of France forbade his subjects to visit Santiago. But by then there were doubts inside Spain about the truth of the legend and the value of having a crusading patron saint when there were no crusades left to be fought. Perhaps, people thought, it might be time for a change, especially as St James's patronage could not be said to have benefited the kingdom during the disastrous seventeenth century. Various challengers were soon proposed, including the Archangel St Michael, St Joseph who was nominated by Spain's Charles II, and St Gennaro, the patron saint of Naples, a city which was then a possession of the Spanish crown. So impressed was he by the liquefaction of St Gennaro's blood that the archbishop of Naples, seconded by the Spanish viceroy, lobbied the king on his behalf.

The most serious and persistent challenger, however, was the recently canonized St Teresa. Early in the seventeenth century the Carmelite monks petitioned the pope to appoint this mystical saint co-patron of Spain with St James. They were supported by the Cortes of Castile and by Philip IV and his chief minister, the Count-Duke of Olivares, who possessed St Teresa's heart set in diamonds,* and whose mother had recovered from a desperate illness after being visited by the saint in Salamanca. In 1627 Pope Urban VIII proclaimed St Teresa co-patron, but the outrage of St James's supporters was so great that two years later the proclamation was withdrawn. The most impassioned defender of St James was Quevedo, one of the greatest of Spanish poets, who declared that 'the holy Apostle, fighting personally and visibly, gave us victories and death to numberless enemies' which he managed to calculate at eleven million Moors killed in '4,700 open and decisive battles'. He added mysteriously, without revealing his sources, that 'Christ wished that only his cousin should be the patron'. Later in the century the Carmelites tried again but were once more rebuffed. The issue did not disappear, however, and during the Peninsular War the Cortes of Cádiz reinstated St Teresa as co-patron.

If Santiago and its saint declined in national importance from the seventeenth century, the following ages saw the challenge and defeat of the city's regional pre-eminence. The spirit of the Enlightenment brushed uneasily against Compostela, and the ideas of the nineteenth century found even less response. Intellectual decadence accompanied economic decline and the loss of political influence. The university, which had once been a centre for humanism, became largely a preserve of the clergy and the families of the nobility. It turned its back on European ideas, rejecting science and even suppressing its chair of mathematics because the subject was considered 'dangerous and useless'. Although the chair was reinstated at the end of the eighteenth century and various other reforms were put into effect, Santiago remained an intellectual backwater: it had no newspaper until the nineteenth century and the few books it published rarely dealt with non-religious subjects. A thousand years after the discovery of the apostle's tomb, the Church retained its stranglehold on the city.

In the nineteenth century Compostela suffered a number of

---

* General Franco used to keep St Teresa's mummified hand by his bedside and took it around with him when he travelled.

knocks at its economy and status which were only very partially offset by the benefits of the railway. The city had long had a reputation for lack of enterprise and an excessive reverence for tradition. For generations there had been virtually no innovations in agriculture, except for the introduction of maize, and the nobles were content to live frugally off their rents and from time to time to build a chapel or a new house. This way of life was evidently considered agreeable because the city's businessmen tried to copy it, preferring to invest their profits in rural property rather than in their businesses. Although this class tended to be politically liberal, it was easily outnumbered by the conservatives, and in the Carlist wars of the nineteenth century Santiago supported the losing side. One consequence of the town's pro-Carlism was the government's decision to make the liberal city of La Coruña capital of the province and transfer from Santiago the law courts and the captaincy-general. The loss of its lawyers and the military establishment was accompanied by the religious disentailments of the 1830s, which decimated the ecclesiastical community. Visiting the city a few years afterwards, Ford described the monasteries as now 'untenanted, rifled sepulchres going to ruin, and adding to the melancholy appearance of this melancholy town, on which the Levitical character is still deeply impressed . . .'.

This series of setbacks ensured that the town did not expand: indeed Santiago is one of the few cities in Spain which had the same number of inhabitants – in this case slightly over 20,000 – in the eighteenth century as it had in 1900. In our own century, however, the population has more than quadrupled, the economy transformed by the establishment of a livestock market and a few factories, the expansion of the university, and the building of the airport and the motorway to La Coruña. In recent years Santiago has even recovered some political influence, serving as the capital of the autonomous region of Galicia set up under the constitution of 1978.

Most of the new residents are housed in the modern suburbs to the south, a fairly horrific area of closely packed apartment blocks which Spaniards from other regions, ignoring similar development in their own cities, point to as an example of 'Galician bad taste'. The parliament building itself, in the dreary avenue named after Franco which descends to the station, is certainly an example of poor taste: the old palace has been vandalized in the name of modernism, its windows knocked out and replaced by single sheets of glass, its old iron railings removed and substituted by hideous triangular pieces of metal. But the passion for the modern is at its worst in the Galician countryside, where among ancient fields and abandoned cottages, bungalows and chalets of vaguely Swiss inspiration have disfigured the landscape. Yet the aversion felt by Galician peasant farmers for their old stone houses, beautiful though they seem to us, is understandable. Until recently rural buildings seldom had electricity and were shared by the farmer's family and his animals. Along the road from Santiago to La Coruña, wrote the future politician Manuel Azaña in 1918, the houses were like slaves' dwellings, with no hint of comfort, hygiene or well-being. This state of affairs barely improved until the 1960s when many Galicians went abroad to work in the factories of Germany and Switzerland and returned some years later with enough money to build themselves a new house on an inherited parcel of land. A man who had grown up in the same building as his father's cows was unlikely to wish to restore a house which reminded him of an impoverished childhood. He preferred to remember the wealth and comfort he had seen in Switzerland and to try to recreate them in his homeland.

Accusations of Galician bad taste are largely refuted by the fact that Santiago is the most perfectly preserved town of its size in Spain. There is no vulgarity in the austere Compostelan houses, those façades of granite with white window frames unadorned but for the closed balconies or miradors on the top floors. With traffic excluded from many of its streets, it is a good city for walkers unless it is raining – which it usually is. Yet even then there is the consolation of the arcaded *rúas* running south from the cathedral: you can walk all but twenty yards of the Rúa Villar along its covered colonnades. The *rúas*, which date from Gelmírez's time, are the secular heart of the city, places to meet or stroll or do business in, the site of small but elegant shops, streets that perform functions for which the main square was not designed; if the blue-uniformed municipal band decides to give a concert on a Sunday morning, it sprawls uncomfortably across

61

one of the *rúas*. The best clubs and cafés also inhabited these streets, and one club is still there, a dingy place with a certain shabby charm, full of red armchairs which have lost their antimacassars, its atmosphere heavy with stale tobacco smoke. It is usually empty but sometimes an old man sits by the window looking lugubriously into the street. On Sundays the staff arranges a row of old basket chairs in the *rúa* under the windows, but nobody sits in them.

Like Toledo, Santiago is a paradise for nightwalkers. In no other Spanish town can you imagine yourself wandering through a past era as you can if you stroll around Santiago at night. The streets and small squares behind the cathedral are deserted and you can walk across them and under the arches without hearing anything but your own footsteps and the light drizzle and the occasional sound of church bells. The silence of the Compostelan night is unlike that of any other Spanish city. Not even Toledo or Córdoba can match it.

Santiago is another rare phenomenon, a Spanish city in which you are always aware of the landscape which surrounds it. Only to the south of the town has the twentieth century obliterated the countryside. In the other three directions fields reach the site of the medieval walls, and later development, usually low and unobtrusive, merely lines the roads to other towns. The country almost reaches the main square, the survival of the orchards to the west of the town hall making the view from the Herradura one of the finest architectural sights in Spain. And the influence of the country can be sensed even inside the city, in the rustic smells of plants and wood fires, in the faces of the peasant women who come in every day with bundles of vegetables to sell, in the bracken sprouting from the walls or the pink and blue wild flowers growing out of the stone of the former Jesuit church.

The inhabitants of Santiago do not take their evening *paseo* in the town centre as other Spaniards do, but many of them go for a stroll in the Herradura (the 'horseshoe'), a beautiful park stretched over a wooded hill to the west of the city. The Alameda, the main walk laid out in the park in the nineteenth century, is divided into three alleys: along the left side walked the clergy, professors and old men, down the middle lane strolled the nobility, and the third path was used by everyone else. The walks are lined with roses, myrtle and blue hydrangeas, the slopes are dominated by hundreds of oak trees, and in each direction there are fine views. The most impressive is to the north-east where, beyond the orchards and low houses, rise the great buildings of the city – the monasteries, the hospital, the town hall and the cathedral – an incomparable skyline which has not changed since the eighteenth century. At the park's highest point is the beautiful Romanesque church of Santa Susana, a place that would be idyllic if a large orange tent housing dodgem cars had not been erected beside it. Even the noise of the toy cars and the screams of their occupants, however, are drowned by rock music pumped from the tent's loudspeakers to every part of the Herradura.

The rainfall in Santiago is three times higher than in London, a rate which deters tourists and seems to depress the spirits of the inhabitants. Some visiting poets, perhaps arriving in melancholic mood, have extolled the light drizzle which resembles a Scottish mist. Lorca evoked the Galician autumn when 'the rain falls slowly and silently on the sweet verdure of the land,' and the Chilean Neruda described the region as 'pure like the rain, salted for ever by its tears'. 'The Galician countryside has gates,' writes a contemporary poet, 'and the drops of rainwater are its keys'. But the rain is not usually a fresh drizzle and few other people have praised it: a poet of the eighteenth century complained that in Galicia every season was winter and every month December. In *La casa de la Troya*, a novel about Compostelan student life, Pérez Lugín claimed 'that it does not rain in Santiago as in the rest of the world. The rain there is a thing of oppression, of enmity, of obsession. A rain without respite, without truce, without hope of sun. It rains and rains and rains, one day and another and another. Who could ever count them? At times it falls lightly, a fine and persistent drizzle; at others it strikes the city with violent downpours, as if the heavens were collapsing on top of the pathetic town. And it never clears. The stones of the street and the ashlars of the façades harmonize with the situation and before the clouds open put on a blackish colour, the infallible sign which announces to the soaked Compostelans the arrival of the enemy. A mortal atmosphere of sadness invades the city.'

The Galician nationalist and historian, Ramón Otero Pedrayo, denied that his compatriots were sad and advised his readers to go to the Alameda to see how happy they were. Nevertheless, the Galicians do look sad – though perhaps less so when promenading along the Alameda – and they frequently admit that they are sad. You can see the sadness in the faces of people gloomily trudging around with umbrellas, you can hear it in the local folk music, in the mournful notes of pipes played on street corners. Perhaps there is even sadness in Galician gardens, dark places of camellias and mimosa, designed to be at their best in winter. Santiago is not a city of smiles or animation. Markets tend to be places of noise and movement, but in the attractive pseudo-Romanesque market of Compostela old women in black with weathered faces sit glumly beside baskets of green peppers and bundles of *grelos*, the dark bitter leaves used for making Galician broth.

This melancholia cannot of course be blamed entirely on the rain. The region's geography, history and agriculture have all contributed to those resigned expressions. Galician cooking is some of the best in Spain, perhaps surpassed only by the Basque, but Galician agriculture could not and cannot support its population. Whereas large estates or *latifundios* were part of the historic problem of Andalusia, the opposite prevailed here: millions of small-holdings or *minifundios* were the chief obstacle to agricultural improvement in Galicia and the north. The Galician had a reputation for hard work, dividing his time between scattered parcels of land, ploughing tiny fields while his wife, with a reputation for even harder work, toiled beside him or tended the family animals. But the land and the system of tenure seldom provided a living and so the Galician became the prototype Spanish emigrant, moving first to other provinces, then to South America and in more recent decades to other parts of Europe. In common with other Celtic regions, most people of Galician descent live outside their homeland.

It is thus perhaps not surprising that the Galicians feel neglected and looked down upon, resentful that the world seems to have passed them by. They are, in the words of the historian Sánchez Albornoz, 'a people on the defensive'. Wellington praised their courage and Dumas extolled their kindness and hospitality, comparing them favourably with the Castilian who was by contrast 'quarrelsome, contemptuous, inhospitable and proud' and worst of all unable 'to abide the French'. But the Galicians know they are not liked, particularly by other Spaniards who have traditionally derided them for their alleged stupidity, boorishness and lack of hygiene. The Castilians, notorious for their jokes at other regions' expense, have made the Galicians a special target, treating them rather like the French treat the Auvergnats and inventing sayings equally unfunny as *'ni homme ni femme, c'est un auvergnat!'*. Referring to the Portuguese, one Spanish writer sneered at them for trying to be English when they were nothing more than Galicians.

The people of Galicia are unlike other Spaniards, especially those south of the Cantabrian mountains. There is a humility and lack of self-confidence which is seldom found elsewhere. They are a phlegmatic people, using few words and gestures, and they seem to have neither the pride nor the passion of their compatriots in other regions. To southern Spaniards they are often incomprehensible: 'one never knows with Galicians' is a phrase you sometimes hear. They like neither affirmations nor blunt negatives, preferring to answer a question with a question of their own. Salvador Dalí believed that Franco could not be explained without understanding his phlegmatic Galician character, and one commentator attributed the dictator's success in governing for so long to his ability to avoid saying yes or no.

To refrain from giving an impression of monolithic melancholy, it should be pointed out that Galicia has provided a large number of political leaders, especially from the Right; that some of Spain's most humorous authors have come from the region; and that, according to those who have done the research, the most voluptuous of Spanish women are Galicians. Nevertheless, even the people themselves admit that their predominant characteristics are *morriña* and *saudade*, melancholy and homesickness. The Galicians' attachment to their land, even if they build horrible things on it, is intense, and their nostalgia when they have to leave it is correspondingly deep. This nostalgia was both shared and expressed by Rosalía de Castro who, according to Gerald Brenan, would have been regarded as the greatest woman poet of modern times had she written in Castilian instead of her native

65

*gallego.** Born in Santiago in 1837, her life might have been designed to produce the maximum amount of *morriña* and *saudade*: illegitimate daughter of a priest and a woman of good family, she was farmed out to a peasant woman, then adopted by her real mother, married to a semi-dwarf who was both unpleasant and unfaithful, forced to live most of her life in Castile which she hated, shunned by Santiago's 'good families' because of her birth, and finally killed by cancer before she was 50.

Many of Rosalía de Castro's most beautiful Galician lyrics were written when she was living in the yellow 'desert of Castile' and witnessing the maltreatment of Galician labourers. 'Galician poetry', she wrote, 'is all music and vagueness, all complaints and sighs and gentle smiles.' And so is her own. She writes of Santiago and Padrón where she grew up, of the light Galician rain, of moonlight on meadows and nightfall over mountains, of past gaiety and present sadness. Above all she writes of nostalgia and regret, the sorrow of the Galician, the pain of separation, the agony of the emigrant.

> ¡Padrón! . . ¡Padrón!
> Santa María . . . Lestrobe . . .
> ¡Adiós! ¡Adiós!

---

* *Gallego* is a language rather than a dialect and is accepted as such by the constitution. Alfonso Castelao, the prophet of Galician nationalism, described *gallego* as a 'son of Latin, brother of Castilian, and father of Portuguese'.

FOUR

Seville

'Sevillianism', declared the distinguished historian, Antonio Domínguez Ortiz, 'is a creation of the sixteenth century.' A colleague, Franciso Morales Padrón, has echoed the idea and taken it further, claiming that Seville and the Sevillians only found their true identity in that epoch. In the Middle Ages, the theory goes, the city was half Moorish and half Castilian. The population was Castilian in race and language, living in an environment created by Moors. Its literature too was Castilian in origin and its art a combination of Gothic and *mudéjar*. The culture was thus a hybrid but not yet a Sevillian synthesis. The true character, the fusion of the ascetic and the epicure, spirituality and sensuousness, Miguel Mañara and Don Juan Tenorio, is a product of the sixteenth and seventeenth centuries.

It is a beguiling theory which provokes questions about the vital or, as the Sevillians would say, *eternal* characteristics of a city. Can they be qualities that are tangible or sensed physically? Many people associate Paris with *Gitanes*, but Paris was obviously Paris long before that acrid whiff was invented. It is surely difficult to speak of a city's typical smell or typical noise when both of these changed at the time equine transport was made redundant by the internal combustion engine. Could Seville really have been Seville in the sixteenth century, before it had experienced so many of the things we now associate with the city, before the arrival of the gypsies, before flamenco dancing, before bullfights had come to resemble anything like the spectacle of today? Perhaps it could, but in that case would it not have been Seville before the Arabs brought the oranges which are now so ubiquitous that the city has more citrus trees than the largest plantation in Spain? Would it not have been Seville even if Carthage had defeated Rome and the elephant had become the normal means of transport?

Seville has several times changed its rulers, its religion and even the race of its inhabitants, yet something has been preserved, something more than mere tradition, transmitted through generations and from conquered people to their conquerors. Characteristics, however intangible they may be, survived conquests, revolutions and physical changes so that modern writers find the same qualities in Andalusia that their classical predecessors discovered 2,000 years ago. Pliny and Strabo described an ambience we recognize today. Byron extolled the beauty of the women of Cádiz in similar terms to Martial seventeen centuries before, despite the fact that there was no racial connection between the *gaditanas* of one era and the other. The Sicilian novelist Giuseppe di Lampedusa was accused unjustly of promoting a climatic interpretation of Sicilian history: in fact he merely claimed that climate was one determinant in the historical development of his island. Climate, allied to vegetation, atmosphere and tradition, has certainly been a determinant in Seville's history, seducing and absorbing its conquerors and turning them into Sevillians. Arabs, Almoravids and Almohads all came out of the desert as puritanical Muslims and all succumbed to an Andalusian existence in which wine was only one of the forbidden fruits that they enjoyed. They became both civilized and corrupted. The Almohads acquired the taste to build the Giralda, the exquisite minaret which still stands beside Seville's cathedral, but simultaneously they lost the power and perhaps also the will to defeat the Spanish Christians.

Seville's allure preoccupied St Teresa who denounced 'the abomination of sins' and 'the crimes against God' which took place there. But she understood the temptations, admiring the nuns who resisted them, and admitted that even she found it more difficult to pray in Seville than elsewhere. 'I did not recognize myself,' she wrote. 'The devils there have more hands with which to lead one into temptation.' Of the five great operas written about Seville, the principal themes of four of them are seduction and sexual infidelity.* But the city's attraction goes beyond its sensuality. It has appealed equally to men from the deserts of North Africa and from the tableland of Castile. For centuries it has enticed travellers from northern Europe who have invariably praised the city and ignored the defects which provoked their contempt in Córdoba and elsewhere. 'Ever since childhood,' wrote Laurie Lee, 'I'd imagined myself walking down a white dusty road through groves of orange trees to a city called Seville.' But the dream has not been confined to foreigners. Spanish emigrants who do not know the place experience nostalgia and a longing to visit it. Even for a family of Asturian origin returning after several generations in Mexico at the end of the nineteenth century, settling in Seville 'was like coming back to something which we instinctively knew belonged to us, but which we had not yet seen. The colours, the perfumes, the movements, the sounds – all seemed so natural; they were the missing link between us and our ancestors, that "something" which means so much and which we had unconsciously longed for.'

The Seville of the Almohads may not have been as great a city as Córdoba at its zenith, but its size was still impressive: the city did not outgrow the four miles of its Moorish walls until the second half of the nineteenth century. The Christian soldiers of Ferdinand III, who 400 years later became St Ferdinand, were astonished by what they found when they captured Seville in 1248. 'No place so wealthy or so beautifully adorned', wrote the king's chronicler, 'had ever been seen before, nor any so populous, or so powerful, or so filled with noble and marvellous sights.' Development in the nineteenth century destroyed much of the Moorish street plan, but in certain districts it still survives. The short Calle de las Siete Revueltas ('Street of the Seven Turns') retains its seven corners in the centre of the city. In his enter-

---

* Mozart's *The Marriage of Figaro* and *Don Giovanni*, Rossini's *The Barber of Seville* and Bizet's *Carmen*. The fifth, Beethoven's *Fidelio*, pursues the opposite theme. Its author, who found *Don Giovanni* deeply immoral, wrote an opera to exalt marital love although he was the only one of the four composers who never married. The Sevillian setting is in any case more or less arbitrary; Bouilly, the playwright, had based the play on an incident in the French Revolution but changed the location to sixteenth-century Spain to avoid problems with the censors. None of the composers, incidentally, had ever been to Seville and only *Don Giovanni* and *Carmen* make attempts, unsuccessful as they turned out, to create a Sevillian ambience. *The Marriage of Figaro*, composed by an Austrian from a play by a Frenchman and sung in Italian, portrays an eighteenth-century society which could have existed in almost any European country *except* Spain.

taining handbook Ford called nineteenth-century Seville 'a purely Moorish city' before contradicting himself on the following page to say 'more than half Seville is Moorish'. Apart from the Giralda, the Tower of Gold and a fragment of the Alcázar, little survives from the period of Moorish rule except for the remains of minarets which have been incorporated into church towers. But as in Toledo and Córdoba, Moorish architecture, the *mudéjar* style, continued to be used for several centuries after the Reconquest. *Ajimeces* and other projections were still built in the narrow alleys, and the *corral de vecinos* – small flats looking on to a central patio, their occupants sharing the well and other facilities – was adopted and extended through much of the city. Little was done to alter the urban structure. No squares or open spaces were created until the sixteenth century, and consequently there was nowhere within the walls to hold tournaments to celebrate the marriage of the eldest daughter of Ferdinand and Isabella in 1490.

The cities in this book have generally enjoyed one or two periods of particular importance or even pre-eminence in Spanish history. Sevillians, however, will claim that their city has been predominant for most of the last 2,000 years and that even when it had to cede the first place – temporarily to Córdoba, permanently to Madrid – it remained the second city until overtaken by Barcelona in the nineteenth century. (The fact that more recently it has been overtaken by Valencia, a city that was – and remains – incomparably less important in the cultural and political history of Spain, is understandably not mentioned.) But the period of its most undisputed supremacy, sustained and enriched by trade with America, was the sixteenth century. *'Qui non ha vista Sevilla non ha vista maravilla'* ('He who has not seen Seville has not seen a marvel') is emblazoned across the skies of sixteenth-century prints. The city, the most cosmopolitan in Europe, was known as 'the Spanish Athens' or even 'the Spanish Venice' for the quantity of its publications. To Fernando de Herrera it was not a city but a world, while to Lope de Vega and others it was a new Babylon. 'Great Babylon of Spain,' wrote Góngora, 'map of all the nations, where the Fleming finds his Ghent and the Englishman his London.' Perhaps the universalism of Seville is best expressed in Manuel Machado's much later lyric on the provincial capitals of Andalusia. To each city he gave one characteristic – the hidden

70

waters of Granada, the flamenco singing of Málaga, the salt-laden radiance of Cádiz – but to Seville he gave nothing because no adjective could sum it up. The last line of the verse is simply 'And Seville'.

The city's population rose dramatically from about 60,000 in 1530 to 150,000 at the beginning of the following century. Immigrants were lured there by the prospect of American silver which, according to the *pícaro* Guzmán de Alfarache, was as common in Seville as copper anywhere else. As a courtier of Philip II explained, the best piece of land in all the king's dominions was that area of Seville which encompassed the cathedral, the royal palace, the house of trade, the oil storehouse, the town hall, the merchants' exchange, the customs house and the royal tribunal. The centre of the city was the Plaza de San Francisco, across which the town hall and the Tribunal still face each other, although its convent and prison have disappeared. Built in the sixteenth century, it was the site of most of the city's spectacles including lengthy *autos da fe* conducted by the Inquisition and the burning of the victims afterwards. Although some smaller squares emerged during this period, the only other space of any size was the Alameda of Hercules, laid out by the Count of Barajas in 1574. Situated in the north of the city, it had previously been a disease-provoking swamp liable to flooding from the Guadalquivir. It was now planted with oranges, poplars and cypress trees and turned into a park. At one end two Roman pillars were erected to bear statues of Hercules, the legendary founder of the city, and Julius Caesar, the mythical constructor of its walls.

The increase in the population led to a building boom in the second half of the sixteenth century. About 2,500 houses were built between 1561 and 1588, principally in the parish of San Vicente and the district of Triana across the river. But very little planning accompanied the construction. Palaces, convents and artisans' houses arose beside each other on the haphazard streets of the Moorish city. There was no attempt to create an aristocratic quarter as the Parisians were preparing in the Marais and later built in the Faubourg St Germain. Great palaces surrounded by miserable slums were perhaps a typically Spanish phenomenon, and not only in Spain. They can still be found in foreign cities which spent long periods under Spanish rule such as Naples, Palermo and Mexico City.

The sixteenth-century houses are more imposing than their predecessors, with windows in the external walls and less bleak façades. But *mudéjar* architecture survived, in the large palaces as well as in lesser buildings. The great Casa de Pilatos, so named because of a fanciful idea that it was based on Pilate's house in Jerusalem, is a wonderful amalgam of Moorish, Gothic and Renaissance styles in which the *mudéjar* predominates. Moorish features also lingered on with the building of *adarves*, alleys with entrances which could be locked at night, and *corrales*; both systems increased nocturnal security and were favoured by ethnic minorities. Even in the nineteenth century architects and town planners were influenced by Moorish ideas of 700 years before: the concept of the *pasaje*, a double line of small houses facing each other across a narrow private lane, is a throwback to the closed alleys of Muslim Seville.

Another nineteenth-century throwback is the *casa de patio*, a Moorish tradition extended and updated for new middle-class houses built often on former monastic property after the disentailment. It is impossible to find a harsh word about the Sevillian patios. Even Borrow, more critical of the city than other travellers, was seduced by them, admitting that 'no situation can be conceived more delicious than to lie here in the shade, hearkening to the song of the birds and the voice of the fountain'. Life revolved, and often still revolves, around the patio, especially in summer when furniture is taken from the warm upper storey and put out in the courtyard and the cooler rooms that lead from it. In the patios, wrote Laurie Lee, 'the rippling of water replaced the coalfire of the north as a symbol of home and comfort'. Antonio Machado's famous autobiographical poem begins with the lines, 'My childhood is memories of a patio in Seville, and a bright yard with lemons turning ripe.'

Most houses of the sixteenth century had a brick-floored patio decorated with tiles and either a well or a fountain with a marble basin. Myrtle, jasmine and citrus trees produced a scented shade to combat the heat, but they were insufficient by themselves, and a canvas awning was usually drawn across the patio at roof level during the hottest hours. Many houses had more than one patio although none matched the thirteen courtyards of the beautiful Viana Palace in Córdoba. Seville's most magnificent example is the great central patio in the Casa de Pilatos. A vast Renaissance fountain stands in the middle of the paved courtyard lined with arcades of marble columns and blue tiles; above the arches are busts of Roman emperors and at the angles of the patio stand ancient statues from Italy. The absence of vegetation contrasts with the lushness of the outer patios, the lilies and box hedges, the figs and giant palms, the oranges, the lemons, the profusion of jasmine and plumbago and *dama de noche* climbing the walls.

Such places deserved to have cultured owners and they often did, although Cervantes reminds us in 'The Jealous Extremaduran' that the city had its share of well-born layabouts, or *señoritos* as their successors are called today. 'There is in Seville an idle pleasure-seeking class of people who are commonly called men about town, a sauntering, sprucely dressed, mellifluous race, always finding means to make themselves welcome at rich men's feasts.' Many aristocrats of the sixteenth and seventeenth centuries, however, were learned men with humanist interests. They held literary salons in their houses, encouraging writers to read their poems and discuss intellectual matters. Much of their wealth was consumed by the collecting of libraries and the patronage of art, a field in which they competed with convents and religious brotherhoods for the pictures of Murillo and his rivals. According to a Flemish Jesuit, the Count-Duke of Olivares had 'an uncontrollable urge to go on adding to [his library] every day' and patronized writers to such an extent that he was nicknamed 'Manlio' after the generous Roman patron M. Manlius Capitolinus. Perhaps the most civilized nobleman of all was Don Fernando Enriquez de Ribera, the third Duke of Alcalá, who maintained a magnificent library and an informal academy of poets, painters and intellectuals at his home in the Casa de Pilatos. Unfortunately he was not allowed to enjoy this life for long because his fortune and his talents were required in turn by Philip II, Philip III and Philip IV. Appointed viceroy of Catalonia, he subsequently became ambassador to Rome and then viceroy of Naples before dying during a diplomatic mission to Germany in 1637.

The culture of the city's élite does not appear to have permeated very deeply the rest of Sevillian society. No other city had such strong contrasts, of opulence and misery, of crime and charity, of sensuality and religious fervour. Gerald Brenan's observation on the Spaniards has a special application to Seville and Sevillians: 'As in their climate and scenery, the half-tones appear to be left out.' Great palaces and Baroque churches opened out on to unpaved, unlit and unhygienic streets which often had appropriately unattractive names such as Horno de las Brujas ('Witches' Oven'), Caño de los Locos ('Gutter of Lunatics'), Mendrugo (this could mean either 'Crumb' or 'Idiot' Street) and, more puzzlingly, Medio Culo ('Half-arse' Street). Seventeenth-century Seville had eight streets called Sucia ('Dirty' Street), an unnecessary appelation which did not imply that the rest were clean but merely that they may have been marginally less filthy. The chief health hazard was the practice of burying the dead in shallow graves within the walls, a custom which produced an appalling stench and vastly increased the risk of disease. The neighbours of the Hospital San Juan de Dios not unnaturally complained of the hospital's habit of burying its dead in the Plaza del Salvador which was used simultaneously as a vegetable market. 'Before the bodies have decomposed, they open the grave for others, they push aside the vegetable sellers' rubbish to dig the holes and they put it back on top afterwards. In winter those riding past sink into the pits and fall off their horses. When the graves are opened the stench is so bad that neither the people in the square nor even those inside the church can bear it.'

Seville was a city of *bullicio*, of noise and crowds and rumbustious movement. It was the home of priests, nobles and rich merchants, but it was also a city of crime and poverty, of a vast underworld of people on the margins of society, of vagabonds, pedlars and branded slaves, of card-players and prostitutes and a multitude of self-mutilating beggars. According to Cervantes, it was a city where you met adventurers at every street corner, and the tough, seedy atmosphere of his Seville was preserved until recently in Triana. The more noble and law-abiding side of this society was portrayed by Velázquez in his early pictures, his *bodegones* or eating scenes, in his water-seller, his old woman frying eggs, his kitchen maid with her pestle and mortar. The rougher side was depicted in the works of Cervantes, who knew a good deal about Sevillian low life, and Lope de Vega, who as a frequenter of taverns and gambling dens knew about this too, although he also wrote more optimistically about love and other things on the banks of the Guadalquivir. Lope was not Sevillian but his blend of sexual promiscuity, intense religious faith and great lyrical talent made him well suited to write about the place.

Seville was very much a city of the *pícaro*, the hungry and usually delinquent youth prepared to travel any road and commit most petty crimes in search of a living. Mateo Alemán, however, was the only picaresque novelist to come from Seville. Although he wrote the most influential novel in this genre, *Guzmán de Alfarache*, he made little money from his writing and was twice confined for debt in the Royal Prison of Seville; during his second incarceration one of his fellow inmates was Cervantes who is alleged to have been inspired to write *Don Quixote* while serving time.

Seville had the largest and best-organized criminal population of Spain, gangs of ruffians, thieves and murderers feeding off the country's wealthiest prey. Extortion was one of their commonest crimes: men who did not pay up might find a pair of horns nailed to their doors and be laughed at as cuckolds by the community. Another trick was to use women to seduce a victim and then to burst upon the couple and, in the guise of the outraged husband, force the 'seducer' to relinquish his purse. These thieves' fraternities formed a prototype mafia with their own territories and regulations, their distribution of loot and their bribery of officials. Monipodio, the 'mafioso' leader in Cervantes's 'Rinconete y Cortadillo', declares that a percentage of their winnings must go to the lawyer 'who defends us in court, the constable who tips us off, the executioner who shows us mercy' and 'the court clerk who ... sees to it that there is no crime that is not a misdemeanour and no misdemeanour that gets much punishment.' In true mafioso style a spurious sense of honour was sometimes grafted on to their behaviour. A stolen purse has to be returned, says Monipodio, because 'the constable who is asking about it is a friend and does us countless good turns every year'. The real Monipodios seem to have enjoyed the same kind of immunity from Church and state as their professional descendants in other places. They used to congregate in the Corral of the Orange Trees which, as it was within the cathedral precincts, could be used as a sanctuary. There they could eat and gamble and receive visitors, and at night they could go out and organize new crimes. Even if they were arrested and imprisoned, they seem to have had a fairly easy time of it. Four taverns, four restaurants and two shops apparently kept them supplied in prison, where they were still able to receive visitors and continue their gambling.

The centre of the underworld was the Compás del Arenal, the area of sleazy taverns and prostitutes' shacks which lay outside the walls between the Triana and Arenal gates. This was the site of the city's official brothel and housed only a small fraction of Seville's prostitutes. Its twenty shacks were owned by religious corporations and the municipality which leased them to various entrepreneurs: the tenant in Cervantes's day was the public executioner. Conditions of acceptance for the women were numerous, although the rules were amended from time to time. The girls had to prove that they were over 12 years of age, that they had already lost their virginity and that they were not called Mary. According to the regulations of 1620, women could not enter if they were married or if their parents came from Seville. They were not allowed to exercise their profession on religious festivals, and every eight days in summer (every fifteen in winter) they had to submit to a medical inspection in case they had caught 'the French disease', a rather odd description of syphilis as it was widely believed for a long time that the Spaniards brought it back from America. In 'Rinconete y Cortadillo' Cervantes describes two whores 'with painted faces, rouged lips, and bosoms whitened with ceruse. They wore serge half-mantles,' he adds, the prescribed headgear for prostitutes who were not allowed to wear hats or ordinary mantles. The half-mantles were supposed to be yellow (although the municipality abandoned this restriction when prostitutes insisted on wearing black) and had to be worn always in public except in church when the women were permitted to wear longer veils.

Various efforts were made to remind the prostitutes of their immorality and to deter them from pursuing their profession. On Sundays they were taken to Mass at a special chapel built by a wealthy woman anxious for their redemption. Other individuals, as well as religious institutions, tried to persuade them to abandon their trade, helping them to marry or enter a convent. Priests were allowed to enter brothels to upbraid the inmates and exhort them to repent, but not for any other purpose. The Archbishop Vaca de Castro organized a picket line outside the Compás, the official brothel, to dissuade potential clients from entering it. This policy was so successful that the brothel was temporarily closed, but its principal effect was to increase the number of prostitutes roaming the streets and, as they were not subjected to medical check-ups, thereby add to the health risk.

Many attempts were made to legislate against prostitution and other crime in Seville. Both the monarchy and the Church demanded the suppression of the Compás, and one bishop even suggested building a convent on its site. They were unsuccessful. So was the decree of 1623, which ordered the closure of any building in which 'women earn money with their bodies', because of the 'abominations and scandals' which took place inside them and because of 'fear of retribution from His Divine Majesty'. Negligence and corruption ensured the failure of this and similar legislation. As contemporary novelists pointed out, every level of Sevillian justice was open to bribery, from Cervantes' 'constable in charge of vagabonds' who according to Monipodio 'is a friend and never comes to do us harm', to the notary and judge who should be bribed, advised Mateo Alemán, by anyone who wanted a favourable verdict. There appears also to have been an official reluctance to allow energetic reformers to interfere with the customs of the city and the prerogatives of its authorities. Certainly the Count of Puñoenrostro, who tried to extinguish corruption at the end of the sixteenth century, encountered such opposition and lack of co-operation from officials that he resigned his post as chief administrator.

If Seville was a centre of crime and sin, it was also a city of charity and extraordinary religious enthusiasm. There is much truth in the remark of the French historian, Pierre Chaunu, that the seventeenth century in Seville was an endless search for God. The Church, wealthy, powerful, a source both of work and of charity, was unquestionably popular, and so was religion. The city's Baroque churches, the rich materials and bright colours of their decoration, their great flowing *retablos*, their ecstatic and tormented sculptures, appealed particularly to the Sevillians and encouraged a participation in religious life which was

77

wider and more intense than in any previous period.

One of the reasons why so much poverty existed in Seville is that beggars and destitute people migrated there because of its fame as a city of charity. Dozens of convents, guilds and religious confraternities competed in displays of philanthropic generosity: one confraternity was established specifically to distribute food to anyone found abandoned or famished in the streets. As the state played a negligible role in the provision of schools, hospitals or poor relief and could be expected to aid its citizens only during an epidemic or some other emergency, the benevolence of the Church and the religious institutions was crucial. The charity of individuals was also important and is symbolized in Seville by the seventeenth-century figure of Don Miguel Mañara. The legend of Mañara, representing the redemption of evil and the triumph of good, is more important to Seville than his real life. According to the story, Mañara was a shameless libertine who stumbled out of an orgy into a funeral cortège and inquired who had died. On being told that it was his own body inside, he decided to renounce his sinful existence and spend his life and his fortune on charitable works. Whatever the truth of the conversion (probably very little), Mañara certainly devoted the second part of his life to charity, in particular to building the great hospital of the Santa Caridad. He was an exemplary figure of the Counter-Reformation, a crusading rejectionist of the Lutheran view of justification by faith alone. In the chapel of his hospital he hung some of the finest of Murillo's religious paintings as well as two notoriously morbid pictures by Valdés Leal, the *Triumph of Death* and the *Finis Gloriae Mundi*, a work which Lorca believed was a quintessential expression of the Spanish preoccupation with mortality. In the chapterhouse, beneath Valdés Leal's portrait of the founder, a quotation encapsulates the harsh message of Mañara: 'This house will endure while people fear God and serve the poor of Jesus Christ, but it will perish as soon as greed and vanity enter its doors.'

The increase in religious feeling in the seventeenth century was highly visible, manifesting its growth in the rash of new Baroque churches, colleges and convents. The number of monasteries and convents almost doubled to forty-three and twenty-eight respectively, and the religious confraternities also increased, ignoring a demand of the Council of Castile that there should be a reduction in their number. Street names were frequently changed, their medieval appelations indicating features, functions or professions being replaced by saints' names. Another indication of the spirit of the century was the books published: the works Seville produced during this period included 1 on mathematics, 2 on geography, 14 on philosophy, 102 literary works, 254 on history and 428 on religious subjects.

The wealth of the Church, its capital assets consisting largely of urban property and its principal source of income being the tithe raised on cereals, was not greatly affected by the economic crisis of the early seventeenth century. According to one estimate, the Church owned 7,000 buildings in Seville, more than two-thirds of the entire city. Apart from providing for its charitable works and its own sustenance, the Church used much of its wealth to build and embellish new churches in a style which in Gerald Brenan's words 'has a power of stirring the emotions and putting the mind into a state of confused exaltation and astonishment . . .'. The impact of Spanish Baroque was described in similar terms by Roger Fry: 'By the very superfluity and confusion of so much gold and glitter, guessed at through the dim atmosphere, the mind is exalted and spell-bound. The spectator is not invited to look and understand, he is asked to be passive and receptive: he is reduced to a hypnoidal condition.' Even anticlerical northerners can find themselves mesmerized by the candles and the chanting and the gusts of incense, the gaze held and the mind compelled by the columns and sculptures of the great gold *retablos* swelling and spreading behind the high altar. The processional figures of Christ and the Virgin – with their agonized features and pathetic expressions – are the most expressive and tangible objects of Baroque sacred art.

Seville's religious painters attracted less popular and emotional reactions than its major sculptors such as Martínez Montañés and Juan de Mesa. The greatest of the city's artists, Velázquez, produced few religious works and spent most of his life in Madrid portraying Spanish society from beggars and drunk peasants to cardinals and the royal family. Seville's finest residential painters, Zurbarán and Murillo, were very different artists although both seem to have appealed equally to the French taste; at any rate,

Marshal Soult and his fellow generals stole dozens of their pictures during the Peninsular War and transported them to Paris. Zurbarán, who was Extremaduran by birth, had none of the exuberance or dramatic intensity of the Sevillian sculptors. He preferred to paint serene and contemplative saints rather than tormented faces in their martyrdom. Much of his work was done for white-habited religious orders such as the Capuchins, and his portraits of these grave, impressive figures – 'une symphonie en blanc majeur' as Paul Guinard called them – are haunting reflections of a humble and ascetic faith.

While Zurbarán appealed primarily to the stricter religious orders, Murillo's attraction was almost universal. In contrast with Zurbarán's simple immobile figures dressed in white or shadowy tones, Murillo used softer forms and brighter colours to create characters who were very much alive. His doe-eyed madonnas and engaging children have nothing mystical about them. He painted what people wanted to look at, using Sevillians as models for his saints and virgins. His favourite subject, perhaps because it was the one most in demand in seventeenth-century Seville, was the Immaculate Conception, which several of his predecessors, including Zurbarán, had also painted.

No other religious issue aroused a tenth of the passion as the belief that the Virgin Mary had been conceived without original sin, and the Day of the Virgin (8 December) is still a public holiday in Spain and one of the country's most important feast days. A distinguished Sevillian historian has described the commotion throughout the city caused by doubts about the Virgin's birth as 'the conceptionist explosion'. The furore began in the early years of the seventeenth century when a Dominican friar rashly declared in a sermon that the Virgin Mary had been 'conceived like you and me and Martin Luther'. The Jesuits turned their theologians against him, the poet Miguel Cid wrote verses to defend her purity, religious confraternities took the voto de sangre (blood vow), and the populace rioted, charging around the streets screaming 'Conceived without original sin!' The 'Marian War' was pursued with vengeful intolerance by the Virgin's supporters: jobs and pulpits were denied to those who did not vehemently uphold her divine conception. When the papal bull defending the conceptionist view arrived in Seville in 1617, the inhabitants surged on to the streets to celebrate with fireworks, bullfights and other entertainments. Similar celebrations took place in 1661, when the papacy authorized a special holiday in her honour, in 1700 when 8 December was made her day, in 1761 when she was proclaimed patron of Spain and the Indies (these festivities lasted a year and half) and in 1854 when the pope declared the Immaculate Conception to be a doctrine revealed by God, later to be counted as one of the rare occasions when the pontiff was claiming to speak infallibly.

Seville's period of religious and artistic glory coincided with the city's swift economic decline. Historians have long argued about the causes of this process. Seville suffered from epidemics and other natural disasters, from wars against England, France and Holland, from the silting up of the river, from the uncertainties and failures of the Atlantic trade. But it had also an inner weakness of its own, an inability to organize itself for the role it was expected to play. Like other great cities, it was an interloping, parasitical place, but its commerce was so much in the hands of foreigners that it was not even a successful parasite. In spite of its monopoly of American trade and the immense advantages this brought it, Seville failed to become either an industrial city or a financial centre in control of its own commerce.

Before 1500 the manufacture of soap was the only industrial activity in Seville with a scale of production above artisan level. Factories were later built to prepare tobacco (in which, as with soap, Seville had a monopoly) and esparto grass, but the city developed no industry to compare, for example, with the textiles of Segovia. Ceramics were an important product in Triana and silk manufacturing employed a large number of people until it was substantially destroyed by competition from Lyon and Milan. The city's most successful goods, however, were made on a small scale in artisans' workshops, which produced items of high quality such as ribbons, gold braid and carriage harness. Unfortunately the prosperity created by this sector of the economy was largely destroyed by the 'sumptuary laws' which Olivares introduced to prevent excessive spending on luxury articles. If citizens could be persuaded not to buy useless items such as brocade or starched ruffs, it was argued, the economy would somehow improve. All that happened, however, was that a lot of people went out of business: in 1648, for example, the population of Seville included 600 unemployed gilders and ribbon-makers. The effect of the legislation on Spanish sartorial fashion remains unclear, but according to Professor Elliott its only lasting bequest was the replacement of the absurd ruff by an uncomfortable cardboard collar called a *golilla*.

Seville had the opportunity, which it failed to take, of becoming the major producer of goods for the New World. It could have manufactured the cloths and fabrics for the Americas, yet curiously it preferred to import materials from other European cities which were merely loaded on to ships at Seville. According to lists of exports from the early seventeenth century, the only major Andalusian product sent to America was olive oil. The problem was not a shortage of skilled labour but the indolence and indifference of those who might have provided the investment. The weapons makers of the Calle Sierpes were capable of producing fine lances, swords and arquebuses, but they could not supply the needs of their own city let alone America. When Cádiz was sacked by Lord Essex in 1596, the Sevillian authorities suddenly realized that their town was completely undefended and could become the next target for the English. As the local small arms industry was so limited, however, a weapons order for 10,000 men had to be sent to Milan. Guns and gunpowder, on the other hand, were manufactured in Seville, although the processes seem to have been hazardous and the products unreliable. The quality of the guns was mediocre, apparently because the Venezuelan copper used was inferior to the Hungarian copper employed elsewhere, while the gunpowder factory in Los Remedios blew up from time to time, causing much damage and once breaking the stained-glass windows in the cathedral.

If Sevillians preferred to develop their city into an enormous market rather than an industrial centre, they should have provided adequate banks and commercial institutions. The Mint, which was the largest in the world, functioned slowly and incompetently. With little to do for much of the time, it was periodically swamped by vast quantities of silver arriving in the American treasure fleets which it was unable to cope with: in order to avoid excessive delays, it therefore minted coins of high denominations which could not be used in shops. The banks performed rather better, partly because they were mainly run by foreigners. Sevillians of the early seventeenth century attributed almost all the evils of the epoch to foreigners in their city, to merchants who imported foreign goods which undercut local products, to outside workers who saved their earnings for their return home, to bankers who appeared even to make the king their prisoner. It was no doubt very annoying that silver mined in the Spanish empire and sent to the greatest Spanish city should end up in the pockets of the Genoese or, even worse, the Dutch with whom the Spaniards were actually at war. But why were the Spanish bankers unable to compete with Genoa and Amsterdam? How did Philip II, the strongest monarch in Christendom, lose against the Genoese bankers when in 1575 he annulled the *asientos* or short-term loans which they had advanced him since 1560? Genoa at that time had lost its great commercial empire in the Black Sea, had neither fleet nor political power of its own, and was moreover in the middle of a violent revolution. Nevertheless it was victorious, forcing the king to retract in 1577 because he was unable to turn to an alternative banking system in Spain or its dominions. It was all very well blaming foreigners for ruining the Spanish economy, but it was less easy to explain why the most powerful Christian empire, with all its resources in America and Europe, should have succumbed so easily to foreign competition.

The traditional scapegoat has been the Andalusian aristocracy, for its alleged refusal to touch any form of industry or trade. No doubt the nobles shared the general Sevillian view that manual labour was degrading, and in some places participation could certainly be a handicap: when it was discovered that Don Pedro López de San Román had joined the military Order of Santiago without admitting he had once owned a wool shop in Seville, he was fined 2,000 ducats, his membership was suspended, and he was exiled to Ocaña. But if they showed less enthusiasm for commerce than did the nobles of Catalonia and the north, they did not share the usual contempt for trade of their counterparts in Castile. Nor did they guard their bloodlines like the hidalgos from the central plains of the *meseta*. As the playwright Ruiz de Alarcón noted, it would have been a miracle to find a Sevillian gentleman without merchants in his ancestry. Besides, it would have been an astonishing act of self-denial to maintain medieval attitudes to commerce at a time when so much silver was pouring into Seville. As two of the city's grandest families, the ducal houses of Medinaceli and Medina Sidonia, even owned sea ports,* they would have been peculiarly stiff-necked not to have traded from them.

Seville suffered less from the reluctance of its nobles to transform themselves into merchants than from the efforts of the men of commerce to become noblemen. The French historian Braudel used the term 'the betrayal of the bourgeoisie' to describe the late sixteenth-century tendency of the European middle classes to abandon trade in favour of investment in land and titles and government bonds. Although it is difficult to talk of a Sevillian bourgeoisie at this period, Braudel's is a reasonable description of a considerable body of businessmen who aspired to an aristocratic existence. As trade slumped and the fear of bankruptcy increased, they invested in safe and prestigious areas such as houses and estates, and bought titles and *hidalguías* from an impoverished Crown. There were Spanish bankers in Seville in the early years of the silver trade, but most of them went bankrupt after the middle of the sixteenth century. From then on the great commercial fortunes of the city were made by foreigners, in particular by the banking houses of Genoa, Florence and Augsburg.

In 1503 the Spanish Crown awarded Seville the monopoly of trade with America which it retained for almost two centuries. Nearly all ships had to cross the Atlantic from Seville, although they could call at Cádiz on the way, and all without exception had to disembark there a year later. These immensely complicated expeditions, which depended for their success on the timing of such things as the Bolivian rains and the hurricane season off Cuba, were regulated by the Casa de Contratación ('House of Trade') set up in Seville. On the whole, Atlantic commerce seems to have benefited the city more in the sixteenth century than later on. After 1610 the trade declined partly because of a reduction in the quantity of silver produced in Peru and partly because the colonists were reluctant to buy from Spain goods which they

---

* Puerto de Santa María in the Bay of Cádiz and Sanlúcar de Barrameda at the mouth of the Guadalquivir.

could now grow or manufacture in America. Sevillian merchants became demoralized, and even disenchanted with silver, especially as most of it ended up in the pockets of foreigners while the portion they were able to save for themselves was often confiscated by the Crown in exchange for government bonds of doubtful value. A good deal of the silver also disappeared illegally, unloaded at night from ships in the mouth of the Guadalquivir and stowed on board vessels waiting to take it to northern Europe. The House of Trade accused the Consulado (the association of merchants in Seville) of participating in the fraud but, as Professor Elliott points out, 'there was fraud and corruption at every level, from the Generals of the fleets to the merchants of the Consulado, and from the officials of the Casa de la Contratación to the Council of the Indies itself'.

Seville had seemed at the beginning of the sixteenth century the obvious place for the American trade monopoly. A major city at the heart of the richest agricultural region of the country, it was ideally positioned for the trade winds needed to take the fleets across the Atlantic. It stood, admittedly, quite far up a winding river and lacked Cádiz's excellent harbour, but it was neither as isolated nor as vulnerable as that port. The English raided Cádiz several times between 1587 and 1702, twice causing considerable havoc, and presumably would have carried out even more raids if the American silver had been stored there. By the beginning of the seventeenth century, however, the disadvantages of Seville were becoming apparent. To begin with, it lacked the skills and the access to deciduous forests needed to develop an impressive naval industry. Philip II tried to buy wood from Poland to build the Armada fleet, and a few years later he was so disgusted by the quality of the ships built in Seville that they were forbidden to take part in the American voyages. Although the prohibition did not last, Seville was never again able to compete with the Basque shipyards: of the thirty-one Spanish ships used in the Atlantic fleets at the beginning of the eighteenth century, twenty-six of them, several of 800 or 900 tons each, were built on the Basque coast, and only five small ones, none exceeding 113 tons, were constructed in Andalusia.

Seville could retain its monopoly without its own ships but not if its river became unnavigable. As vessels became larger, their entrances and exits at the mouth of the Guadalquivir became increasingly hazardous, and many foundered on the notorious sand-bar, formed mainly of silt, at Sanlúcar. Some captains left Seville without their cargoes which they then loaded, dangerously, in the open sea. Others preferred, at even greater risk, to chance the sand-bar. In 1625 an official from Jerez catalogued the gambles which had not come off. In one incident Don Luís de Córdova, who had been forced 'to postpone his departure from the river for two months because when there was enough water there was no wind, and when there was enough wind there was no water', subsequently set off only to be 'drowned with two thousand men who went to the bottom of the sea with seven galleons containing two millions worth of gold and silver and 150 bronze artillery pieces'. An even worse disaster took place in 1660 when almost the entire fleet of Roque Centeno was lost at the sand-bar. Various measures were proposed to improve the situation such as digging canals or widening the mouth of the river, but eventually it was decided that cargoes should be loaded and unloaded at Cádiz. The decision, reasonable and perhaps inevitable though it was, effectively ended Seville's period of greatness.

Various natural disasters, however, had done much to batter the city before the Consulado and the Casa de Contratación were moved to Cádiz. Fires and earthquakes were comparatively mild tribulations. Drought and flood were more common, often following each other so that months of hunger would be succeeded by incessant rains, as in 1683 when floods wrecked a third of the city's houses. Seville was inundated on seventeen occasions in the sixteenth century and almost as many times during the following fifty years. One of the worst incidents took place in January 1627 when the river waters poured through the gates and flooded the entire city. According to one chronicler, 3,000 houses were ruined.

Although floods caused the greatest amount of material damage, they did not compete with disease as a slayer of Seville's population. Bubonic plague attacked the city on six occasions during the first quarter of the sixteenth century and in 1507 it is recorded that 1,500 victims were buried in a single week in the parish of La Magdalena. Worse still was the effect of the plague of 1649, which killed almost half the population, leaving 65,000 survivors to inhabit a city which had changed its personality. According to Professor Chaunu, Seville was no longer Seville after 1649 but a city which had lost its spirit and movement and preserved only its name. It was no longer the city of Cervantes and Lope de Vega, no longer the colourful, rumbustious goal of the *pícaro*, no longer the open cosmopolitan city of adventurers eager to make their fortunes there or in the New World. It became a city turning in upon itself, a superstitious and demoralized place, the city of Murillo's beggars, the city of Valdés Leal and the macabre *memento mori* he left on the walls of the Santa Caridad.

Like the other cities in the first half of this book, Seville experienced long periods of decline in the eighteenth and nineteenth centuries. It became a duller and more provincial town, writes Professor Domínguez Ortiz, with 'neither great saints nor great sinners; both Don Juan and Mañara had disappeared from the scene'. In the eighteenth century the streets were condemned as unlit, dangerous, dirty (rubbish was collected once a month) and full of ruined houses. Few urban improvements were attempted even during the five-year residence of Philip V and his court, although many houses had to be rebuilt after the earthquake of 1755. The municipality of Seville, which was always parsimonious with its public works, still refused to build a bridge across the Guadalquivir. Although other cities had possessed stone bridges for hundreds of years, Seville had to make do with a bridge of boats linking it to Triana until the nineteenth century.

It was typical of Seville that in this age of inertia and decay it should build (with state funds) the tobacco factory, the largest building in Spain after the Escorial and perhaps the largest industrial structure in Europe at that time. This impressive and beautiful building, where 2,000 tobacco workers including 'Carmen' once worked, is now the university. Other major exceptions to eighteenth-century sloth are the magnificent bullring (where Carmen's lover was performing while she was being killed outside) and the restoration of the Alameda of Hercules in the north of the city. The Alameda has had a mercurial history. Drained and planted in the sixteenth century, it later degenerated into an evil-smelling wasteland full of stagnant pools of effluent from a nearby dyeing factory. Replanted in the eighteenth century and embellished with marble fountains and two more columns to match those supporting Julius Caesar and Hercules, it became a site for outdoor concerts in summer and the fashionable place for Sevillians to take their evening stroll. By the twentieth century it was on the way down again, although an Andalusian writer in the 1950s described its 'happy and colourful crowd hurrying by' and claimed it was 'one of the places where one can most accurately capture the tone of Sevillian life'. Nowadays it is an ill-kept place lined by buildings of shoddy concrete and surrounded by hopeless streets in which prostitutes sit waiting on wooden chairs, licking ice-creams in the sun.

The nineteenth century saw more radical changes to the city's appearance, notably the destruction of the old walls with the exception of the Macarena entrance in the north. Much of the development of the southern end of Seville was inspired by the presence of the Duke of Montpensier, son of the last king of France, and his wife, sister of the then queen of Spain, who went to live in the city in 1848. They restored the old nautical college of San Telmo for their residence and planted the gardens that later became the María Luisa park. Nearby, the authorities converted the Prado de San Sebastián into the site of the April *feria* or horse fair, and in the centre of the city they created Seville's only large square by knocking down the convent of San Francisco and constructing the Plaza Nueva. Nevertheless, there was no development on the scale of that taking place in Madrid or Barcelona, no vast extensions of geometrically arranged boulevards pulling the middle classes out of the old city. The population of Seville increased slowly, allowing most of the new inhabitants to be housed within the area of the medieval town.

Seville in its decadence retained characteristic features of its past. Misery and bad hygiene lived elbow to elbow with the elegance of earlier days. The period provides photographs of overcrowded *corrales*, dozens of women and barefoot children jostling around the communal wells, but it also gives us images of the country's most aristocratic society, of the Montpensiers and foreign royalty in San Telmo, of Queen Isabel's afternoon parties for the infantas in the gardens of the Alcázar, of the lines of fashionable carriages revolving slowly around the Paseo de las Delicias and the María Luisa park. Borrow was unfair to describe

the Sevillian upper classes as 'upon the whole the most
foolish of human beings, with a taste for nothing bu
amusements, foppery in dress, and ribald discourse'. I
was by any standards a leisured society, living off its re
the *latifundios*, huge estates which their owners seldo
and where they never lived. Gerald Brenan was h
probably justified in refusing to call this aristocracy 'feud
grounds that 'feudalism implies a sense of mutual obliga
has long been entirely lacking in Spain'.

Seville stays closer to its traditions, admirable and o
than most cities. Its calendar, that procession of feast
festivals that goes from Holy Week via the *feria* and the
Christmas, is sacred. The jukeboxes of its cafés play t
music by local groups such as Los Romeros de la Puel
than endless international rock. The children do not all c
go 'disco-dancing' but prefer to practise the beautifu
called *sevillanas*. Its citizens have perhaps an excessive
their city, convinced that it has no equal on earth. 'The l
gave you', sang one poet of Seville, 'was so strong and
that if I had given it to God, I would have gone to heav
pride, which is in many things justified, comes with
insularity, amounting almost to indifference to the outsi
which provoked Ortega's terrible judgement of Sev
'first-rate city with third-rate inhabitants'. The writer
Formica, who was brought up there in the 1920s and
town, more justly described the 'Sevillian sin' as a
curiosity for anything from outside which is not r
shooting, bulls or the countryside'. This insularity, how
be refreshingly unpretentious. Only an Andalusian p
write, as Manuel Machado did, that he would rather ha
good *banderillero* than a bad poet.

The virtues and defects of the Sevillian gentleman, a
species nowadays but still sometimes to be seen in a
suit, his hair smoothed back with old-fashioned oil c
under a felt hat, have been immortalized in a poem by M
brother Antonio.

> Don Guido has died,
> in his youth a gallant reveller

and something of a bullfighter;
in old age extremely devout.
They say he kept a harem,
this gentleman of Seville,
that he was a skilful rider
and an expert at chilling
manzanilla.
When his fortune dwindled,
it became his obsession
to ponder about settling down.
And he settled down
in so Spanish a way
by marrying a great heiress,
by touching up his coat of arms
and speaking of the traditions
of his house,
but staying silent about
loves and scandals.
A great pagan,
he became a member
of a holy confraternity;
and sallied forth on Holy Thursday
with a candle in his hand
– that roisterer! –
dressed as a Nazarene.
Today the bell tells us
that tomorrow they will take
good Don Guido to the cemetery.
Good Don Guido, you have already
gone, and for ever . . .
Someone will say: What did you leave?
I ask: What have you taken
to the world where you now are?
Your love for tassles
and silks and gold,
and the blood of the bulls
and the smoke of the altars?
Good Don Guido and your luggage,
Safe journey! . . .

90

Don Guido's degree of religious devotion is common today. If Seville no longer has the fervour of the seventeenth century, neither does it breed the anticlericalism of the Second Republic. Many churches still celebrate mass fifty times a week to sizeable congregations which do not consist solely of elderly widows. The men may be outnumbered, but they do not stand together at the back, chatting or wandering in and out of the west door. Nevertheless, it would be hard to exaggerate the social import- ance of religion in Seville. Even men who are agnostics retain a parochial, almost tribal loyalty to their confraternities. The whole city goes on to the streets in Holy Week to celebrate a festival which is partly Christian and partly pagan but in no sense an exhibition of self-conscious folklore. Hundreds of men proudly shoulder the immense weight of the *pasos* bearing Christ's effigies, thousands tramp in solemn procession after them wear- ing bizarre uniforms, and many non-participants put on their blazers and tie-pins to cheer them as they pass. The women dress up too: from Holy Thursday onwards the entire female popula- tion wear black mantillas and jostle each other in the streets to touch the *pasos* going by. This often delirious adulation – surely the most spectacular and blatant worship of graven images in Christendom – might almost be interpreted as a Sevillian act of defiance of those Reformation leaders who doubted the reality of Christ's Presence in the Eucharist. The Presence, the people are proclaiming, is not only in the communion but also in the images.

The city has over fifty confraternities with an average mem- bership of about 2,000. Even though some men are members of more than one, the number represents nearly half the adult male population of Seville. Membership of a confraternity may depend on a man's parish or his class or even his colour. The city's upper classes have traditionally gravitated towards the Jesús del Gran Poder and the Quinta Angustia, while the Cristo del Calvario is an ancient confraternity for mulattos and the Cristo de la Salud is for gypsies. The Esperanza Macarena has usually drawn its followers from the poor *barrios* of the north but its brotherhood has also included some of Spain's greatest bullfighters. Joselito was the *hermano mayor*, or 'elder brother' of this confraternity, although his great rival Belmonte belonged to the Esperanza de Triana.

Many confraternities were founded in the sixteenth century and conformed to the Council of Trent's decrees on the worship of images and the mortification of the flesh. The processions of the Tridentine period must have been lugubrious affairs, the brothers flagellating themselves through the city, but they became more cheerful and more popular in the following century. The abolition of the 'blood penitence' and the sculpting of the great effigies transformed the processions into the triumphant Baroque festivals which they remain today. The Virgin *'Dolorosas'* dressed in black originated in the sixteenth century; the far commoner images of Mary swamped by velvet, lace and gold brocade are of Baroque inspiration.

Sevillians sometimes admit that the Holy Week processions are the only things they can arrange efficiently. The organization is certainly a feat. The Virgin of the Macarena, for example, leaves her church at midnight and, after a thirteen-hour journey to the cathedral and back, returns the following afternoon at one o'clock precisely. During that time she, her miles of hooded brothers and her escort of young men dressed up in toy armour to represent Roman legionaries, will snake slowly through the city along a set route trying to avoid the large number of other processions also making their way to the cathedral. A piece of bad timing, for which a guilty confraternity will be fined, or an inopportune shower, can cause havoc.

Each confraternity normally has two *pasos* representing the agony of Christ and the suffering of the Virgin Mary. The first is usually a crucifixion although Christ is sometimes portrayed carrying the cross or with another figure, Simon of Cyrene for example, or the Roman centurion poised with his lance. For more than an hour before the beginning of each procession, the streets and squares around the church are thronged. People lean out of windows and balconies to obtain a view. Before the *pasos* appear, brothers of the confraternity, dressed as 'Nazarenes' in rather sinister-looking hoods and robes, pour out of the church. Depending on their affiliation, they wear black, white or coloured garments; some of them go barefoot bearing crosses, others carry candles. Eventually priests and officials of the confraternity appear, followed by the first *paso*, which is greeted by noisy applause. It comes juddering out of the door, borne by a number of sturdy and largely invisible *costaleros* whose movements are controlled by orders from a senior figure called a *capataz*. It is his duty to ensure that the *paso* does not hit the church door or collide with other obstacles during its trek around the city.

A band plays various marches during this performance, but once the *paso* is out in the open it stops and everyone is silent. A stout elderly man appears on a balcony and sings a *saeta*, a short ecstatic verse sung in the flamenco manner, and then the *paso* sets off towards the cathedral, stopping frequently to allow the *costaleros* a short rest and a drink. It is followed by many more Nazarenes and about half an hour later the process is repeated with the *paso* of the Virgin. She receives an even noisier reception when she appears, swaying slightly, bedecked with candles and orchids, the tips of her silver carriage lightly grazing the church doors. Sometimes she receives a special escort: at the church of San Vicente, for example, she is accompanied by a detachment from the Guardia Civil which regards her as its protector. In the square the Virgin will also be awarded a *saeta*, perhaps this time sung by a woman, who will exalt from another balcony 'this lighthouse of our lives'.

The contrasting sides of the Sevillian character are starkly on display during Holy Week, especially early on Good Friday when few people go to bed before nine in the morning. As the austerer confraternities pass by – the Silencio, the Gran Poder – the crowds seem cowed by the heavy incense, the funereal music, the interminable lines of black-gowned Nazarenes. But the silence gives way to shouts as the Macarena comes past, her beauty inspiring cries of '¡guapa! ¡guapa!', and to more cheering as her rival, the Esperanza de Triana, is carried by at dawn. The most revered images, representing opposing extremes, are the Macarena and the Jesús del Gran Poder. The figure of Christ, sculpted by Juan de Mesa, is housed in the church of the beautiful parish of San Lorenzo. Although protected by a sheet of glass, a small hole has been cut around the saviour's heel so that women may touch or kiss it while their husbands kneel and make the sign of the cross. The tragedy in the features is difficult to convey: the tortured brow, the agony in the eyes, the mouth opened by pain. No visual image could express more vividly the suffering of Christ's journey to Golgotha. 'The paradox of the Passion and

Calvary', as J. M. Pemán observed, '– defeat and victory; humility and power – is all there in this piece of powerful carving.'

The Macarena, radiant with jewels and a gold crown, is lauded all around the city for her beauty. But she too has a tragic face: those sculpted tears seem to have only just fallen from her heavy-lidded eyes. One year she was decked out in mourning for the death of her *hermano mayor*, Joselito, who was killed in the bullring at Talavera at the age of 25. She still wears the emeralds he gave her, and among her treasures she keeps relics of other bullfighters, Ignacio Sánchez Mejías who was fatally wounded at Manzanares, and Manolete who was killed in the obscure ring at Linares. In 1936 her church of San Gil by the Macarena gate was burned, but she was rescued by members of her confraternity and hidden away. After the Civil War a new church was built which now possesses both the Virgin and the tomb of Queipo de Llano, the general who captured Seville for Franco and then ordered a murderous repression of republican supporters in Andalusia.

The Macarena's appearance, her history and the sorrow she represents, do not arouse expressions of grief among Sevillians but feelings of joy and enthusiasm. Her return after her marathon journey in the early afternoon of Good Friday is cheered by ecstatic crowds and more cries of '¡guapa! ¡guapa!'. Doña Concha, an elderly grandmother who has a flat overlooking the church, invites her friends and family to a huge lunch to celebrate the Virgin's return. It would be difficult to find a more Sevillian gathering, for Doña Concha's grandsons include a footballer and a bullfighter, and her daughter is a retired flamenco dancer. After the Macarena is back inside her church, two more grandsons arrive in dusty Roman uniforms after their thirteen-hour tramp around Seville. The exploits of Doña Concha's family – bulls, goals, baptisms, weddings – have been recorded by camera and are displayed on the walls. But the principal photograph on each wall is a portrait of the Virgin wearing the emeralds of Joselito.

Foreigners who read about Holy Week in Seville or even visit the city at Easter without local friends, will probably be puzzled by the whole performance. What exactly is the point, they may wonder, of six days and six nights of so many similar processions, so many tortured Christs and resplendent Virgins, so much identical music, so many thousands of men treading ponderously through the city dressed like a cross between the Wizard of Oz and the Ku Klux Klan? And what do the young *costaleros* achieve, apart from sore backs and stiff necks, by taking these immensely heavy images from their churches to the cathedral and back again? If you go in the right circumstances, however, the monotony of the event dissolves, the processions become more than just a spectacle, and you begin to understand something of the city's character and composition. You start to differentiate between the various confraternities and the different *barrios* and then you begin to have an idea of the human geography of Seville. Above all you understand that you are seeing a people united not in the re-enaction of some piece of dead folklore but in the celebration of a ritual which in spite of its great age is still regarded as tremendously significant.

Outsiders may be equally puzzled by the next great event in the Sevillian calendar, the *feria*. It is perhaps typical of the city that it should be held after Holy Week rather than before, when the religious ceremonies might have acted as a penitential purgative after so much unabashed hedonism. The *feria* is a comparatively new festival, a horse fair celebrated for the first time in 1848 that rapidly became a vast social event, an excuse for thousands of people to dress up and see each other constantly for the best part of a week. It used to be held in the Prado de San Sebastián, where the Inquisition once burned people, but it outgrew the space and has recently been moved to a desolate area beyond the hideous suburb of Los Remedios on the other side of the river. On paper the *feria* seems rather ridiculous. You go there in the early afternoon, have lunch at about seven in the evening, dinner at two in the morning and go to bed at six. In between you parade up and down long lines of striped tents called *casetas* where you greet people you know and drink a lot of sherry with them. If you are lucky you may be invited to go for a drive in someone's carriage or lent a horse to ride, but you can only walk about on it because there is no place for a canter. After a few hours you get a bit bored and wonder what all the fuss is about, but then somehow Seville's sensuous magic begins to work. You feel drugged by the scents and the sherry and the smell of jasmine, by so much beauty and hospitality, and you start to make new friends and end up in unexpected places, at an impromptu flamenco concert sung in a *caseta* at four in the morning or in the patio of a beautiful house where people you have never met before have invited you to a party.

The *feria* and Holy Week are examples of unchanging traditions in a city which has suffered too many physical changes in the last thirty years. The population in 1900 was no larger than it had been in 1600 – slightly less than 150,000 – but in our century it has multiplied by at least four times. Until 1960 the urban structure remained largely unaltered. Immigrants from the province built themselves shanty-towns of *chabolas* which surrounded the city with a belt of misery. But the old town survived, dominated as ever by convents and noble palaces (Seville still has more convents than any other diocese in Spain). And amongst the great structures of the Church and the aristocracy, the *pícaro* would still have felt at home in the taverns, brothels and gambling dens of the city.

After 1959 the Franco regime practised liberal economic policies while remaining politically authoritarian. This combination had a disastrous effect on Spain's architectural heritage because speculators, who were often friends or relations of government ministers, could behave as they liked without fear of confrontation with pressure groups or democratically elected councillors. Laws that should have protected old buildings were inadequate and disregarded. Clandestine destruction went unpunished and nothing was done to prevent owners from letting their houses fall into such disrepair that they had to be demolished. A regime which justified its existence – and the Civil War it fought to establish itself – by reiterating the need for Spain to return to its past glory, thus actively collaborated in the destruction of much of its physical glory. During the last fifteen years of the dictator's life many of Seville's great palaces, most scandalously that of the Medina Sidonia family, were torn down to make way for spectacularly ugly development such as the Calle Imagen and the Plaza del Duque. And the devastation was not confined to certain areas but permitted to spread to any part of the city where it might be profitable. No attempt was made to preserve an ambience slowly built up over centuries. As a local pop group complained in a song in 1972, the new buildings could wreck a Sevillian square as violently as pistol shots at a plaster saint. The presence of white concrete cubes of flats beside ancient parish churches – San Isidoro, San Nicolás and San José were all victims of this mania – testifies to a philistinism unique in Seville's history.

José Hernández Díaz, a man of wide learning who during his long career was author of various books on Seville's artistic heritage, rector of the university and mayor of the city in the 1960s, published in 1936 *A Study of the Religious Buildings and Monuments of Seville Sacked and Destroyed by the Marxists*. As the journalist Antonio Burgos points out, it is a pity Hernández Díaz did not write a companion volume entitled *A Study of Religious Buildings Sacked and Destroyed by the Francoists* or a sequel with a similar title recording the recent activities of the city's socialist municipality, because even in the 1990s the councillors see little merit in convents and like to replace them with post-modernist buildings with a vaguely Sevillian flavour, buildings that are not as ugly as the glass and concrete structures of the 1960s but which are certainly out of place in the centre of the city. Burgos, who for years wrote a daily column in the *ABC* under the name Abel Infanzón, trying to alert Sevillians to these dangers, was too polite to suggest the most appropriate title for a book by Hernández Díaz: *A Study of Seville's Buildings Sacked and Destroyed by My Command When I Was Mayor of the City*.

Although the vandalism was usually carried out for profit, it was often sanctioned by officials such as Hernández Díaz who did not themselves stand to gain. They believed that 'progress' required the demolition of old houses, however attractive they might be, and their replacement by larger and more 'relevant' buildings. It was no use pointing out that Seville was surrounded by flat countryside where the new construction could take place; modernism must come to the centre, or the city would become a museum (as if Seville could ever become a museum). The monuments must be preserved, of course, or at any rate the important ones, the cathedral, the Alcázar and so on, but every-thing else was expendable. The arguments in favour of 'progress' were often ludicrous. It was asserted, for example, that old buildings should not be restored if they could be regarded as symbols of repression. The *corrales*, inhabited by many families sharing the courtyard and other services, were often squalid and overcrowded but no worse than modern shanty-towns and

97

certainly more personal than the friendless high-rise blocks of the suburbs. In any case they could have been modernized so that fewer families lived in them and each one possessed its own bathroom. Nevertheless, the 'progressives' believed that the restoration of the Corral del Conde, however beautiful it could be made with its wooden balconies overlooking the courtyard and fountain, would be 'obscene', like restoring a gas chamber or the stakes of the Inquisition. The municipality agreed with them and ordered its demolition.

The Corral del Conde was in fact saved, after a good deal of wrangling, by the young Duke of Segorbe, a member of the Medinaceli family. Over the years he has rescued large areas of old Seville, buying and restoring scores of semi-ruined buildings. The survival of so much of the old city owes shamefully little to official bodies and a great deal to individuals like Segorbe and Burgos and the historian Morales Padrón. They understood that every city is greater than the sum of its monuments and none more so than their own. Seville may have had the most valuable twenty acres of Philip II's dominions but it had a further thousand acres of medieval city as well. It has the most wonderful cathedral in Spain, the most beautiful royal residence, some of the finest noble palaces, yet its vital qualities are not here but in the bleached streets, the orange trees, the fountains of small squares, the flowers in tiled courtyards. Visitors to Seville may afterwards forget every church they have seen except the cathedral, but they will always remember the ambience. As Sacheverell Sitwell once wrote, 'there is no other town in Europe, save Venice, where every small alley is so typical of the whole city'.

Seville is still Seville in spite of the damage inflicted on its body. And its spirit survives unbeaten by the twentieth century. In this city, wrote Aubrey Bell, 'the most curmudgeonly pessimist will be seen smiling; the miser loosens his purse-strings'. Visitors will understand what V. S. Pritchett meant when he said that 'pleasure seems to walk with one like a person, when one is alone'. They may even experience Gerald Brenan's 'explosion of euphoria which expressed itself in the writing of a sheaf of poems'. And they will surely agree with the judgement of Théophile Gautier who observed 150 years ago that 'Seville lives entirely in the present; memory and hope are the pleasures of unhappy races, and Seville is happy; she plays, while her sister Córdoba appears to brood gravely, in solitude and silence [upon her] vanished splendours.'

Seville still lives in the present, spontaneous and irrepressible, refusing to make plans. Its spirit, captivating and almost tangible, is all around you, in the German shepherd dogs sunning themselves on narrow pavements, in the gypsy trumpeter of the Calle Feria, in the pots of geraniums decorating green balconies in a hundred different streets. It is in the street names themselves, those which express sorrow, 'Bitterness', the 'Lost Child', the 'Seven Pains of the Virgin', and those which celebrate life, the streets of 'Air', 'Water', 'Sun', 'Pepper'. It is in the women whitewashing the fronts of their houses before the Macarena passes by, and in the handicapped children who are taken in wheelchairs to view her in her church. It is in the quality of light, in the sun dappling the cobbles through branches of orange trees, in the sound of water dripping from a marble fountain, in the shops of the Calle Sierpes displaying rows of bright flamenco dresses for little girls to wear at the *feria*. Its inhabitants say Seville is eternal and, in spite of the efforts of philistines to prove otherwise, it is a justifiable claim.

At the Universidad Fray Luis de Leon, Salamanca

FIVE

Salamanca

In the later Middle Ages Salamanca belonged to that select group of cities whose other members were Oxford, Paris and Bologna. It was one of the great European universities and contained some superb architecture to reflect the fact. The city was known as *Roma la chica* ('Little Rome') and sometimes also as 'the Spanish Athens'. To Lope de Vega it was the 'well of knowledge', the 'miraculous fount' of wisdom which might justifiably despise the ancient Greek city. Even in 1812, with the university decayed and much of the town destroyed by Napoleon's armies, Salamanca could enchant some of Wellington's officers and lead them to make comparisons with Oxford.

The city has some of the finest Spanish architecture of every period from the twelfth to the eighteenth centuries. It has a magnificent Romanesque cathedral and a very fine Gothic one as well, a Plateresque university façade which is rivalled only in Alcalá de Henares, and Baroque buildings equalled only in Santiago. In addition it has the most beautiful square in the country, the Plaza Mayor. The golden local sandstone, which in Unamuno's words encloses the soul of the city, has inspired a good number of imaginative descriptions. To Edward Hutton it was 'the colour of a Gloire de Dijon [rose] just before it drops its first petal'. To the Belgian writer t'Serstevens, it changed colour to amber or mango and was thus impossible to paint. According to Unamuno, who was rector of the university at the beginning of this century, the stone is naturally soft and 'after quarrying can be cut like cheese with a knife'; with time and oxidization it acquires its 'warm colour of old gold'.

Many of Spain's cities preserved a certain continuity, of tradition, of culture, sometimes even of population, through the invasions of Romans, Visigoths, Arabs and Castilians. Salamanca preserved very little of its distant past because it was refounded and resettled after the Reconquest. At the beginning of the twelfth century Raymond of Burgundy, son-in-law of Alfonso VI, arrived with miscellaneous groups of settlers who included Franks, Portuguese, *mozárabes* and natives of the nearby town of Toro. A wall was built encompassing various hamlets and 260 acres of land, the largest urban space in Christian Spain at the time, although considerably smaller than Moorish Seville or Córdoba. Despite the arrival of the military orders in the thirteenth century, followed by the major religious communities, it was never, however, the most populous of Castilian cities.

Medieval Salamanca's main features were its Romanesque churches and the tower houses of the nobility. Few examples of either survived the great building periods which followed. Only a couple of towers, which once gave the town a skyline similar to San Gimignano's today, still exist, and only one of them had much military value; the delightful Gothic octagon, the Torre del Clavero, was largely decorative. Of the thirty-three parish churches from this era, only five remain, including the little church of Santo Tomás Cantuariense (St Thomas of Canterbury) across the street from the Baroque splendour of the Calatrava College. Its foundation only five years after Becket's murder and three years after his canonization is an indication of the unity and internationalism of Latin Christendom at the time.

Salamanca's great architectural age lasted more than 250 years, beginning with the Casa de las Conchas ('House of Shells') in the last years of the fifteenth century and ending with the completion of the Plaza Mayor in 1755. During that period dozens of churches, convents and colleges were erected in golden sandstone. In no city in the world, the French traveller Auguste-Emile Begin noted in the middle of the nineteenth century, had he seen such a density of fine monuments. But neither, he added, had he seen so many buildings unfinished or ruined, a rather uncharitable observation from a member of the commission entrusted with the publication of Napoleon's letters and therefore someone who should have been aware of the damage caused by Napoleonic troops in Salamanca.

The sixteenth-century Plateresque style, peculiarly Spanish and difficult to define, achieved some of its finest works in Salamanca, possibly because the soft sandstone is susceptible to intricate carving. 'Plateresque' means 'like silver work' and the name suggests the intensely detailed craftmanship employed on the façades of its buildings. Scholars describe the style as a fusion of Gothic, *mudéjar* and Italian Renaissance, but observers can instantly recognize Plateresque work without necessarily being able to identify its origins. It is entirely ornamental, unrelated to the structure or proportions of the buildings it decorates, and has no function except to please and impress. Sometimes it looks artificial, like elaborate stucco, but at its best it is both delicate and imposing. Several palaces and colleges in Salamanca have Plateresque façades yet none can compare with the entrance of the university. In this superb display of controlled exuberance, angels and demons compete with Venus, Hercules, the pope and his cardinals, contorted animals and much royal paraphernalia. Above the doors are stone portraits of Ferdinand and Isabella, and above them, flanked by the twin-headed eagle of the Habsburgs and the one-headed eagle of the Aragonese kings, are the arms of Charles V. Given the extent and variety of his royal blood, it is not surprising that this is a highly complicated escutcheon, accommodating the arms of Castile, Leon, Aragon, Navarre, Sicily, Naples and Granada quartered with those of Austria, Burgundy, the Tyrol, Brabant and Flanders.

Many buildings in Salamanca combine features of both Gothic and Plateresque to the confusion of local writers, who find it difficult to know how to categorize them, and to visitors who find a Plateresque palace in one guide-book described as Gothic in another. Two religious buildings combining these styles in the south-east of the city are the convent of Las Dueñas, which has one of the most beautiful cloisters in Spain, and the impressive monastery of San Esteban, final resting place of that scourge of the Calvinist Dutch, the third Duke of Alba. Another is the new cathedral, built in the sixteenth century because the chapter considered the old one to be 'very small and dark and low' and inappropriate for the imperial age. The second version, however, did not replace the first or, as in Santiago, encase it in a new shell. It was merely attached to the smaller and more interesting

Romanesque church, obscuring parts of it in the process, so that the city ended up with a double temple.

The Spaniards were still building Gothic cathedrals more than a hundred years after Brunelleschi had completed his Renaissance dome in Florence. The persistence of Gothic and Plateresque architecture in Salamanca delayed the appearance of the Baroque, although the later style in turn lingered on to trespass on decades which in other countries were devoted to neo-classicism. The process was not, however, repeated because the Spaniards never grew to like the severe classical forms admired in England and elsewhere in the eighteenth century. They had had their period of architectural austerity under Philip II, when Herrera built the Escorial and the town hall in Toledo, and it had not been popular. The Bourbon monarchs later patronized neo-classical architecture in Madrid, but examples of it in the provinces, such as the façade of Pamplona cathedral, are isolated. Salamanca itself possesses many Baroque buildings, including the Clerecía, the remarkable Jesuit church which took nearly 150 years to build and was only completed a few years before the Jesuits were expelled from Spain in 1767, but it has only one major neo-classical structure, the Anaya College opposite the cathedral, a building so Italianate that it seems quite out of place in the city.

The neo-classicists railed impotently at the triumphant Baroque architects. Jovellanos, who personified the Spanish Enlightenment, dismissed the altars of José Benito Churriguera as 'monsters conceived by poor taste and aborted by ignorance', a view later echoed by Ford who condemned the Salamanca architect as 'the heresiarch of bad taste . . . whose name is synonymous with absurdity in brick and mortar'. José Benito was one of three brothers who gave rise to the term 'Churrigueresque', a highly detailed and exuberant style subsequently so exaggerated by their followers that the word was later used as an insult to dismiss the more florid fancies of Spanish late Baroque. The brothers moved from Barcelona to Madrid and then to Salamanca where they worked on a large number of buildings including San Esteban, the Calatrava College and the new cathedral. Alberto, who was the youngest of the three, designed the Plaza Mayor on the site of the old market-place. Like the earlier squares of Valladolid and Madrid, it is a rectangular space designed to host spectacles surrounded by balconied houses with plenty of room for the spectators. The buildings are symmetrical and nearly identical except for the town hall, in the middle of the north side, which is taller and more ornately decorated than the rest.

The Plaza Mayor is the most lively and welcoming square in Spain. Its architecture, the colour of its stone, the animation at all times of day and for much of the night, give it a perennially warm feeling. The inhabitants of the city spend much of their lives in their square, especially in the evenings when the lanterns under the arches are lit and the golden colour of the stone becomes still more luminous. They walk round and round, through the arcades or out in the open, thousands of old and young, talking, gesticulating, greeting friends at the tables of outdoor cafés. When you hear the warm rumble of so many voices you understand why Unamuno called the Plaza Mayor the 'chief place of gossip and the main school of idleness in the city'. But he loved the square, frequented one of its cafés, the 'Novelty', and thought it superior to the Place des Vosges. 'What arcades!' he exclaimed on seeing the Parisian square. 'They are poorer, narrower, lower and more rustic than those of the Plaza Mayor in Salamanca.'

The medieval city had three distinct zones. The southern housed the cathedral and the university and the people who directed these institutions. The northern contained the homes of labourers and artisans, and the middle possessed the commercial centre and the palaces of Salamanca's seventy noble families. The town's aristocrats were great builders, and not only of their own dwellings. Many of the churches and colleges were built by leading clans such as the Monroy, the Maldonado and the Fonseca; sometimes noblemen also left instructions in their wills for monasteries to be erected on their property. Such charity was no doubt often designed to facilitate the journey of the donor's soul. Teresa Alfonso left enough money to feed 50 poor people for 40 days after her burial and to continue feeding 500 more on the thirtieth day of each subsequent month; but she also stipulated that 5,000 masses must be said for her in the course of the following four years. A member of the Monroy family went even further, insisting in his will that no less than 20,000 masses were to be said for his soul.

Salamanca owed its great prestige in Spain and abroad to the

105

university founded in 1218 by Alfonso IX. In 1254 it was enlarged by Alfonso X, 'the learned', who took a strong interest in the foundation and doubled the number of professors. Although not formally administered by the Church, the university had tight ecclesiastical links, especially with the archbishopric of Santiago, to whose diocese Salamanca had been joined in the twelfth century. A number of the city's early bishops and many of the university's first professors came from the chapter of Santiago. In spite of this connection, however, the university followed the path of Bologna rather than Paris, opting for canon and civil law in preference to theology. This emphasis on an administrative rather than a philosophical education was a characteristic of Salamanca for much of its history.

For the first 200 years of its existence the university had no public buildings of its own and used the cathedral precincts for its activities. Even after the building of its main schools (Escuelas Mayores) in the fifteenth century, certain customs were retained out of respect for tradition. Until the nineteenth century exams were held in the Santa Bárbara chapel and degrees were awarded in a side aisle of the new cathedral. The classrooms, arranged around the patio of the Escuelas Mayores, were built at the end of the fifteenth century and have changed little since then: the room in which the poet and scholar Fray Luis de León was arrested by the Inquisition in 1572 – and to which he is supposed to have returned four years later to complete his interrupted lecture – retains its rows of bleak and uncomfortable benches.

Salamanca had four of Spain's six prestigious *colegios mayores* (the others were in Alcalá and Valladolid). Founded between 1401 and 1521, they provided many of the civil servants for the increasingly powerful Castilian state. In the course of the fifteenth and sixteenth centuries, the university also gained twenty-five lesser colleges and could boast a total of seventy professorial chairs. The student population also increased, the number of matriculations doubling from 2,500 in 1500 to 5,000 by 1546.

We know a fair amount about university life at this time from the memoirs and other documents of students. At the most privileged level was Olivares, who went to Salamanca at the age of 14 with a retinue of nineteen servants including a tutor, four footmen and eight pages. The father of the future statesman insisted that his son should attend mass every day, receive communion on feast days and give a tenth of his expenditure to charity. He was to take a degree in canon and civil law, improve his Latin and divide most of the day between attending lectures and studying his notes. He was allowed to talk to his lecturers for a short time in the cloisters but had to avoid chatting with idle students. His recreations consisted of croquet or ninepins before lunch and a little reading afterwards. Whether or not Olivares obeyed these rules, he retained, as his biographer Professor Elliott points out, a passion for books and a nostalgic affection for Salamanca. Elected rector as a student in 1603, he recalled the incident forty-two years later on his death-bed, and his last words were 'When I was rector, when I was rector!'

'Get along, and don't start arguing with me,' a graduate of the university tells Don Quixote's housekeeper. 'You know that I am a Bachelor of Salamanca, and there is no better bacheloring than that.' Real students were no doubt equally proud of their university and its academic distinction, but we know less about their work than about various extra-curricular activities. From the beginning there was a good deal of violence, and Alfonso X was forced to instruct the bishop to imprison rioting students or expel them from the city. Confrontations between the town's inhabitants and students of the university were frequent and led to serious casualties: forty-six people were killed in brawls during the first nine months of 1640.

Salamanca was famous for its taverns, a reputation it justly preserves today. The town maintains an incredible density of bars, many short streets containing eight or nine of these establishments which always seem to be full. In the 1980s, according to municipal statistics, this town of 167,000 inhabitants possessed over 700 bars and cafés. But if medieval drinking traditions have continued unbroken to the present day, the students' gambling habits appear to have been curtailed. Card-playing was banned at the university but few people seem to have observed the regulation. In his picaresque novel *El donado hablador* Jerónimo de Alcalá satirizes Salamanca's craze for gambling in a scene in which two competitors for a university chair each appeal for the students' votes. The first proclaims his learning and suitability for the post and points out that his opponent is a man academically inferior

107

who has wasted his time and talents in gambling. In his reply the second competitor admits that his rival is intelligent and virtuous and confesses that he does indeed know how to gamble. 'Therefore I beg you', he tells the students, 'that those who do not know how to gamble do not vote for me, while those who do know favour me with their choice.' Needless to say, the second candidate wins the election without a single vote cast for his opponent.

The students' fighting, drinking and gambling were not of course unique to Salamanca. Nor was their whoring, about which much can be learnt, including the names and prices of individual prostitutes, from the diaries of an Italian student called Girolamo da Sommaia. We also learn that a good many of these prostitutes were married with complaisant husbands, although at the same time there was a lucrative market for young girls. In 'La tia fingida' ('The Bogus Aunt'), a story which may have been written by Cervantes, the 'aunt' travels to Salamanca confident that she can sell her 'niece's' virginity for the fourth time. It seems that in this city prostitution was not a trade which carried much of a stigma, although it is doubtful if many people reacted like the father of a later age who, when told how his daughter earned her living, said, 'Ah, prostitute! What a relief! I thought you said Protestant.' But a line had to be drawn somewhere, and in Salamanca it was drawn at Lent. Forty days before Easter all the prostitutes in the city were rounded up and rowed across to the opposite bank of the River Tormes. There they had to live until Easter Monday when a flotilla of boats manned by hordes of drunken students set out to bring them back again. The day, known as the *Lunes de las Aguas* ('Water Monday'), became one of the great bacchanalian feasts in the Salamanca calendar.

By the early sixteenth century Salamanca was the centre of humanist teaching in Spain and the foremost printer of books. In 1535, it is said, there were fifty-two printing houses and eighty-four bookshops. The university also had a magnificent library guarded by a notice threatening to excommunicate anyone who lost or damaged its books. The influence of the Renaissance could be felt in Salamanca earlier than in other Spanish cities. The first chair of Greek in the country was established in 1480, and by that date several Italians were teaching at the university. Salamanca could also claim to have founded Spanish political thought. In the sixteenth century Spain had to contend with moral and political problems which no other country, except possibly Portugal, was yet troubled by. The question of empire, the role of Christian missionaries, the problems of domination and slavery, were all discussed in Salamanca, particularly in the teaching of Francisco de Vitoria. It was Dominicans from Salamanca, apparently, who first objected to the brutal treatment of American Indians.

Salamanca received eulogies even from men who were not its students. An Italian humanist called the city 'mother of all virtues and all teaching' while Jerónimo de Alcalá, who had studied at Valencia, described it as 'mother of all the geniuses of the world and princess of every science'. Lope de Vega also extolled the city and was much influenced by it, describing himself in one poem as 'a student of love by its riverside rather than at its celebrated university'. Salamanca's influence reached beyond Spain to Europe, where several of its professors played important roles in the Council of Trent and, more extensively, in America. In 1551 Charles V agreed to the request of Peruvian envoys that he should found a university in Lima with the same privileges as those enjoyed in Salamanca. A few months later a university in Mexico was founded along the same lines, followed later in the century by similar establishments in Bolivia, the Dominican Republic and Ecuador. Even more universities, affiliated to Salamanca and heavily influenced by its graduates, were set up in Latin America during the following 200 years. By the beginning of the nineteenth century they had reached the astonishing total of thirty-eight.

At the height of its prestige Salamanca was a tolerant university. In spite of its imprisonment of Fray Luis de León, the Inquisition was weak and the city never witnessed a single *auto da fe*. The theories of Copernicus, rejected by the Church and banned in European universities such as Paris and Tübingen, could be studied at Salamanca. But the university became less tolerant towards the end of the sixteenth century and less open to foreign ideas. Moreover, its function began to change, the educational emphasis on humanist teaching diminished and the institution reverted to what its founder Alfonso IX had intended it to be, a school for administrators and bureaucrats. All other subjects declined in competition with law, because a law degree was regarded as a passport to administrative and judicial posts in Spain and America. According to Dr Kamen's statistics, nearly three-quarters of Salamanca's students in 1595 were studying civil or canon law. The 35 per cent who had studied Latin in 1555 had declined to 9 per cent, the students of Greek and Hebrew had disappeared altogether and the chair of mathematics was often vacant.

More professorial chairs were created in the seventeenth and eighteenth centuries, but their occupants were widely acknowledged to be lazier and less able than their predecessors. Simultaneously, the students became fewer and more insubordinate. Towards the end of the eighteenth century a light reformist breeze flickered across the university, bringing with it some French ideas and influencing a few of the students who later became politicians in the Cortes of Cádiz. But the institution itself was unaffected: resistance to change now seemed to be its principal preoccupation. When Philip V's government suggested the possibility of establishing a new chair of mathematics, the university opposed the idea, one senior member declaring that the subject was useless and its textbooks the work of the devil. Later in the century, Charles III's ministers tried to introduce various reforms but the university reacted so strongly against them that some of its colleges were closed down for their obduracy.

Lower educational standards were well exemplified by the decline of Latin. Gerald Brenan repeats the story of the eighteenth-century Cardinal Borja who, when someone spoke to him in Latin, replied that he did not understand French. The cardinal's inability even to read Latin was witnessed by the Duke of St Simon at the marriage of the Prince of Asturias and Mademoiselle de Montpensier. 'The worthy prelate could not manage it at all; he read out loud, and all wrong: the almoners corrected his mistakes, he scolded them and began afresh; again they had to set him right till at last he became really angry and shook them by their surplices . . .'. The following day the cardinal had similar problems saying Mass, and a few weeks later St Simon observed him making a hash of the baptism of the Infante Don Felipe. At this ceremony he insulted not only the almoners but also two bishops who tried to help him.

Norberto Caimo, an Italian friar who visited Salamanca in 1755, was horrified by the Latin spoken there. After hearing a couple of doctoral dissertations, one of them discussing the possibility that Nebuchadnezzar had been turned into an animal, he concluded that the Latin was 'the most barbarous, the most detestable and the most stupid that one could ever hear': it was 'an extraordinary mixture of Spanish and Arabic words Latinized and muddled together'. If they spoke Latin like that in Salamanca, he wondered, what must it be like in places where there was no university? According to Caimo, the problem stemmed from the Spaniards' decision to abandon the study of Roman writers such as Terence and Cicero in favour of various saints who may have been irreproachable as far as piety and morality were concerned but who were not necessarily masters of Latin. A more fundamental problem, he concluded, was the way of thinking taught at Salamanca which encouraged students to concoct pointless, artificial ideas at the expense of rational thought.

The decline of the university was accompanied by the decline of the town and the exodus of noble families in search of positions at court in Madrid. By the middle of the eighteenth century many of their palaces were inhabited only by stewards of aristocratic estates. The population continued to drop, falling from over 25,000 in 1561 to 17,000 two centuries later and 11,400 in 1820. Foreign travellers agreed that the town was dirty and depressing. To Richard Twiss it had 'a melancholy aspect' while the French Baron de Bourgoing found it 'one of the saddest cities in Europe'. The university, according to William Dalrymple in 1774, 'has not a most flourishing aspect; most of the colleges appear as if they had been lately wasted and ruined by a ravaging army'.

Less than forty years later, a ravaging army really did lay waste the colleges. The list of buildings destroyed by Marshal Marmont's army in 1812 is terrible: most of the districts of San Blas, San Bartolomé and San Vicente, several parish churches, various monastic buildings including the beautiful Romanesque convent of San Vicente, and about a dozen colleges, among them the Colegio de Cuenca, the most beautiful Gothic building in the city, and the Colegio de Santa María de los Angeles, razed after the French had carted away 13,000 volumes from its library. Three convents on the edge of the city were turned into forts and then

111

further damaged by British artillery fire. Wellington exaggerated when he said the French had destroyed half the city's convents and four-fifths of its colleges, but the south-western areas were certainly devastated and have not recovered even now; one quarter has been known since then as 'los Caídos' ('The Fallen'), a name it still deserves. After Marmont's behaviour, it was not surprising that when Wellington entered the city he was kissed by its female inhabitants wherever he went. 'The people of Salamanca', he wrote after his defeat of Marmont, 'swear that my mother is a saint; & the daughter of a Saint, to which circumstances I owe all my good fortune!!!' There had been a similar episode in India, he recalled, when the Mahrattas decided she must have been a Mahratta.

The observations of visitors in the nineteenth century are predictable. Ford found 'the western portion of the ill-fated city [was still] a heap of ruins' and the Spanish novelist Alarcón listed a. dismal catalogue of districts that were dead, ruined, depopulated, flooded or merely ugly and desolate. One French traveller was surprised by the enormous number of pigs wandering around, 'like dogs in our country', while another noted the inadequacy of the university's libraries and laboratories. The students had declined to less than a tenth of their original number and could now be counted in hundreds. They seem to have preserved some spirit, however, for Ford found them 'full of tags and rags, fun, frolic, *licence*, and guitars. Their peculiar compliment is the throwing their cloaks of shreds and patches on the ground, for well-dressed handsome women to walk over.' George Borrow, who was in Salamanca taking 'measures that the Word of God might become generally known in this celebrated city', did not regret the decline of the university for he believed the world had derived no benefit from its 'scholastic philosophy'. But he found the place magnificent in spite of the silent halls, the grass growing in the courts and the depredations of Marmont. 'How glorious are its churches, how stupendous are its deserted convents, and with what sublime but sullen grandeur do its huge and crumbling walls, which crown the precipitous bank of the Tormes, look down upon the lovely river and its venerable bridge.'

Salamanca in its desolation still had romantic admirers. René

Bazin was indignant that certain inhabitants should even dream of an industrial future. The city, he asserted, must be spared that destiny for its mission was spiritual rather than commercial. Ilya Ehrenburg, an acolyte of Stalin, held similar views. The university was so beautiful, he wrote, that he could not understand how anyone could study pathology or civil law there. It was a place built for contemplation and poetry. But the man who most loved Salamanca even in its wretchedness, the man who identified himself so closely with the city that to his contemporaries he seemed to embody the place, was Miguel de Unamuno.

Philosopher, essayist and poet, Unamuno was one of the leading members of that tormented group of intellectuals known as the 'generation of '98'. A Basque by birth and upbringing, he went to Salamanca as a young man in 1891 and stayed there for the rest of his life except for some years of exile in the 1920s. His statue stands in front of the Convento de las Ursulas opposite his house in the Calle Bordadores,* a powerful, slightly hunched figure with a combative, almost manic expression and a jutting beard. It is a fine sculpture which well portrays the character of this restless, dogmatic, egotistical man, perennially wrestling with the problems of religious faith and national decline. Unamuno was a man of contrasts, well described by a friend as 'cultured and primitive, modern and medieval, mystical and scientific, with the fervour of the apostle and the sagacity of the pícaro'. He was a great arguer, unable to compromise, compelled to disobey even minor conventions if he disagreed with them; as ties seemed to him completely useless, he refused to wear them. On political questions he was equally dogmatic and critical of all governments. He opposed Alfonso XIII and he opposed the dictator Primo de Rivera who sent him into exile. Returning with the Second Republic, he also turned against that and briefly supported Franco's insurgency. After a few weeks he opposed the rebels as well, an extremely dangerous thing to do in a city which had recently become Franco's headquarters.

Unamuno's last public appearance was at a meeting held to celebrate 'the day of the race' (12 October) in the university hall

---

* This is the house he moved to in 1914. The Unamuno museum beside the university is in the house where he lived when he was rector between 1900 and 1914.

113

three months after the outbreak of the Civil War. Various leading Francoists made angry speeches denouncing the republic, and the event degenerated into propaganda and slogans. The motto of the Foreign Legion, *Viva la Muerte* ('Long live Death!'), was shouted, followed by other mindless cries and much fascist saluting of a photograph of Franco. At the end Unamuno, who had been reappointed rector after his exile, stood up to make the closing speech. To an audience almost delirious with Francoist fervour, he said frankly what he thought of the previous speeches, what he thought of the Foreign Legion's slogan (he called it 'repellent'), and a good deal about what he thought of the Legion's founder, General Millán Astray, a crippled one-eyed fanatic who was sitting close to him. After listening to a complicated passage in which Unamuno stated that 'a cripple who lacks the spiritual greatness of a Cervantes is wont to seek ominous relief in causing mutilation around him', Millán Astray shouted out, *'¡Mueran los intelectuales!'* ('Death to intellectuals!'). Despite roars of approval from Falangists in the audience, Unamuno continued his speech. 'You will win, because you have more than enough brute force, but you will not convince. For to convince, you need to persuade. And in order to persuade you would need what you lack: reason and right in the struggle.' When he had finished, certain legionaries began waving their guns in his direction and Unamuno might have been lynched if Franco's wife, Doña Carmen, had not taken his arm and led him out of the hall. That night he was expelled from his club and shortly afterwards stripped of his rectorship. He died a few weeks later on the last day of the year, dying in Ortega's words of 'sickness of Spain'. His last speech had been worthy of any life.

When Unamuno arrived in Castile in 1891, he was overcome by nostalgia for the green damp hills of his native Vizcaya. But he soon came to prefer the dry austere landscape of Salamanca. The Basque countryside was like different notes on a flute; the Castilian plains were like the full and solemn note of an organ. Vizcaya was the seed, he later wrote, and Castile the fruit. But initially he was worried that he would go downhill in Salamanca, lapsing into an existence of provincial idleness. If after two years in the city, he wrote, his friends learnt that he was playing cards every day, spending two or three hours each afternoon in the

Plaza Mayor and taking siestas, they should give him up as a lost cause. But if he spent his time studying, thinking, writing and arguing in public on cultural matters, he would be better off there than in Madrid. His friends disagreed and Ortega tried to persuade him to live in the capital. But Unamuno was adamant. Madrid was sterile and uncultured, he thought, and like all great cities it depersonalized the individuals who went to live there. When the Valencian novelist, Blasco Ibáñez, told him that Paris and the rest of the world were what really mattered in their century, his listener replied, 'No, give me the plaza in Salamanca. It's worth more than all of that.'

Unamuno became obsessed by his adopted town. 'Sa-la-man-ca!' he said, 'How good those four full syllables sound, all with an "a", the most serious of vowels'. He never tired of writing about the place and referred to it repeatedly as 'my Salamanca'. In his poems and prose he employed imagery which indicates his view of the organic nature of the town: *alto soto de torres* ('tall thicket of towers'), *encina plateresca* ('Plateresque oak'), *selva de talladas piedras* ('forest of carved stones'), *vieja ciudad campesina, aldeana, noblemente aldeana, con sus torres del color dorado del trigo* ('ancient rural city, rustic, nobly rustic, with its towers the golden colour of wheat'). The poet Guerra Junqueiro told Unamuno he was lucky to live in a city where you could wander dreamily along so many streets without disturbing your dream. The solitude of Salamanca was vital to Unamuno. 'One hardly notices the passing of time,' he wrote; its tranquillity enabled one 'to hear oneself think'.

Unamuno managed to fit a great deal into his Salamanca routine. He had hours for lecturing, for reading, for writing letters, for poetry, for his newspaper articles, for long walks and incessant conversations. His friends recall Unamuno striding out after lunch, not like most of the inhabitants to the Plaza Mayor, but to the Zamora gate and out into the countryside, or along the banks of the Tormes to La Flecha, the orchard where Fray Luis de León wrote his ode *La vida retirada*. The soul of Spain, he believed, could be found in the Castilian landscape, in the severe frontier provinces which had once divided Moors and Christians. So he tramped tirelessly across it with his friends, interrogating shepherds and farmhands whom he encounterd and noting the new words and expressions that he heard. Castilian cities, he declared, contained 'the poetry of the centuries' while the Castilian countryside guarded the spirit of the race.

It is now rather hard to find much national spirit among neglected fields and abandoned villages, just as it is difficult to dream undisturbed amid 'the poetry of the centuries' of Salamanca's streets. The stone and the architecture should make Salamanca the most beautiful city in Castile. But decay and development have robbed it of that unity which can still be found in towns like Toledo or Segovia. No city with Salamanca's quality of monuments should have so many ugly new buildings or so many derelict old ones. Ruined houses still collapse in the centre of the town: of the four sides of the proudly named Plaza de los Leones, three are badly dilapidated and the fourth is the cathedral. As for development, the juxtaposition of old and modern may be inevitable in a city in which little was built between the Baroque period and our own era, but the new buildings, too high, too brash and too densely packed, demonstrate remarkable insensitivity to the ambience. Below the Clerecía, the vast former Jesuit college which now houses the Pontifical University, the three Salamancas meet, the monumental, the modern and the miserable. For down the hill from the Baroque towers and the modern blocks is the Barrio Chino, the most dismal red-light district imaginable. Barefoot children play in the rubble, emaciated dogs sniff at garbage and at street corners a few thin, ill-looking women stand, incapable even of raising a wink or a smile for passers-by.

During the course of this century the university has expanded and the city has undoubtedly become more prosperous, but both have been achieved at an appalling and unnecessary cost. Between 1900 and 1981 the population of Spain doubled, the population of Salamanca province rose very slightly, but the inhabitants of the city increased by six and a half times. The quiet provincial town of 25,000 which Unamuno had known when he was first appointed rector became the second city of Old Castile with a population of 167,000. Salamanca could have absorbed the pressure from the new inhabitants, who were mainly immigrants from rural districts, by housing them all in new suburbs and restricting traffic in the centre, as the Tuscans successfully managed in towns like Lucca and Siena. But the opposite happened.

116

Modern blocks were built in the historic quarters on uprooted gardens and flattened houses, and roads were widened for the increased traffic. In the despairing view of the urban historian, Chueca Goitia, it was folly to open more and more routes to absorb more and more traffic; the city should not have been destroyed to help the motor car but the motor car restricted to save the city.

The Franco regime's early plans for Salamanca, although in certain respects Utopian and rather absurd, would have been very much better for the place than the chaos which ultimately emerged. The Urbanization Plan of 1939 defined the city as an 'indestructible unity' based on Catholic thought (which prevented it from becoming an amorphous conglomeration as in 'liberal' countries), on the *'genius loci'* (which meant it should obey 'interior laws' determining its character) and on its organic nature (because like a human body it had different parts with different functions). Apart from further gobbledegook about Salamanca's future as an 'imperial city', the planners decided the town should have a belt of woodland around the old city, a park to the east and another to the west, and new houses decreasing in height towards the periphery so that the furthest buildings from the centre would be cottages of one storey. This proposal to integrate the city with the countryside was never attempted, however, and in 1944 it was superseded by the less pretentious Plan of Paz Moroto.

The new plan was more practical, proposing among other things the inevitable Gran Vía, the closure of the Plaza Mayor to traffic, and the 'sanitization' of the Barrio Chino, which was considered scandalously close to the university and the hospitals. Architectural standards were to be maintained with the aim of 'preserving the state of affairs which allows the centre of Salamanca to be described as a sonnet in stone'. The Plan of Paz Moroto was not much more successful than its predecessor, and the parts which were carried out tended to be those which interested the developers. Spain was still too poor for grandiose plans. The reason why the country has so little fascist architecture, the reason why Madrid lacks the imperial follies attempted by Mussolini in Rome, is that it was bankrupt when fascist ideas were dominant. By the time Spain was again rich enough to build, the Falangist Party had been discredited and the economy liberalized.

The growth of the Spanish economy after 1959 coincided with a disastrous relaxation in planning controls. Modifications to the existing regulations in 1961 and a new plan for Salamanca in 1966 were encouraging to speculators, and the ending of height restrictions effectively condemned unprotected low buildings in the centre to demolition. In 1963 a government decree issued by the ministry of industry urged private enterprise to stimulate the economy by building hotels, factories and apartment blocks without worrying too much about planning procedures. Those who objected to so much demolition and construction, often carried out illegally, were told they were obstructing the development of the country; not that there was anyone to object to, because Spain had no such thing as a National Trust or a Society for the Protection of Ancient Buildings. The unelected government and the unelected town halls held all the power and could disregard their own rules with impunity. Along the isthmus leading to the port of Cádiz, for example, the municipality allowed the construction of apartment blocks of ten storeys in an area it had reserved for bungalows.

Salamanca used to have one of the best silhouettes in Spain, but from the Madrid road little more than the Clerecía and the cathedral tower can now be discerned above the tall red-brick blocks erected on the site of the medieval walls. Fray Luis's orchard at La Flecha has been eaten up and the view of the river is ruined by the ugliest parador in the country. Inside the city the new buildings are almost uniformly hideous except for the Gran Vía which, although driven in Haussmann fashion through the middle of medieval parishes, is at least built of stone and seldom exceeds four storeys in height. There is nothing to be said for the concrete zone north of the station, and its ambience is not improved by the fact that its treeless streets are named 'Cedars', 'Camellias', 'Cypresses' and so on.

In the twenty years prior to 1986, according to official municipal statistics, more than 8,000 of the 13,000 dwellings built before 1936 were destroyed – a statistic which would destroy most comparable cities. The fact that it does not quite destroy Salamanca indicates the quality of the surviving monuments. But it means that walking around the streets can be a depressing experience, inciting regret for the lost beauty and anger at the people who let it happen. When you see one palace transformed into a bingo hall, another turned into a telephone exchange, a third demolished to make way for a bank, you feel that the town council's claim to be guarding the 'patrimony of humanity' is perhaps a little bogus.

Cadiz, looking out to the sea

SIX

Cádiz

Not many people visit Cádiz nowadays. The ancient port attracts few Spaniards and fewer foreigners, who when they do go are disappointed to discover it is not 'typically Andalusian'. They do not find a town of low white houses, nor a Holy Week of delirious display, nor even a strong bullfighting tradition. Unlike Seville, it has not been the home of high grandee families nor the goal of *pícaros* and beggars. But neither has it bred great painters or writers of its own, although Murillo worked there at the end of his life and died shortly after falling off some scaffolding in the Capuchin church.

If Seville is like a concave mirror, enlarging Spanish virtues as well as Spanish defects, Cádiz is the opposite. It diminishes or even conceals its qualities. Although there is much beauty in its streets, Cádiz is a shabby and decayed place today, a provincial town no longer among the top twenty cities of the country; even in its own province it has been overtaken in size by Jerez. Spaniards recognize its past importance, but the place has never imprinted itself on the Spanish psyche. There is no whiff of the conquistadors in Cádiz (although Columbus embarked on his second transatlantic voyage from there), no Quixotic nostalgia, no musty aroma of St Teresa or the Inquisition. It is one of the most influential cities in Spanish history yet ill-known and unhailed because it is regarded, above all by Spanish conservatives, as the promoter of unSpanish values. When General Franco proclaimed that he had 'liquidated the nineteenth century which should never have existed' because it was 'the negation of the Spanish spirit', he was condemning ideas and movements which had originated in Cádiz, ideas which in his eccentric reading of

Spanish history had turned the country into the 'bastardized, Frenchified and Europeanized Spain of the "liberals"'.

Cádiz's earlier historic role is of course well known. Its position, its harbour and the trade winds made it a natural port for its rulers as well as a natural target for their enemies. Founded by Phoenicians just after the Trojan War, Cádiz is probably the oldest city in Europe, but there is a theory which would make it older still: according to Edwin Björkman, it may even be the site of Atlantis. An important port under the Carthaginians and Romans, it declined under the Visigoths and Moors before resuming its role after the Reconquest. For a long time it was almost certain to be attacked in any war fought by the Spaniards. Drake's 'singeing of the king of Spain's beard' in 1587 and the sack of the town by Lord Essex in 1596 are familiar episodes: Cervantes wrote a sonnet about the second raid, mocking the cowardice of the Spanish commander, the Duke of Medina Sidonia, who arrived triumphantly on the scene 'with duly measured step' long after Essex, who ransacked the place and burnt sixty-five ships, had departed. Less familiar is Sir Edward Cecil's embarrassing expedition in 1625 when his men landed near Cádiz and discovered large quantities of wine in some farm buildings. They proceeded to drink so much of this that they became militarily useless and had to be re-embarked before they were annihilated.

The town assaulted by Drake and Essex, however, was a small port with 6,000 or 7,000 inhabitants. A hundred years later it had multiplied four times; by the end of the eighteenth century it had a population of over 70,000 and was the richest, as well as one of the largest, of Spanish cities. It was in Cádiz not Barcelona that Spain's first modern middle class emerged, and it was Cádiz which produced so many of the things later anathematized by General Franco. It can be argued that the city was the birthplace of the modern Spanish state with its free press, its liberalism and its nationalism; it was perhaps also the birthplace of that Latin American nationalism which led to the break-up of the empire. A distinguished local historian, Ramón Solís, has claimed that Spanish political dialogue originated in the Calle Ancha, the imposing street where politicians used to meet informally during the years of the Cortes of Cádiz (1810–13). Although that dialogue, especially during the debates on the constitution, tended to be inflated and rhetorical, and although it was short-lived at the time and only occasionally and for brief periods resuscitated before 1977, it was an important and influential precedent for what Franco called the forces of 'Anti-Spain'. The Cádiz constitution of 1812 remained for more than a century and a half an inspiration for Spain's beleaguered liberals.

Cádiz and Seville were rivals from the fifteenth century and are physically very dissimilar. Yet they also complement each other, and the later history of the port cannot be understood without the history of the great inland city eighty miles up the Guadalquivir. The old Cádiz that we see today, the eighteenth-century town, is in a sense an extension of Seville: it consists of buildings, which in the normal course of events would have appeared in Seville, erected in the place where the American trade monopoly had gone. That is why eighteenth-century houses are so hard to find in Seville. For ten years after the discovery of America, Cádiz and Seville competed for the Indies trade. Perhaps the outcome would have been different if Columbus had been able to sail from Cádiz in 1492, but the port was then full of ships deporting Spain's Jewish population, and he sailed from Palos instead. In the event Seville was given the monopoly of American trade in 1503 and soon after began to expand. The subsequent loss of that monopoly, which has already been discussed, condemned Seville to a long period of decline just as its transfer down the Guadalquivir inspired more than a century of growth in Cádiz.

In 1680 Cádiz became the port for the loading and unloading of ships on the Atlantic voyages. The administration of the Indies trade, however, remained in Seville, a cumbersome arrangement which persisted until the trading house and the merchants' association were moved to Cádiz in 1717. Even then Seville fought a rearguard action, claiming against all the evidence that the sand-bar at Sanlúcar was not particularly dangerous, and in 1725 the city prevailed upon Philip V to transfer the administration back to Seville. Its triumph, however, was brief. Cádiz sent an emissary to the royal court to point out the absurdity of the new plan and the king was quickly persuaded to annul his decree.

Cádiz was prospering in 1670, when the French consul described its commerce as 'the greatest and most flourishing in Europe', although the volume of Indies trade had greatly declined during the century, and in spite of the fact that most of that trade was in foreign hands. As an emporium and financial centre, Cádiz managed to profit from a system which was of little benefit to the rest of the country. According to French observers, only 5 per cent of the goods shipped from the port were actually Spanish. Foreign merchants also controlled much of the import trade: at least half the American bullion, unloaded in Cádiz harbour and put on non-Spanish ships, never entered the country at all. Then there were the problems of corruption and smuggling which further reduced the benefits of the trade for Spain. A frequent ploy of ships' captains was to put ashore at a French or Portuguese port, where they could evade customs duties, and subsequently claim that pirates, bad weather or enemy ships had driven them there.

The eighteenth century was Spain's American century. No longer compelled to play a role it could not afford, a role created by accident when one man inherited the Habsburg and Burgundian domains as well as Castile and Aragon, Spain could free itself from the European entanglements which had turned out so disastrously in the middle of the seventeenth century. Although no longer a great power, a fact disguised by the French alliance and the presence of the Bourbons on the throne, Spain retained a great empire. In spite of the problems of governing vast colonies on the other side of the Atlantic, there was no serious challenge to Spanish rule in the American viceroyalties. And in spite of the problems of smuggling, the monopoly and foreign participation, the transatlantic trade prospered. Cádiz continued to be the principal beneficiary. The system of a single-port monopoly remained unquestioned for most of the century and more than four-fifths of the Indies shipping resisted the temptation of subterfuges and returned each year to Cádiz.

In 1778, however, the Spanish government abolished the monopoly and opened American commerce to all ports in the country. There was consternation among the merchants of Cádiz who believed they would be ruined by the decision. 'They have received a severe shock,' noted a Wiltshire vicar, the Reverend Joseph Townsend, travelling to the city shortly afterwards, and there had been 'many failures'. Notwithstanding the shock, he added, commerce in the town was flourishing. After all, Cádiz still had the advantages of its position and its harbour, as well as the experience and expertise it had gained in its century of monopoly. Glutted American markets did lead to a business collapse in 1786, when the vicar was there, but recovery was fast and the following decade was more prosperous than any in the town's history. As the most efficient of the Spanish ports, Cádiz was bound to thrive in a free trading system, and its decline after 1796 was caused not by competition but by wars with Britain.

The execution of Louis XVI in 1793 had prompted Spain to fight the French revolutionary government, a disastrous involvement which ended in 1796 when the country changed sides and declared war on Britain. This was an even more disastrous decision, costing Spain part of its fleet off Cape St Vincent and the permanent loss of Trinidad. The war against the Third Coalition, in which the country was an unwilling ally of Napoleon, was more fatal still and resulted among other things in the destruction of the Spanish navy alongside the French at Trafalgar. For Cádiz both wars were catastrophes. The first conflict cost the city 186 ships and the majority of its trading houses, and in the second the remaining trading houses went bankrupt along with more than 50 insurance companies.

If Spain's role as a French ally had lost Cádiz its British and American trade, its alliance with Britain from 1808 naturally resulted in the end of its commerce with France and those parts of Europe (most of the continent) under French control. But in this desperate period, when its citizens knew that even after the war their city would never regain its pre-eminence, Cádiz enjoyed its moment of glory as the centre of political Spain, the bastion of national resistance and the birthplace of the Spanish constitution. Appropriately enough, in view of the damage France had caused the city, all this was made possible by French negligence. Joseph Bonaparte delayed his southward march in order to take Seville, and by the time Victor's troops had reached the Cádiz area, Albuquerque's Spanish forces were safely behind the port's impressive fortifications. Supplied by British ships and protected by British cannons, the besieged consequently had a much easier time of it than the besiegers.

Cádiz in this epoch was much admired by Lord Byron, who extolled both its appearance and its valour. Arriving in 'sweet Cádiz' a few months before the siege, he declared it to be 'the first spot in creation . . . The beauty of its streets and mansions is only excelled by the loveliness of its inhabitants.' To his correspondents he announced that Cádiz was 'the prettiest and cleanest town in Europe' (London was 'filthy in the comparison'), 'Seville a large & fine city', and Gibraltar 'the dirtiest and most detestable spot in existence'. In *Childe Harold's Pilgrimage* he praised the city's performance during the siege in a verse which somewhat over-simplified the nature of the struggle.

> Adieu, fair Cádiz! yea, a long adieu!
> Who may forget how well thy walls have stood?
> When all were changing thou alone were true,
> First to be free and last to be subdued:
> And if amids a scene, a shock so rude,
> Some native blood was seen thy streets to dye:
> A traitor* only fell beneath the feud:
> Here all were noble, save Nobility;
> None hugg'd a conqueror's chain, save fallen Chivalry !

Later writers competed with extravagant imagery in their descriptions of the city. To Richard Ford Cádiz may have been 'shaped like a ham' (presumably on the map rather than from the sea) but it nevertheless sparkled 'like a line of ivory palaces'. Théophile Gautier thought of it as 'an immense crown of silver filigree' with the cathedral dome appearing 'like a silver-gilt tiara set in the midst of it'; the town's whiteness, he added, was 'as pure as silver, milk, snow, marble and the best crystallized sugar'. Edmondo De Amicis also found it the whitest city in the world: it was the colour of milk whereas Córdoba and Seville were merely as white as paper. There were also some ornithological analogies. To De Amicis Cádiz resembled a seagull after a swim while Gallenga saw it as a swan, 'its stately rows of buildings bearing a resemblance to the bird's half-unfolded wings as it struggles to

---

* The 'traitor' was General Solano, the city's governor murdered by rioters at the beginning of the anti-French uprising.

emerge from the waves'. Even at the beginning of this century, in its most unfortunate period, Cádiz could inspire a British journalist to call it 'a Spanish Venice, cut in straight white streets, like the slices of an iced cake'. A generation later, Laurie Lee described it from a distance as 'a scribble of white on a sheet of blue glass, lying curved on the bay like a scimitar and sparkling with African light'. On closer investigation, however, he found it an appalling place, 'a rotting hulk on the edge of a disease-ridden sea, its people dismayed [and] half-mad ...'. This excessively unsympathetic view was no doubt influenced by those the young author encountered in Cádiz, 'sailors, beggars and pimps', 'the blind and the crippled, the diseased, the deaf and dumb', people 'who lived by trapping cats and dogs and roasting them on fires of driftwood', a man howling on a tenement rooftop 'who was pretending to be a ghost in order to terrorize the landlord and thereby reduce the rents'.

Spanish descriptions have been more favourable. Manuel Machado summed up Cádiz in two words, *'salada claridad'* ('salt-laden clarity') while to J. M. Pemán the street corners were like the prows of ships and the town's balconies like the poops of old galleons. A popular image sees Cádiz as a white handkerchief waving farewell to a sailor.

The city poeticized by these writers belongs to the eighteenth and early nineteenth centuries. The municipal museum's fine architectural model, made of mahogany and ivory in 1777, shows how little Cádiz has altered in the last 200 years. The changes in the old city have been largely confined to buildings in the port and along the seafront, as well as to the sites of a few convents which were demolished in the last century to make way for squares. The urban grid to the west of the cathedral has remained almost intact, the long white streets meeting at right angles and carrying on to the sea. Much of the building was designed to lessen the impact of the east wind, for Cádiz is the windiest city in Spain. Whether or not this had much effect, several writers have remarked on the wind's role in forming the characters of the inhabitants. 'Few places are more healthy than Cádiz,' observed an eighteenth-century traveller. 'Yet when the *solano*, or south wind, blows, which comes to them over the scorching plains of Africa having only the intervention of a strait, all the passions are inflamed, and during its prevalence, the inhabitants, who are most irritable, commit every species of excess.' Native writers, on the other hand, have blamed the east wind for 'that indolence and exhaustion which overtakes us whenever the sultry levanter approaches', while Pemán believed it was responsible for the large number of eccentrics in the city.

The buildings are more varied than the streets although they invariably manage to produce a homogeneous effect. The houses are usually Baroque with a number of neo-classical and Isabelline (mid-nineteenth-century) mansions in the most prosperous streets. The vast, decaying Baroque cathedral, built in the eighteenth century, has been treated with almost universal derision, especially by the English. To the eighteenth-century vicar, the Reverend Joseph Townsend, it was 'heavy and disgusting' and a 'disgrace to taste', while to Ford it was full of 'detestable daubs' and its plans were 'so bad, even for that corrupt Churrigueresque period, that no-one, in spite of many attempts, has been able to correct them'. This criticism is arrogant and unfair, as is Sacheverell Sitwell's dismissal of the cathedral as 'only interesting because Haydn wrote music specially for the chapter'. There is grandeur and dignity in the building, especially in the curves of the façade, although it is indeed unfortunate that the bottom half should have been constructed in a warm brown stone and the top half in a cold white one.

Ideas formed by travellers in other Spanish cities are often revised when they visit Cádiz. It is undisputed, for example, that the Baroque in Spain is very greatly superior to the neo-classical. Anyone who walks through the lanes of a medieval town and suddenly comes across a vast pillared façade, pompous, awkward and out of place, will agree. But in Cádiz with its later, more regular street plan, the neo-classical is the more distinguished of the two styles, at any rate for public buildings. The town hall, the customs house, the headquarters of the military governor and much similar architecture unseen in other parts of Spain are as impressive as they are unexpected.

The houses of Cádiz are similarly unique. You only have to take a boat across the bay to Puerto de Santa María to be reminded what other Andalusian towns are like. The houses in Cádiz are taller than elsewhere, with dark unwelcoming patios. 'Each house stands on tiptoe,' observed Gautier, 'peeping inquisitively over its neighbour's shoulder, and raising its head above the thick girdle of the ramparts. And since this does not always suffice, almost all the terraces have a turret or belvedere at the corner, sometimes crowned with a little dome.' The height of the houses reflects the lack of space and their uniformity indicates the tightness of the town's building regulations; owners who erected extra storeys were frequently ordered to demolish them by the municipal authorities.

The uniformity of the houses reflects another un-Andalusian quality: the lack of extreme class distinctions. Obviously some streets were smarter than others, just as some houses were lavishly decorated with marble and others adorned simply with miradors and iron railings. Naturally, too, there were many people with capital and many more without, many who could afford to live in their own houses and many others who lived a communal existence in the *casas de vecinos*. But the differences were small compared with Seville and Córdoba. The nobles of Cádiz formed a merchant aristocracy, many of them of foreign, particularly Italian, descent. Unable to live off rents from estates they did not possess, they were forced into commercial or military careers. Presumably this made them less vain and ostentatious than Andalusian grandees elsewhere. Certainly they lived more modestly. Instead of inhabiting great palaces sprawling over several courtyards, the nobles of Cádiz usually had terraced houses of four floors and a single patio which was seldom used. They lived on the second floor with their servants above them and the two lower floors reserved for store-rooms and offices.

In 1809 Byron called Cádiz the cleanest town in Europe, but a generation earlier Richard Twiss had observed that 'all the streets in Cádiz are narrow, crooked, badly paved and filthy' while Henry Swinburne declared that 'except the Calle Ancha, all the streets are narrow, ill-paved, and insufferably stinking ...'. The accusations of narrowness and crookedness are unfair and can be refuted by looking at the same streets today or examining the city model in the municipal museum. But the dirtiness was real. 'The swarms of rats', observed Swinburne, 'that in the nights run about the streets are innumerable; whole droves of them pass and repass continually, and these their midnight revels are extremely troublesome to such as walk late . . .'. Neither he nor Twiss were impressed by the Alameda on the north-western seafront, although that had not yet become the fine promenade it is today. 'The sea air prevents the trees from thriving', remarked Swinburne with prophetic inaccuracy, 'and destroys all hope of future shade'. Twiss had a graver charge, finding the Alameda 'much resorted to by ladies of easy virtue . . . the only place in Spain where I find such barefaced licentiousness and libertinism'.

By the time Swinburne's criticisms were published in 1787, however, Cádiz had been transformed by zealous local government. 'For their pavements,' remarked Townsend, 'for the cleanliness of their streets, for a well regulated police . . . [the inhabitants] have been indebted to their late governor, Count O'Reilly.' Anyone who visited the city at the turn of the century found it clean, attractive and prosperous, particularly the Calle Ancha and the Plaza San Antonio, regarded as the right places to stroll and meet people and discuss politics, and the Calle Nueva and the Plaza San Juan de Dios, which formed the commercial centre. It was by any standards a civilized town with institutions such as the Academy of Noble Arts and the Faculty of Medicine, one of the first medical colleges to function in Spain. Visitors compared Cádiz favourably with Madrid, especially wealthy Creoles who were amazed to find the capital of the empire so much poorer and dirtier than their own cities. Cádiz's inhabitants were also surprised by the difference. At the beginning of the nineteenth century the politician Alcalá Galiano found the shops and cafés of the port far superior to those of the capital. Madrid was at that time ugly, he recalled later, with little luxury and less hygiene; the houses were miserable, their balconies and railings left to rust whereas those in Cádiz were painted green. The dirty and opaque window panes in the larger city contrasted with the clean and clear glass used in the southern town. Even the bottles were different, colourless and elegant in Cádiz, black and ugly in Madrid. The prosperous port, he noticed, was full of mahogany tables, but even in the highest social circles in the capital one could find pine tables painted to masquerade as mahogany.

Cádiz was a city which set trends. It was there that coffee overtook chocolate as the most popular hot drink, and it was probably there that modern office hours, at any rate the long morning culminating in the three o'clock lunch, were first observed. Not that everyone went to offices or stayed in them until lunchtime. Alcalá Galiano recalled the wealthy classes strolling about the Plaza San Antonio, smoking and chatting, until the church bell struck three and they all went off to eat. During the evenings a good deal of time was spent in the cafés, which appeared in Cádiz before anywhere else in Spain. There men could talk or play billiards or read the newspapers, although more drinking was probably done in taverns such as the celebrated beerhouse in the Calle de Flamencos Borrachos ('Street of the Drunken Belgians'). One very Spanish institution, the *tertulia* or meeting of friends swapping intellectual *bons mots* day after day across a café table, was much in vogue in Cádiz. Women, who were not allowed to enter cafés and had to meet in *confiterías* instead, instigated their own form of *tertulias* based on the French *salons*. These affairs, usually taking place in the house of an intelligent, domineering, sometimes even cigar-smoking hostess, had their origin in Cádiz and were later adopted in Madrid.

Cádiz was a cosmopolitan, outward-looking city with a tradition of tolerance. The Inquisition there was weak and its inhabitants had little difficulty finding books by Voltaire, Rousseau and other banned writers. At one time in the 1830s, wrote George Borrow, 'two missionaries from Gibraltar, Messrs Rule and Lyon, during one entire year, preached Evangelic truth in a Church at Cádiz. So much success attended the efforts of these two last brave disciples of the immortal Wesley, that there is every reason for supposing that, had they not been silenced and eventually banished from the country . . . not only Cádiz, but the greater part of Andalusia, would by this time have confessed the pure doctrines of the Gospel, and have discarded for ever the last relics of popish superstition.' The significant thing about this passage is not Borrow's indignation nor his fantasy that Andalusia could have been converted to Methodism, but the fact that the two missionaries had been allowed to preach at all in a country that had long been the most intolerant of heresy in Europe. It is doubtful if they could have done so with safety outside Cádiz.

The town's open, liberal character had been heavily influenced by foreigners. Pemán called it an 'American and Genoese city' symbolized by the mahogany imported from the tropics and the

131

marble brought from Italy. The quantity of *retablos* and grand Baroque doorways made with Italian marble indicates the extent of Genoese influence. The Latin American penetration was even more pervasive and can still be seen in the architecture of buildings such as the beautiful women's hospital, the street names (Paraguay, Venezuela and so on), the statues of Bolívar and fellow heroes, and the endless plaques put up by Americans to salute Cádiz (and the other way around). The city was the meeting-point between Spain and its empire and retains a strong American flavour: when Lorca visited Havana he described it as a larger and hotter Cádiz. An historian's description of the port as 'a piece of America inserted into Spain' is not as whimsical as it sounds.

Trade with America was the reason why so many foreign merchants came to live in the city, where their principal role was to re-export goods imported from their own countries. Ninety per cent of the English silk stockings which arrived in Cádiz, for example, were sent on to Mexico or South America in the later seventeenth century. The same was true for the larger volume of French trade. According to a contemporary estimate, less than a seventh of the leading trading companies in the 1670s were Spanish: the others were Genoese, French, British, Flemish, Dutch and Hanseatic. At the beginning of the eighteenth century about 10 per cent of the town's population was foreign, a proportion which rose in the following decades faster than the increase in population. By 1791 there were some 9,000 foreigners in a city of 75,000 inhabitants. The largest groups were French and Italians, but the numbers of these and other nationalities fluctuated with wars and changing alliances. In 1801, when Britain and Spain were at war, there were only six Englishmen in Cádiz.

According to a local historian, the inhabitants owed their enthusiasm for fine arts to the Italians, their ideas to the French, and their views on education to England, where many of their sons were sent to study commerce. The French influence on the theatre was pronounced, although on political thought it seems to have been limited. The intellectuals of Cádiz may have read Rousseau but very few supported the French Revolution. The English constitutional tradition, by contrast, was widely admired and was reflected in the preference for dressing in British rather than French clothes. Much appreciated, too, were the kilts of the Scottish troops in the Peninsular War, although these do not appear to have been imitated by the natives. Nevertheless, Cádiz had an ambivalent attitude towards England, inspired by memories of the British fleet and competition from British commerce. Not everyone appreciated Wellington when he arrived at the end of 1812, although his horse received a smart gold net embroidered by the ladies of Cádiz and he was greeted by a crowd chanting *Ahe Marmont, onde vai Marmont,* a mocking anti-French song composed in the port after the battle of Salamanca. Nor did Wellington's sense of humour go down well when he took various aristocratic women to supper at a ball and closed the doors to prevent their husbands joining them. The failure of the nobles to protest against such boorishness, declared an outraged historian, was proof of the decadence of their class.

If Wellington found the women of Cádiz particularly attractive, he was merely following a trend begun nearly 2,000 years earlier when Martial praised the women for their sensuous, swirling dancing. Ford described Roman Cádiz as 'the centre of sin and sensual civilization', and declared that the women of the modern town had 'retained all their former celebrity; they have cared neither for time nor tide'. Their movements, he added, were considered by 'grave antiquarians' to be unchanged since Martial's day, although presumably both Ford and the antiquarians were aware that there was no ethnic connection between the two populations: Cádiz was resettled after the Reconquest in the thirteenth century with people from the northern city of Santander.

A few curmudgeonly travellers failed to be enchanted by the women. Richard Twiss described them as 'Macaroni ladies' who wore 'yellow powder in their hair, which to me appeared nauseous and unbecoming', but more typical observers admitted their attractiveness at the same time as they deplored their behaviour. 'Female virtue', wrote Henry Inglis in 1831, 'is a thing almost unknown and scarcely appreciated. It is with difficulty and pain we can bring ourselves to believe that in a civilized country there should exist a state of society in which that purest gem, female modesty, bears no price . . .'. He said he 'could give innumerable examples of the depraved state of morals in Cádiz' but had decided not to sully his pages with the details. Ford was equally reticent. He admitted the women were charming and fascinating and that Cádiz was 'rather the city of Venus, the mother of love, than of the chaste Diana', and then added without elucidation that 'the lower orders have borrowed from foreigners many vices not common in the inland towns of temperate and decent Spain'.

Most Englishmen were delighted to find that the women of Cádiz were so unlike their own women at home. Their 'finely-rounded limbs', wrote Sir Arthur de Capell, 'contrast very agreeably with those sharp, angular points which one is so apt to come in contact with in our own country', while Byron proclaimed that 'the women of Cádiz are as far superior to the English women in beauty as the Spaniards are inferior to the English in every quality that dignifies the name of man'. They were irresistible, he told his mother, with 'long black hair, dark languishing eyes, *clear* olive complexions, and forms more graceful in motion than can be conceived by an Englishman used to the drowsy listless air of his countrywomen.' Other connoisseurs were much impressed by their walk. A traveller at the end of the nineteenth century declared that Cádiz seemed 'a sojourn fit for the gods' populated by women who had 'all the gait and bearing, the grace and dignity, of terrestrial goddesses'. This walk was apparently unique and had its own name, the *piafar*. According to Ford, the *piafar* had 'been distinguished by Mrs Romer, a competent judge, from the "affected wriggle of the French women and the grenadier stride of the English, as a graceful swimming gait". The charm is that it is *natural*; and in being the true unsophisticated daughters of Eve and nature, the Spanish women have few rivals.'

As far as I can see, the *piafar* no longer exists. At any rate it is now as difficult to detect a special walk in Cádiz as it is to discern a special beauty in the women. Since Byron's day, alas, the city has become a place of steadily decreasing interest. Later nineteenth-century travellers felt bored almost as soon as they arrived. 'One tires of Cádiz in a day or two,' wrote the man who talked of terrestrial goddesses. 'It is a town without a country.' Augustus Hare made the incredible remark that, apart from the picture Murillo was painting when he injured himself, there was 'literally nothing else to see in Cádiz'. In the 1830s Borrow found 'many splendid shops, several of which are in the style of Paris or London,' and at the same time Ford described the town as 'well built, paved and lighted'. In spite of the *piafar*, however, Cádiz was 'a shadow of the past' and 'as a residence . . . dull', for it was 'but a sea-prison' and had 'small attraction to the scholar or gentleman'. Besides, its officials were tiresome and unhealthy. 'It is carrying a joke some lengths,' complained Ford, 'when the yellow cadaverous Spanish *health* officers suspect and inspect the ruddy-faced Britons . . . bursting from a plethora of beef and good condition.'

Alcalá Galiano, who returned to Cádiz in 1844 after a long absence, was shocked by its decline and could no longer compare it favourably with Madrid. Each era seemed to bring a new disaster to the decaying city: the wars against England, the war against France, the removal of the Cortes in 1813, the independence of southern America, the defeats of 1898 and the loss of the remaining colonies, the more recent decline in ship-building and consequent unemployment. Yet Cádiz is still an important port and the principal link between Spain, North Africa and the Canary Islands. Its bay still has a naval industry although this is shared with Rota, La Carraca, Matagorda and San Fernando. It also has a large dry dock, a huge cold storage plant and various food-processing industries which give employment to immigrants from the province who live in stumpy tower blocks along the isthmus leading to the city.

Old Cádiz is still there, its streets a little tattered and neglected now, its houses peeling and faded. The gardens and squares are still luxuriant, crammed with bougainvillaea and swaying palms. As in Gautier's day, 'Two colours, blue and white, alone assail the eye', and the brilliance of the light, the sea almost permanently reflecting the sun, remains in the memory of the visitor. Cádiz in its tribulations still retains its charm, but it is no longer 'a sojourn fit for the Gods' and its terrestrial goddesses no longer walk the *piafar*.

The port, Barcelona

SEVEN

Barcelona

From the wooded summit of Montjuich you can see the different ages and faces of Barcelona. To your right are the dockyards and wharves of the port, to your left the pine-covered slopes and villas of Tibidabo and Pedralbes. In between is the largest city on the Mediterranean, former capital and commercial centre, head-quarters of a medieval empire, first industrial city in Spain and reluctant political deputy to Madrid. The vertical lines indicate the diverse history: the Columbus monument, the factory chimneys, the medieval Gothic towers of the church of Santa María del Mar, and the twentieth-century Gothicized spires of the Sagrada Familia.

Montjuich itself is almost a microcosm of a past whose contrasting epochs of glory and gloom are more pronounced than in the histories of comparable cities. Its castle has at different times been Barcelona's watchtower, lighthouse, fortress and execution ground. A number of Francoist sympathizers were shot here at the beginning of the Civil War and a larger number of republicans at the end of it. Lluís Companys, the president of Catalonia's autonomous government, the Generalitat, was captured by the Gestapo during his exile and handed over to Franco. He was shot by a firing squad after taking off his shoes and socks so that he would die touching the soil of Catalonia; on his death certificate his executioners stated that the cause of death had been an internal haemorrhage. But although a stone commemorates the place where Companys fell, Montjuich today naturally emphasizes the city's cultural and recreational character. Its long wooded hillside contains a raucous funfair, the principal stadium for the 1992 Olympics and the delightful gardens of the Palacete

Albéniz. At its centre, below the summit, are the surviving buildings of the 1929 international 'Expo', including the Pueblo Español, an amusing attempt to display all of Spain's regional styles in a single 'village', and the Palacio Nacional which houses the Museo de Arte de Cataluña, an incomparable museum whose chief glory is the large number of Romanesque frescos transported from decaying Pyrenean churches in the early years of the century.

Barcelona's mercurial history has been largely a consequence of its hostile relationship with Castile, an enmity displayed by warfare, long sieges and a contemptuous dislike of Madrid – a feeling which is well reciprocated. Foreigners, like the Spaniards themselves, have found it difficult to be neutral in the rivalry between the two cities; most of them, indeed, have admired Barcelona as much as they have disliked Madrid. Now that a political solution to Catalan nationalism has been found, the rivalry between the two cities is at its most intense in the football arena. Barcelona ('Barça') and Real Madrid usually dispute the league championship between them but, as in Glasgow, there is also a sectarian struggle within the city itself because the rival Barcelona team is called Español, a club Catalan nationalists could hate for its name alone. Catalans have long boasted that their city is the most European in the Iberian peninsula, and it is only with reluctance that they will admit that it is also Spanish.

The stereotypes Catalans and Castilians have created for each other persist today. *Madrileños* still complain that Catalans are smug, narrow-minded, avaricious and mean: I have heard diplomats from the capital denounce one of their colleagues as 'typically Catalan' because he was more interested in money than culture. The Catalans see themselves, however, as progressive, hard-working and European, and they claim that Barcelona has more in common with Paris than with Madrid. To them the Castilians are arrogant and lazy, unwilling to dirty their hands with work. Of course these stereotypes have never been less true than they are today, and intelligent people reject them. But somehow they persist, often subconsciously, and the rivalry and grievances persist also. There is a certain pettiness about it even at the highest cultural level. Barcelona's excellent Picasso museum presumably hopes to attract the majority of its visitors from

138

Europe and other parts of Spain. But the labels describing the pictures are not printed in English or French or Spanish, only in Catalan, a language very few foreigners and non-Catalan Spaniards can read. It is a pointless gesture which merely suggests that Catalonia is rather provincial after all.

The rivalry can be traced back to the Christian surges southward against the Moors. As the historian Pierre Vilar observed, 'Spain of the Reconquest disintegrated rather than cohered', and the drive down the peninsula was three-pronged. As early as 801 Barcelona was recaptured and the 'Spanish march' established, but for nearly three centuries (during which the city was sacked by al-Mansur) there was little further progress against the Moors. By the time of Huesca's capture in 1096, the Castilians were much further south and had taken Toledo; by the middle of the following century the newly independent kingdom of Portugal had reached as far as Lisbon while the Catalan-Aragonese* forces were stuck at Tortosa, 140 miles further north. But in the first half of the thirteenth century the Aragonese conquered the Balearic islands and Valencia, though they were prevented by a treaty with Castile from extending further south to Murcia.

The kingdom of Aragon gained less land from the Reconquest than Castile, but its new territories were richer and more cohesive than its rival's. By the thirteenth century it had become a powerful state with Mediterranean possessions and a prosperous commerce. The extent of the prosperity can still be seen in the Barrio Gótico, the old quarter of Barcelona, a city which had some 40,000 inhabitants before the Black Death and was perhaps the largest in the peninsula. It is an area of tall houses and narrow streets and palaces with courtyards and grand external staircases. Its finest feature is the Gothic architecture of its churches with the strong horizontal lines, octagonal towers and austere, undecorated spaces in their façades that make them so different from contemporary buildings in the rest of Spain. Yet while it is remarkable to find such a well-preserved core in a vast, largely nineteenth-century city, the Barrio Gótico has little of the charm

---

* The union of Catalonia and Aragon took place in 1137 when Ramón Berenguer IV, Count of Barcelona, married Petronila of Aragon. Their descendants were known as kings of Aragon.

of other medieval towns. Perhaps it is the fault of the high buildings of dull brown stone or perhaps it is because the area is now mainly shared between tourists and down-and-outs. It would be delightful to sit in the Plaza Real were it not for the large number of lurching drunks who seem to live there, just as it would be agreeable to walk in the nearby sidestreets if they were less frequented by drug addicts injecting themselves.

The city's prosperity in the thirteenth century came mainly from its seaborne commerce. It is often said that Barcelona has its back turned to the Mediterranean, and in a famous ode the native poet Maragall asked his city why it 'fled from the sea'. It is true that the architecture does not seem to 'embrace' the water as it does in Cádiz or San Sebastián. It is true, too, that the city had no maritime conception unlike Venice, for example, which created itself from the sea and then expanded on the mainland; Barcelona established itself on land and later discovered a marine vocation. Moreover, it is true that the town has a poor natural harbour which, in spite of numerous improvements, remained well below the standard required by a great sea port. Nevertheless, Barcelona's wealth in the early Middle Ages was largely a consequence of the expansion of its maritime commerce, a process assisted by Pisan and Genoese immigrants of the eleventh century who brought with them the nautical skills and knowledge of their native cities. The growth in maritime activity was accompanied by the development of a banking system and a woollen-textile industry which transformed the city and its region. In the words of Catalonia's distinguished historian, Jaime Vicens Vives, 'this feudal, peasant, Romanesque people of other times gave way to a brilliant and expansive society of colonizers and merchants'. Why this happened is not entirely clear: the Catalans themselves ascribe their success to hard work and enterprise, and it is difficult to find arguments to refute them.

Commercial expansion soon translated itself into imperial power. The Aragonese drive south against the Moors in the thirteenth century was accompanied by naval expeditions resulting in the conquest of Majorca, Sicily and Minorca; the kingdom was even strong enough to compel France and the papacy to recognize its sovereignty in Corsica and Sardinia. Early in the following century Aragonese troops defended the Byzantine Empire against the Ottomans and then carved out various territories in Greece for themselves to govern. The energy and the conquests were impressive, but it would be hard to claim that the resulting 'empire' was a great success for either the conquerors or the conquered. Historians of Sicily have failed to uncover great benefits brought to the island by Aragonese rule. Minorca's Moorish population was removed and enslaved, but few Christian volunteers could be found to settle in its place. And the attempt to colonize Sardinia turned that island, as Felipe Fernández-Armesto has observed, into Aragon's Ireland. The colonialist adventures, he concludes, which were largely financed by Barcelona's merchants, probably did the city more harm than good.

Imperialist overreach was not the only reason for the decline of Aragon in the fourteenth and fifteenth centuries. The Black Death, followed by recurrent plagues from the 1360s to the 1470s, commercial rivalry with the Genoese, agrarian revolt and long civil wars drained the kingdom of its wealth and energy. By 1469, when the marriage of Ferdinand and Isabella paved the way for the union of the crowns of Aragon and Castile, the balance between the kingdoms had altered: Aragon was tired, weak and underpopulated whereas Castile was at its most confident and dynamic. The timing of the union thus consigned the Aragonese to a subordinate role during Spain's 'golden century', a position they resented later as the balance swung back in their favour. Both Catalan nationalism and Barcelona's dislike of Madrid owe much to the circumstances of the union.

Catalans are apt to think of the following centuries, leading up to the industrial revolution, as an almost unbroken catalogue of Castilian repression and neglect. They look at the thirteenth and nineteenth centuries as their eras of glory and tend to see the intervening periods as featureless ages punctuated by heroic attempts to claim their just rights from Castile. The first blow, particularly damaging to Barcelona, was the removal of the court which was now linked to Isabella's and travelled between Seville, Granada, Toledo and Valladolid before ending up in Madrid. Since the royal house of Aragon had become extinct at the beginning of the fifteenth century,* Barcelona had been rather

---

* Ferdinand of Aragon did not belong to the indigenous royal family of Aragon. His grandfather Ferdinand of Antequera, who was chosen to fill the empty Aragonese throne in 1412, was a member of the Trastámara dynasty and a brother of Henry III of Castile.

neglected by its new dynasty of Castilian origin, but the permanent departure of the court after Ferdinand and Isabella was a more drastic loss. Later it gave rise to the idea of Barcelona as the 'widowed' city, bereft of its rightful role, an imperial capital robbed of its imperial destiny.

Aragonese resentment was doubtless compounded by other problems. By the beginning of the sixteenth century Barcelona's maritime trade had dropped to such an extent that its vessels rarely sailed further than Marseille or the Balearic islands. The coast was virtually undefended, savaged by corsairs from France or Algiers. Commerical life, heavily damaged by the expulsion of the Jews, had greatly declined, and it was hardly surprising that merchants should prefer to invest safely in land than risk money in perilous enterprises overseas. In 1562 the city's shipyards were so run down that Philip II had to order much of his fleet to be built in Italy; in an attempt to revive them, he brought various caulkers, carpenters and masters of galleys from Genoa to instruct the Catalans in their lost skills.

Yet Barcelona could not be described during this period as a poor city. Don Quixote praised it, in spite of his mishap while jousting on the beach, and so did most travellers. Indeed, throughout the period of Barcelona's supposed neglect visitors were praising its cleanliness, the magnificence of its palaces and the beauty of its gardens. Furthermore, its population increased, doubling from 32,000 at the end of the sixteenth century to 64,000 by 1650. Thereafter there was admittedly a decline, the epidemic of 1651, the siege of 1652 and various other disasters reducing the figure to about 50,000 at the end of the century.

The beginning of Aragon's economic recovery coincided with the end of Castile's dynamic period and led to attempts by both kingdoms to redefine the relationship between them. The Aragonese wanted to reassert their federal and autonomous traditions while the Castilians wished to persuade their partners to play a more active and responsible role in defence of the Crown's other dominions. In practice this meant an increase in the amount of soldiers and taxes provided by Aragon. The failure of the king's chief minister Olivares to achieve this led to a deterioration in relations that finally caused a revolt in which the Catalans proclaimed their allegiance to the French king. The rebellion ended with the capture of Barcelona in 1652, but only after a long war in which Portugal managed to secede permanently from Spain.

Two generations later Catalonia and Castile were fighting again, on opposite sides in the War of the Spanish Succession. The French Bourbon claimant, Philip V, offered to respect the *fueros* or liberties of Catalonia, but the Catalans rejected him and his offer and fought for his Austrian rival instead. By the time Barcelona was captured in 1714, after another lengthy war, Philip was in no mood to preserve Catalonia's institutions: Barcelona's university was removed, its city council dismantled and the *fueros* abolished. Catalans have regarded these acts as the height of their repression by Castile, worse even than the predations of Olivares, but the harshness of their treatment seems to have been exaggerated afterwards. Indeed there was probably more indignation from later generations than there was at the time.

The most visible sign of Bourbon repression was the building of an enormous fortress, the Ciudadela, on the edge of the city. To make way for it, 800 homes had to be demolished and their 4,000 inhabitants moved at the city's expense to a new district by the port, La Barceloneta. The Ciudadela's vast ramparts in the shape of a pentagon turned out to be militarily useless and were captured by surprise by the French in 1808. But its ostentatious presence naturally turned it into a symbol of repression, and the Barcelonese longed to get rid of it. In 1841, in an incident described by an historian as 'one of the first symptoms of the rebirth of the Catalan spirit', a city official pulled down the first stone shouting 'Victory for Catalonia and Barcelona!' A partial demolition followed, to the fury of the government which declared that the action constituted treason and punished those responsible. Further unrest was succeeded by further repression: the regent, General Espartero, finally bombarded the city into submission, imposed a huge fine, ordered a large number of executions, and told the inhabitants to repair the obnoxious fortress. It was not until 1869, when the Catalan General Prim was prime minister, that they were allowed to begin knocking it down again. Thereafter the Ciudadela was ingeniously transformed into a park housing the 'Expo' of 1888 and a number of museums. The old arsenal has since undergone several metamorphoses, transformed first into a royal palace, then a museum of art and archaeology, then the seat of the Catalan parliament during the Second Republic, and subsequently the Museum of Modern Art. Part of it now once again contains the regional parliament.

At the end of the eighteenth century the Reverend Joseph Townsend described Barcelona as 'one of the most delightful cities in the world'. Other travellers endorsed the view, appreciating the climate and vegetation as well as the fine buildings. Yet it was still a small city in spite of industrial growth in the eighteenth century and the building of numerous cotton mills. It was not much larger than the thirteenth-century town and only in the port district of La Barceloneta had it expanded beyond the late medieval walls. Yet there were considerable changes taking place within, which increased after the disentailment of religious property. It is difficult now to imagine seventeenth-century Barcelona, but it was then almost as much a 'convent-city' as Toledo or Seville. The Ramblas, for example, which with its diversity and movement embodies the city's contemporary spirit, was at the time lined by the monastic buildings of Jesuits, Carmelites, Augustinians and several other religious communities.

The Ramblas began its existence as a stream dividing religious houses on its western bank from the city walls on its eastern. By the middle of the eighteenth century it had become the city's main street, lined with a double avenue of elms and poplars. Later, acacias and oleanders were added and in 1859 the famous plane trees were planted; planes remain the most important species of tree in Barcelona, although in certain areas the palm predominates. Some of the monasteries came down at the beginning of the nineteenth century, the rest after 1835. They were replaced by markets, squares, large houses and streets. In 1822 the liberal ministry in Madrid handed the Capuchin monastery to the municipality, which intended building a square dedicated to national heroes in its place. As soon as it was demolished, however, the succeeding reactionary government decided it should be restored as a monastery. Nothing much was done until the disentailment of 1835 when plans were drawn up to build a theatre and a pair of huge glass galleries on the site. These also fell through and eventually the Plaza Real was erected, a beautiful arcaded square adorned with palms and later with lanterns designed by Gaudí.

By the second half of the century the ancient stream and ecclesiastical district had become the Ramblas we know today, the street of the Opera and the Calle de Fernando (in the past sometimes referred to as 'Barcelona's Regent Street'), the street of fountains and florists (the painter Casas met his future wife among them), the street of caged-bird sellers, the street of lust and movement and painted street walkers. One of the most well-known spots is the Canaletas fountain where the water was once so good it was said that anyone who drank from it would never leave Barcelona. As the local writer Vázquez Montalbán points out, however, the fountain must have lost its magic. In the 1950s the great Argentinian footballer Di Stefano was photographed drinking its water when he seemed about to join Barcelona. A few months later he was playing for Real Madrid.

The Ramblas remained the centre of the city until the middle of the nineteenth century when the government finally gave Barcelona permission to knock down its walls. The citizens, who suspected that the state had preserved them not only for military reasons but also from an atavistic desire to repress Catalonia, eagerly set about demolishing this obstacle to their city's growth. In 1859 they adopted a plan by the architect Ildefons Cerdà to build a vast extension to the north and east which would increase the city's size by a factor of ten. It was the largest urban project in the history of Spain, and most of it was completed. Geometric regularity is the most obvious feature of this extension which is known as the Eixample: 200 kilometres of new streets each 20 metres wide, widths of 30 or 50 metres for the most important avenues, and square blocks 113 metres long between street corners. To the Catalan historian, Josep Pla, the uniformity was tedious and depressing, but the monotony of the project is relieved by architectural variation and the long diagonal streets.

With the construction of the Eixample, the centre of the city moved north, to the Plaza de Cataluña and the Paseo de Gracia beyond. The most elegant shops left the Calle de Fernando (which has gone badly downhill since: a McDonalds and a Kentucky Fried Chicken now guard its entrance on the Ramblas) and installed themselves in new premises in the Paseo de Gracia. Some of the best bars moved as well: the 'Bar la lune' abandoned the Plaza de l'Angel in the old city and re-established itself in art nouveau splendour beside the Doré cinema on a corner of the

Plaza de Cataluña. The Paseo de Gracia's western pavement, where pedestrians could catch the morning sun, became the most fashionable promenade in Barcelona: photographs from the turn of the century show it ludicrously overcrowded while the opposite pavement is almost deserted. People liked to stroll too among the palms of the enormous Plaza de Cataluña where Barcelona's most prestigious hotel, the Colón, was situated. Once the social centre and political meeting place of the city, the hotel has unfortunately disappeared. It became the headquarters of the Communist Party in the Civil War, its façade covered by enormous portraits of Lenin, Marx and Stalin, and its site is now occupied by the Banco Español de Crédito. The square remains the centre of the city but the palms and the cafés have gone. Seven large but architecturally undistinguished banks now loom above the traffic and the reduced gardens in the middle.

The growth of Barcelona in the nineteenth century was prodigious. A population totalling a mere 100,000 in 1826 had doubled by mid-century and reached 533,000 by 1900. Most of the new inhabitants were migrants from the countryside coming to work in the city's new factories. They formed the first industrial working class in Spain and suffered the same evils of the age as their counterparts in other European cities: child labour, malnutrition, overcrowding and tuberculosis. Cholera epidemics killed 3,500 people in 1834 and 5,600 twenty years later. In fact living conditions in Barcelona were probably worse than elsewhere in Europe. Until the building of the Eixample, the population density was more than five times that of London. A report on the city's housing in 1890 expressed surprise that human life could survive at all in such conditions.

Social reforms were opposed by those who pointed out that Barcelona's population was being constantly augmented by people who evidently found living there preferable to an existence of hunger and unemployment in much of the rest of the country. It was certainly true that most of them could find a job, a room to live in, and enough food (potatoes, bread and fried cod) to survive. But an industrial crisis at the end of the century caused earnings to drop and led to a political radicalization of the working class. Until then there had been little public support for anarchism, a movement which seemed to consist mainly of individuals prepared to chuck bombs at generals or an opera audience. But from the beginning of this century anarchism grew in popularity, stimulated by a government which invariably over-reacted after events such as the 'Tragic Week' of rioting in 1909. Barcelona became an increasingly violent place, a city of bombs and church-burning, of large-scale riots and heavy-handed repression afterwards. The government paid gangsters to hunt down anarchist leaders, and the anarchists retaliated. Between 1919 and 1923 there were more than 700 political assassinations in Catalonia.

In spite of the violence, Barcelona's middle classes continued to prosper and build extravagantly along the streets of the Eixample. Much of their wealth had come from the textile industry. At the beginning of the nineteenth century the city swarmed with small cotton mills employing between them some 10,000 people, but large-scale production did not begin until after 1832, the year of the construction of the Bonaplata mill and of a tariff law banning imports of cotton textile manufactures. The building of the Bonaplata mill, which was the first Spanish factory to have one of Watt's steam engines, has been considered the beginning of Barcelona's industrial revolution. Within thirty years half of Spain's looms and nearly all its spindles had been mechanized. But Catalonia's manufacturing industry extended in other directions as well, perhaps most dramatically in the production of corks. The cork trees of Gerona are of high quality, particularly suitable for beer and sparkling wine, and Catalonia was able to expand its exports of corks from 300 million in the middle of the nineteenth century to over 3 billion by the end of it.

Barcelona's industriousness and vigour impressed visitors. It was 'a city of the North', observed Edward Hutton, 'full of restlessness, an unnatural energy, haunted by the desire for gain, absolutely modern in its expression,' although it was also 'full of mean streets and the immense tyranny of machinery'. In the 1880s another English traveller described Barcelona as 'combining the business of mill and shop, of warehouse and dock ... of Liverpool and Manchester in one,' a comparison which in those days was a compliment to Barcelona. But in fact Catalonia's industry could not compete either in scale or efficiency with Lancashire's: in 1907 there were fewer than two million spindles in the whole of Spain compared to more than forty-three million in Britain, and without the tariff even these would not have existed. Barcelona compared well with the rest of Spain but poorly with the rest of Europe. Its feeble stock exchange and inadequate banking system certainly hindered manufacturing, as did the lack of coal and iron in Catalonia, but at the end of the century there was a failure of entrepreneurial initiative as well. Protectionism may have been necessary in a country as backward as Spain, which by 1906 had the highest tariffs in Europe, but it conveniently absolved the industrialists from the need to modernize in order to compete with foreign manufacturers. It gave Barcelona's textiles a free hand inside the country but effectively prevented them from finding markets outside.

The lack of self-confidence displayed by the Catalans in international trade was not reflected in their behaviour at home. Barcelona's bourgeoisie was industrious and dynamic and lived well. Although open and tolerant in comparison with Madrid, it could not, however, be described as a liberal society: as late as 1880, for example, it was opposing the government's decision to abolish slavery in Cuba, one of the last of Spain's colonial possessions. According to Vázquez Montalbán, this 'wise and cynical' class had its fair share of baseness and cruelty, and was certainly ruthless in defence of its interests. At home it lived in conditions of ostentatious opulence, proud of a cosmopolitanism which differentiated it from Madrid. Paris was its magnet and principal model, although from other parts of Europe – from almost anywhere except Castile – it also sought social and cultural patterns to emulate.

There is a fine tradition of Catalan seafood cooking, which does not consist only of the ubiquitous *bacalao* or codfish, but Barcelona's smart restaurants have seldom used it. Italian pasta, particularly cannelloni and macaroni, was introduced in the eighteenth century and became popular, but was soon overtaken by French cuisine. Restaurants at the end of the nineteenth century were built in French style and served French food; not only the menus but even the details on them and the addresses of the restaurants were printed in French. An English traveller recorded that the cafés were 'as grand and sumptuous as those of Paris'. They were certainly enormous: the Café Novedades in the

Paseo de Gracia had 23 billiard tables, 88 waiters and other staff, and 160 tables in the café.

In the 1880s fashionable women in Barcelona wore such tight skirts that they sometimes tied their knees together to prevent them splitting the material as they walked. Whether or not this particular custom came from France, the inspiration for most female dress was French. Men's fashion, however, looked to London and was supplied by tailors such as 'Old England' in the Calle Pelai. Only artists with their long hair and large floppy hats remained loyal to Paris and its version of Bohemia. At the end of the nineteenth century it was almost obligatory for them to go to the French capital, settle for a period in Montmartre and succumb to the influence of the Impressionists and Rodin.

Musical cosmopolitanism meant becoming a partisan of Verdi or Wagner, whose operas were performed at the Liceo opera-house in the Ramblas. If the Italian's music appealed more to Barcelona's ears, the Catalans found in Wagner heroic visions of a mythical past which seemed particularly appropriate to their own quest for a national identity based on ancient glory. Wagnerian motifs started to appear on furniture, sculpture and even articles on the dressing-table. The German composer was perhaps as unlikely a hero for the Catalan bourgeoisie as he was for the radical proletariat, but both classes found inspiration in his work. The novelist Baroja witnessed anarchist choirs singing Wagner on the slopes of Monte Tibidabo.

The cultural centre of Barcelona society was the Liceo, the largest opera-house of its period after La Scala. Built in 1844 on the ruins of the Trinitarian monastery, it burned to the ground in 1861 and was rebuilt and reopened a year later. It was a fashionable meeting place as well as an opera-house and indeed it became fashionable even before it was built: the management was able to sell all the first-floor boxes at vast prices before a spade was applied to the site. One of its attractions was the club at the back with the Casas paintings and exuberant decoration which miraculously survived the Civil War. Another was the famous fancy-dress balls which opened with a waltz followed by a rigadoon and a mazurka. A good deal of time and ingenuity was spent copying the clothes of remote historical figures to comply with the strict censorship of contemporary costumes. Article 5 of the rules governing the balls stated that nobody was permitted to wear magistrates' suits, religious garments or military uniforms, presumably because the intention of the wearer could only be subversive. Even more subversive would be dressing up in clothes of the opposite sex: anyone doing so, warned Article 6, would be expelled immediately. The balls declined towards the end of the century, but the Liceo is still an important opera-house. Some of the boxes have remained in the hands of the families which bought them, and they preserve a rather mid-nineteenth-century ambience. People walk in and out during performances, talking and greeting one another, without provoking a chorus of shushing.

Catalonia's economic strength fuelled the rise of cultural and political nationalism in the region. Its intellectuals and business-men may have looked to European models for transforming feudal Spain into a modern state, but they also sought inspiration in their own past. Madrid and the central government were hated not only for their incompetence and neglect of Catalonia, but also for the policies which had allegedly led to the impoverishment of Catalan culture. People looked back to the government of the old kingdom of Aragon – less centralized and more democratic than Castile's – and remembered the things that went with it, the language, the commerce, the architecture, the Mediterranean empire. A movement known as the *Renaixença* or Catalan Renais-sance began, symbolically at least, with the publication of Ari-bau's 'Ode to the Homeland' in 1833. Claimed as the first poem written in Catalan since the sixteenth century, it was soon followed by the 'Ode to Barcelona' in which Rubió i Ors extolled the city's beauty but lamented that in its 'widowhood' its palaces had no function. The resurgence of Catalan as a written language accelerated, stimulated in 1859 by the revival of the famous literary competitions of the Middle Ages, the *Jocs Florals*.

The most important field for the medieval revival was architecture. The men of the *Renaixença* sought an architectural style which combined the glories of the Catalan past with modern, progressive ideas appropriate to an industrial age. As neither the European Renaissance nor the Baroque had played much part in Barcelona's development, and as the neo-classical was too recent and too closely implicated with the Bourbons, they obviously had to explore further back for an inspirational style. The city's first neo-medieval building, Rogent's university of 1860, was Romanesque, but subsequent architects blended Gothic traditions with new technology and contemporary European ideas to form Barcelona's most original architectural movement. Known in Catalan as *modernisme* and flourishing from about 1880 to the First World War, it has in fact little to do with 'modernism' elsewhere. There are obvious similarities with art nouveau and the Arts and Crafts Movement of William Morris, yet it nevertheless forms a distinct style of its own. Like Morris and Ruskin, its proponents thought machines were dehumanizing and so they promoted the revival of medieval artisan skills. Yet they were not averse to technological innovation and used it skilfully in their attempt to create a modern architecture to reflect the past and future glory of Catalonia.

Unlike its sister movements in France and England, *modernisme* was not a small minority movement. Its political and patriotic dimensions meant that it was accepted by a large proportion of Barcelona's bourgeoisie, particularly by the newest and most energetic members of this class such as the Güell family, which became Gaudí's principal patron. *Modernisme*'s influence on the city is thus much greater than the influence of Morris in England, Charles Rennie Mackintosh in Glasgow or Otto Wagner in Vienna. Moreover, it was used not only for houses but for purposes as diverse as shops, fountains and mausoleums; Barcelona's south-eastern cemetery is full of *modernista* tombs and sculptures. In the 1970s the city still had more than 800 shops built in this style, many of which survive today. A few cafés of the period have also resisted the temptation to gut their interiors to make way for a dreary aluminium bar.

One of the principal features of *modernisme*, in architecture as well as sculpture, is the predominance of curves over lines: in the sinuous façade of La Pedrera, Gaudí's celebrated building in the Paseo de Gracia, there is not a single straight line. Other features include the widespread use of mosaics, red brick, stained glass, ceramics and flamboyant sculpture. The leading exponent of the *modernista* school was not in fact Gaudí, whose work and architectural theories strayed outside the movement, but Domènech i Montaner, an architect and politician who as a young

151

man wrote a manifesto proclaiming the need to create a Catalan architecture. Domènech i Montaner epitomized the *modernista* tendency to study the distant past while experimenting with new techniques. He praised modern technology and iron structures yet he persuaded a collaborator to go to Italy to study ancient mosaics and he himself travelled to the Valencian countryside to question an old potter about his craft. A prolific architect, whose first *modernista* building was the café-restaurant for the 1888 'Expo' (and which is now the zoological museum), his most remarkable work is perhaps the Palau de la Música Catalana, Barcelona's principal concert hall. Begun in 1905 as an auditorium for the Orfeó Català choir, its exterior looks as if a *mudéjar* palace, a number of vaguely classical pillars and St Pancras Station had been stirred in the same pot and then reassembled and turned upside down. The interior also shocks at first, but after a while, perhaps aided by the music and the excellent acoustics, the mosaics, the stained glass and the delirious stone carving harmonize together and combine to seduce the listener.

Modernista architecture spread to Gerona and other parts of Catalonia and also to Valencia and Palma de Mallorca. But it is rare to find it outside the borders of the old kingdom of Aragon, and isolated examples such as Gaudí's palace in León seem ostentatiously out of place. There was unlikely to be much affection in the rest of Spain for a style which claimed to embody Catalanism, least of all in Madrid and the Basque country, the only places where a bourgeoisie capable of building on a large scale existed. Yet there was hostility also in Barcelona to so audacious and extravagant a style. Even at the height of the fashion many families avoided it, preferring to live in solid, respectable, Frenchified villas in Sarria or Tibidabo. By the 1920s the reaction against *modernisme* had become almost unanimous in the city. A new, mainly literary movement known as *noucentisme* ('Nineteen hundredism') tried to introduce classical rules, and the subsequent rationalist style set about straightening out *modernista* curves. In 1929 there was even a move to demolish the Palau de la Música, which was denounced as 'a monument to the ostentatious vanity of an epoch overloaded with illusions'. The following year Salvador Dalí defended *modernisme* as 'supremely creative bad taste'. Yet he found few supporters and, although

152

the Palau survived, many other buildings were pulled down. The distinguished contemporary architect, Federico Correa, remembers that during his childhood walks up the Paseo de Gracia his nanny always turned around before they reached La Pedrera so that they would not have to see 'that exhibition of bad taste'. To the eyes of the era, the other side of the street was even worse: that extraordinary concoction of buildings by Gaudí, Domènech i Montaner and Puig i Cadafalch was disparaged as the *manzana de la discordia* ('apple of discord').* Gaudí's work was reviled abroad as well as at home. 'Not even in the European architecture of the period', declared Gerald Brenan, 'can one discover anything quite so vulgar or pretentious' as Gaudí's unfinished church, the Sagrada Familia. Evelyn Waugh, however, was more charitable and even advocated the completion of this soaring fantasy. 'I do not say that if I were rich I could not find a better way of devoting my fortune,' he wrote in 1930, 'but I feel it would be a graceful action on the part of someone who was a little wrong in the head to pay for its completion.'

Catalan nationalism, the *modernistas'* political creed, enjoyed varied fortunes during the first forty years of this century. In 1913 its political representatives persuaded the Madrid government to grant the region the *mancomunidad*, which gave them a measure of control over their schools, social services and communications. This was abolished in the 1920s by the dictator, General Primo de Rivera, who was highly unsympathetic to regionalist movements. He also banned Catalan from being taught in schools and suppressed even minor manifestations of Catalan feeling such as performances of the *sardana*, the famous national dance which seems as dull and as pointless to an Englishman as cricket no doubt seems to a Catalan. The nationalists had better luck with the Second Republic, receiving an autonomy statute in 1932 which Spanish conservatives denounced as 'a crime against Spain'. It gave the Catalans their own government, the Generalitat, with control over most local issues, and proclaimed Catalan as an official language of the region. The statute did not go as far as the nationalists wanted, and in the revolt of October 1934

---

* There is a play on words in the description because *manzana* also means a block of buildings.

Companys, the president of the Generalitat, proclaimed the 'Catalan state within the Federal Spanish Republic', a hopeless gesture which ended a few hours later in ignominy and imprisonment for Companys. The autonomy statute, however, was popular in Catalonia and ensured the region's loyalty to the republic in the Civil War.

Loyalty to the republic turned Barcelona into a revolutionary city, a city of posters and slogans, of collectivized shops and gutted churches, of elegant hotels transformed into the headquarters of Marxist political parties. The red flags of the communists (known in Catalonia without irony or intended euphemism as 'United Socialists') competed with the red and black banners of the anarchists. The houses of rebel supporters were looted, private cars were commandeered and daubed with initials – CNT, FAI, UGT, PSUC and so on – announcing the political identity of the driver and his passengers. The Ramblas and the long streets of the Eixample saw frequent demonstrations, military marches, funeral processions, the moving farewell parade of the International Brigades and La Pasionaria's rousing last speech to them.

The revolutionary atmosphere was exhilarating to foreign observers, who enthused about the sight of armed workers strolling about. 'In Barcelona,' wrote John Cornford, the young communist poet who arrived in the city shortly after the outbreak of war, 'one can understand physically what the dictatorship of the proletariat means.' To him it seemed to mean that 'the mass of the people . . . simply are enjoying their freedom' by, among other things, 'sitting in the cafés which used to belong to the bourgeoisie'. George Orwell, who reached the city a few months later in December 1936, was impressed by the sense of equality. 'Waiters and shop-walkers looked you in the face and treated you as an equal. Servile and even ceremonial forms of speech had temporarily disappeared.' Barcelona's bootblacks had been collectivized and their boxes painted in anarchist colours. Barbers' shops displayed anarchist notices 'solemnly explaining that barbers were no longer slaves. In the streets were coloured posters appealing to prostitutes to stop being prostitutes.' Above all, declared the English writer, 'there was a belief in the revolution and the future, a feeling of having suddenly emerged into an era of equality and freedom. Human beings were trying to behave as human beings and not as cogs in the capitalist machine.'

To Orwell's disappointment, this atmosphere had evaporated by the time he returned to Barcelona the following April. Strangers had abandoned the instant use of *tú* and 'comrade' and returned to the more formal *Usted* and *Señor*. The beggars were back and there were bread queues in the poor districts. Uniformed waiters and cringing shop-walkers had returned also. 'The smart restaurants and hotels were full of rich people wolfing expensive meals' and the cabarets and brothels had reopened. The new atmosphere reflected the changing balance of power between the numerically inferior communists, their hand strengthened, however, by Russian weapons and support inside the government, and the more revolutionary anarchists, whose zeal was seldom matched by military or organizational efficiency. Within a month of Orwell's return, armed conflict inside the republic broke out in Barcelona, prompted, apparently, by a ludicrous incident involving an operator at the telephone exchange which was under anarchist control. The President of the Republic, Manuel Azaña, was having a telephone conversation with the President of Catalonia, Lluís Companys, when the operator cut in to tell them to stop chatting because telephones should be used to discuss more interesting and important matters. According to a senior official of the Generalitat, the interruption finally convinced the government to agree to communist demands to take action against the anarchists. The telephone exchange was assaulted in early May, followed by several days of street fighting and the assassination of a number of leading opponents of the Communist Party.

Franco launched his offensive against Catalonia at Christmas 1938 and, following the collapse of the republican army, Barcelona fell at the end of January. The city suffered the usual brutal repression inflicted by the victors on every town which they captured, but like Bilbao and the Basque country it received additional punishment from a centralizing government because of its regionalism. In Francoist eyes its sins were threefold – communism and separatism as well as republicanism – and castigation could not be confined simply to the execution or imprisonment of those who had opposed Franco's rebellion. The essence of Catalanism, in particular the language, was to be stamped upon.

At the end of the war the Falangist director of propaganda, the

155

poet Dionisio Ridruejo, was sent to Barcelona to 're-educate' the Catalans and integrate them into mainstream Spanish (that is, Castilian) culture. Unfortunately he did not understand very clearly what his superiors wanted and he arrived in the city with a load of Falangist propaganda written in Catalan. Refused permission to distribute it, he gave up the project and returned, ill and disheartened, to Burgos. Afterwards he recalled the 'closed-down institutes, the translated commercial signs, the proscription of language teaching, and the cities and towns full of impertinent exhortations: "Talk in Spanish!" "Speak the language of the empire!" etc.' Many years later Ridruejo protested to Franco that the regime was treating Catalonia like a foreign country under occupation. He left the Falange in 1942, became a social democrat and devoted the rest of his life to a courageous and persistent opposition to the regime. He should have been one of the leaders of democratic Spain and it was a tragedy for the country that he died, prematurely, a few months before Franco.

The dictatorship prevented Catalan from being taught in schools or used in newspapers or magazines. At Barcelona University the chairs of history, literature and Catalan were all suppressed, and when in 1952 a chair of Catalan and Catalan literature was finally permitted, it was located in the University of Madrid! (In the same year the Basques were given a chair for their language in the University of Salamanca.) Catalonia also suffered from economic discrimination. The government understandably decided to help the development of backward areas in preference to those already industrialized, but its policy in Catalonia was evidently to hinder rather than simply ignore the economy. Once other areas had caught up with the region, ran Franco's curious argument, the Catalan problem would disappear. The government took measures to ensure that the Barcelona stock exchange did not function properly, and it refused to provide sufficient electricity supplies, with the result that Catalan industry was often paralysed by power cuts. According to Ridruejo, Catalans who wished to set up or invest in new industries were frequently told they could only do so outside Catalonia.

One of the most petty and ridiculous of the regime's policies was to change a large number of Barcelona's street names. Within weeks of the city's capture, a commission was set up to propose

156

'the changes of names of streets and squares . . . with the aim of honouring the heroes and martyrs of the Homeland and eradicating the memory of the hordes who passed through Barcelona, staining it with the names of foreigners and undesirables . . .'. The Diagonal was thus named after Franco and the Gran Vía (like its counterpart in Madrid) after the dead Falangist leader, José Antonio Primo de Rivera, although in fact the town's citizens continued to refer to the streets by their earlier names. Other alterations included renaming the Carretera de Montjuich after the Blue Division (which fought alongside Germany in Russia), and the relegation of the Catalan cellist Pablo Casals, who found his street named after General Goded, the leader of the failed uprising in Barcelona in 1936. Later, when Jose María de Porcioles was mayor of the city between 1957 and 1973, more changes were made. Various streets were called after prominent Falangists but others, like the Avenida Gaudí, were given Catalan names. Some alterations were particularly puzzling, such as the replacement of the Calle Marco Antonio by the Calle Marco Aurelio. 'What was it about Mark Antony', asked the authors of one urban study, 'which displeased the mayor or whoever demanded the change? Perhaps he did not approve of Antony's suicide or his love affair with Cleopatra? Or can the truth be that Señor Porcioles is an admirer of the stoicism of Marcus Aurelius?'

The republican defeat cost Barcelona many of its leading architects. Torres Clavé died on the Ebro front; his collaborator Sert and several of his colleagues were forced into exile. Their fate, however, was a human tragedy rather than a great loss to Barcelona for several of them were disciples of Le Corbusier and had adopted an appalling scheme known as the Macià Plan. In the 1920s Le Corbusier had put forward his mercifully unsuccessful project to demolish the entire Parisian district of Les Halles and replace it with eight monstrous tower blocks leering over the Seine. His followers urged a similar plan in the 1930s which would have ruined much of Barcelona. Visitors to the London exhibition 'Homage to Barcelona' in 1986 were able to look at the design and see what a lucky escape the city had. (Marseille was less fortunate, suffering an awful *unité d'habitation* from Le Corbusier in the 1950s.)

Barcelona's deliverance from the avant-garde was followed by what Oriol Bohigas has called 'blackmarket architecture', a phrase which reflects the shoddy speculative building of the dictatorship. Most of the new construction took place in the 1960s and was characterized by undistinguished commercial buildings in the centre, such as the banks in the Plaza de Cataluña, and ugly cheap apartment blocks in the suburbs and the satellite towns. 'To repair Barcelona,' declares Oriol Bohigas, 'one would have to destroy almost everything built under Franco,' a point not invalidated by either the exaggeration or the impracticality of the scheme. It is impossible to speak of an architectural style in this period; certainly there was no attempt to construct anything remotely identifiable as Catalan. The policy of the Porcioles administration was to allow private enterprise to build whatever it liked virtually wherever it liked so long as it respected the prerogative of the motor car. Not surprisingly, the city of his era sometimes gave the impression of turning into a giant car park.

The municipality's principal problem during the dictatorship was the housing of immigrants from other regions of Spain. There had been a long tradition of migration to Barcelona, thousands of people coming from the south in search of work, crammed into third-class railway carriages; they arrived, in the words of Vázquez Montalbán, 'with a wooden suitcase in their hand and centuries of sun and failure in their face'. Those who appeared in the decade after the war, some 100,000 of them, found nowhere to live and so built themselves shacks in shanty-towns outside the city. Subsequently they came in greater numbers. Between 1950 and 1970 the population of the Barcelona conurbation increased by nearly 2 million, mainly through immigration; in the 1960s there was a net influx of 600,000 people, a large majority of them Murcians or Andalusians.

Little attempt was made to integrate these southerners with the Catalan working class. Many were sent to live outside Barcelona in poorly built satellite towns such as San Ildefonso, a ghetto of 60,000 people living in tiny apartments in uniform ten- or twelve-storey blocks of flats. The place had virtually no amenities, recreation grounds or green spaces, and its services were minimal. Indeed, San Ildefonso epitomized the title of a book on the immigrants, *Donde la ciudad pierde su nombre* (*Where the City Loses its Name*), except that it was worse than anonymous, for it was also a wasteland of broken hopes. Citizens of Barcelona sometimes complain that the immigrants are stubborn because they refuse to assimilate and insist on remaining Andalusians. But how can they become Catalans, how can they learn to like *pan y tomate* or dance a *sardana* or wish to support the Barcelona football team if they live together in a place such as San Ildefonso, which is alien not only to them but to Catalonia as well?

In spite of the repression, the bad modern architecture and the problem of immigration, Barcelona was, as in previous periods of adversity, quick to revive. Indeed, the stupidity of the government's policies helped the city to thrive as a centre of opposition. If children could not learn Catalan at school, then their parents made a greater effort to teach it to them at home. If Catalanism could not be discussed in the media, then clandestine groups prepared its resurgence in private. If Maragall's 'Hymn to the Catalan Flag' could not be sung in public, members of a theatre audience might risk arrest and a beating-up to sing it illegally. Even if people found the *sardana* a boring dance to perform, holding hands in a circle and interminably shuffling steps, it could acquire an exhilarating dimension if done as an act of defiance outside the cathedral.

A campaign in 1959 against Luis de Galinsoga, the Francoist editor of Barcelona's newspaper, *La Vanguardia*, demonstrated the strength and solidarity of revived Catalanism. Galinsoga, whom the government imposed upon the unfortunate paper after the fall of Barcelona, despised Catalonia: during the Civil War he had even suggested in a newspaper that it should suffer the fate of Carthage, '*Delenda est Catalonia*'. More than twenty years later he had an argument in a Barcelona church with a priest who was preaching in Catalan (which he was allowed to do one Sunday a month). After an abusive exchange, Galinsoga left the church shouting that all Catalans were excrement. The remark echoed across Barcelona, and a boycott of *La Vanguardia* was organized: orders were quickly cancelled and advertising withdrawn. As the campaign continued and grew in strength, the Madrid government met to discuss the matter and concluded reluctantly that Galinsoga would have to resign.

In the 1960s Catalonia's cultural resurgence was exemplified by singers such as Raimon and Serrat, and by the large increase in the number of books published in Catalan. Censorship still existed, however, and in 1968 the minister of information prevented Serrat from taking part in the Eurovision song contest because he intended to sing in Catalan. But by then the region had recovered its self-confidence and there was a new optimism about the political future after Franco's death. Unlike the Basques, the consensus among Catalans, combined with their cultural revival and the strength of their traditions, gave them the confidence that they would be able to recover their rights without resorting to violence.

By the end of the dictatorship Barcelona could justly claim to be the cultural capital of Spain. It had the most publishers, the best concert halls, the finest art galleries after the Prado; even the architects had improved and were the best in the country. The city was at the forefront of the campaigns for the democratization and modernization of Spain. When charges were brought against a woman accused of adultery (a female crime under Franco's regime), 10,000 women demonstrated on the streets of Barcelona, many of them carrying placards announcing that they too were adulteresses: '*Jo també soc adúltera*'.

In July 1974 Franco became seriously ill with phlebitis and handed over his powers as head of state to his designated successor, Prince Juan Carlos, grandson of the last king of Spain. It is said that the citizens of Barcelona responded to the news by buying large quantities of champagne. The dictator recovered, however, and the champagne was either drunk or kept in the fridge for another sixteen months; at any rate, when he finally did die, Barcelona's shops ran out of the stuff. Perhaps the citizens thought they were toasting a new era which would preserve their cultural and economic ascendancy as well as achieve political rights they had not known since the fifteenth century. But something went wrong. They did indeed gain democracy and an autonomy statute granting Catalonia its own parliament and government; moreover, their linguistic and national rights were ensured by the 1978 constitution. Yet it soon became apparent that Barcelona's cultural triumph over Madrid had been a temporary victory. The capital had suffered for many years because it was the home of an over-centralized, over-bureaucratic and anachronistic regime. Freed from Francoism, the cultural and economic vigour that had characterized Barcelona under the dictatorship suddenly appeared in Madrid. Spaniards without special loyalty to either city would in 1978 have gone to Barcelona to pursue an artistic career; a decade later they would have preferred Madrid. Contrary to most predictions, Barcelona today is a rather provincial city, while Madrid is one of the most dynamic capitals of Europe.

Fishermen's Port, San Sebastian

EIGHT

San Sebastián

The fortunes of San Sebastián have been determined by its position on the sea, its position near the French frontier, its position amidst some spectacular scenery, and its position in the Basque country. The first and third factors have usually brought the city good luck, while the benefits of the second and fourth have been outweighed by accompanying vicissitudes. Each factor has in turn been dominant, shaping the city's character to its own requirements so that the place which began as a port later acquired the aspect of a garrison town before becoming Spain's most fashionable resort and then a centre for both Basque industry and Basque nationalism.

For more than a century the sea at San Sebastián has been associated with the beach and the regattas, but the fishing and commercial links with the Atlantic are far older, and it is said that the immigrants' most nostalgic memories of their city are of its docks and wharves. This attachment to the sea has been symbolized by Eduardo Chillida's powerful metal sculpture on the rocks at the foot of Monte Igueldo. The product of intermittent labour between 1952 and 1978, Chillida called his work *El Peine de los Vientos* (*The Comb of the Winds*) to suggest the combing of the Atlantic rollers before they enter the elegant bay of La Concha. Unlike Barcelona, San Sebastián has loved the sea, not only for commercial purposes but also for sport, for relaxation and for the enhancement of its urban landscape. The city has the most striking marine views in the land. Queen Victoria, the first British sovereign to visit Spain,* was much impressed by the beautiful position and the picturesque streets.

---

* Charles I visited the country when he was Prince of Wales and Charles II during his exile.

From the Middle Ages fishermen from San Sebastián were crossing the Atlantic to catch cod off Newfoundland. Later they crossed the ocean to hunt whales as well. Whaling became an important industry for the Basque sailors, especially in the seventeenth century when the pursuit was extended to the waters of Greenland. In 1625 an expedition from San Sebastián and Pasajes, a small port a few miles to the east, consisted of 41 ships with 298 launches and 1,475 men. Whales did, however, sometimes come closer, and in 1611 the hunters decided to build a watchtower to spy on them from the heights of Monte Ulia outside San Sebastián. One such arrival was particularly fortunate. In 1643, during the Thirty Years War, a fleet was assembled at St Jean de Luz to burn Pasajes, but a whale providentially appeared, causing the commanders to abandon hostilities and set off in pursuit.

The fishing wealth turned San Sebastián into an important commercial centre in the Middle Ages: its merchants even traded in sterling when Gascony belonged to England. Fishing also boosted the shipping industry so that by the end of the sixteenth century the San Sebastián shipyards were the most important in Spain: a majority of the great ships of the Armada were constructed there. Subsidiary factories were also set up, producing sails, oars and, according to one local historian, the best anchors in Europe. The docks too must have been impressive because in 1617 Philip II used them as a model for the new harbour he wished to build at Gibraltar. San Sebastián's commerce was no doubt helped by a nobility which did not share the contempt for trade of the Castilian hidalgos. When at the end of the sixteenth century a Basque candidate for the military Order of Santiago was accused of having had a 'mechanical trade', his witnesses declared that 'all the citizens of San Sebastián, even if hidalgos, have mechanical trades and live by them'. He won his point and joined the order.

Towards the end of Habsburg rule the city suffered from competition with the rival Basque city of Bilbao, which tempted away much of its maritime traffic. But the eighteenth century saw a resurgence, especially after the creation of the Guipuzcoan Company of Caracas, which had its headquarters in San Sebastián, and the later termination of Cádiz's trade monopoly with

America. By then, however, the city had acquired a new role as the nation's principal fortress facing France on the western Pyrenean frontier. It thus also acquired a garrison and camp followers and an impressive set of fortifications. These developments caused innumerable problems for the inhabitants, especially when a French army loomed near. The French besieged the city on several occasions and after the last siege, in 1823, remained in occupation for five years.

None of the hostile French armies, however, did as much damage as the 'friendly' British one which looted and set fire to the place in 1813. San Sebastián already had a disastrous history of fires. The town had burned to the ground in 1266, and successive rebuildings had been destroyed in 1278, 1338, 1361 and 1397. It was burned again in both 1433 and 1524 after being abandoned by its inhabitants fleeing the plague. Following another blaze in 1489, Ferdinand and Isabella insisted that all the houses must be rebuilt in stone, but this does not seem to have been very successful and in any case a few years later some districts were burned by the town's citizens to prevent their capture by the French. A further fire was started in 1575, when lightning hit the gunpowder store in the castle, followed by three more conflagrations in the seventeenth century and two further ones in the eighteenth. None, however, compared in scale with the fire started by the British army and its Portuguese allies.

In the summer of 1813 Wellington decided not to risk crossing the Pyrenees while French garrisons remained in San Sebastián and Pamplona. The Basque port was ably defended by General Rey who repulsed the first English assault in July and held the town until the last day of August. When the British troops, after suffering heavy casualties, finally breached the walls and entered the city, they went berserk, sacking and looting for three days until almost nothing was left: of more than 600 houses, only 36 remained together with 2 churches and the beautiful convent of San Telmo. The inhabitants naturally felt aggrieved to have lost their city without having gained anything in return. Other cities had suffered, they pointed out to the government the following year, by resisting the 'tyrant' and 'demonstrating the heroic ancestral virtues of the Spaniards'. But the 'glorious, immortal' consolation of self-sacrifice was denied to San Sebastián which

165

had been 'destroyed by the inhumanity of our own allies'.

Wellington was accused of allowing the town to be sacked in order to destroy its commerce with France. In fact he had tried to prevent damage to San Sebastián, specifically forbidding a bombardment of the city because it would be 'very inconvenient to our friends the inhabitants, and eventually to ourselves'. Moreover, on the day the town fell he had shown tact and goodwill to his Spanish allies by *refusing* to help them fend off a French counteroffensive on the heights of San Marcial close by. Wellington had never been impressed by Spanish troops or their generals (it was his brother Henry who remarked that one of them was very popular because he had won a battle and lost only seventeen), but he understood the psychological importance of a purely Spanish victory at San Marcial. 'Look,' he told the Spanish officer begging for reinforcements, 'if I send you the English troops you ask for, they will win the battle; but as the French are already in retreat you may as well win it for yourselves.'

The British commander was not personally to blame for the destruction of San Sebastián, although his refusal to accept responsibility afterwards was certainly insensitive. The real culprits were what he called 'our vagabond soldiers' who had lost so many of their officers in the storming of the city that they became uncontrollable. The British have long proclaimed the superiority of a volunteer army over a conscript force, but the superiority applies only to the fighting; its behaviour at other times is likely to be worse. As Wellington remarked in a passage containing his most famous phrase, 'the conscription calls out a share of every class – no matter whether your son or my son – all must march; but our friends . . . are the very scum of the earth . . . People talk of their enlisting from their fine military feeling – all stuff – no such thing. Some of our men enlist from having got bastard children – some for minor offences – many more for drink.' A Spanish writer, discussing the British siege later in the century, came to similar conclusions. Volunteer armies were largely composed of men of violence who enlisted to avoid arrest for previous crimes. They might fight well but their behaviour in victory was likely to be more savage than 'the most ferocious of wild beasts'.

The British ferocity did at least give San Sebastián's citizens the opportunity to design a fine new town along their devastated promontory to the south of Monte Urgull. A number of plans and counter-plans were proposed over the following years, but the city which eventually emerged is an harmonious and attractive piece of urban planning. The buildings, largely the work of the Aragonese Silvestre Pérez and the local architect Ugartemendía, are sober neo-classical edifices such as the old town hall in the Plaza de la Constitución, a structure which put an end to the tradition of erecting Baroque town halls in the Basque country. Its architect, Silvestre Pérez, was later lauded by the city's official chronicler as the man who 'restored to architecture its pure and beautiful nakedness, eliminating so much excessive and over-decorated "carnavalesque" adornments . . . which hid the dignity of its forms and the nobility of its expression'. Another important factor in the town's rebuilding was the strict enforcement of its planning regulations. Heights, façades, windows, even eaves and cornices, were rigorously controlled. An architect who disobeyed the regulations would be banned from directing another project for two years for the first offence, six years for the second, and permanently if caught a third time.

The expansion of San Sebastián was halted in 1833 by the outbreak of the first Carlist War, a long and complicated conflict in which British volunteers and the British navy made some slight restitution for the earlier disgrace by helping the inhabitants defend their town: high above the city on the northern slopes of Monte Urgull, a small, ill-kept but very poignant cemetery holds the remains of the British who died there. After 1840 San Sebastián started to grow again, inspired largely by improvements in communications. The journey from Madrid took fifty uncomfortable hours in a diligence, an expedition likely to deter even the most enthusiastic admirer of the Basque coastline. The building of the Madrid–Irún railway, however, and the opening of the station in San Sebastián in 1864, made the journey effortless and popular. The city had a thousand or so summer visitors in 1850 but 90,000 a generation later.

The first obstacle to the city's enlargement was the continued existence of its fortifications which had been restored after 1813. Although military experts pointed out that these were virtually useless in modern warfare, they were not finally demolished until 1864. Thereafter the expansion or *ensanche* could spread southwards along straight regular streets between the bay and the River Urumea. The *ensanche* was bounded to the north by the Alameda, a wide boulevard dividing the older town from the new development, and to the south by an avenue originally named after the queen, then after 'liberty' and subsequently after Spain by Francoists who found the word *libertad* subversive; it is now once again, however, the Avenida de la Libertad. The architect, Antonio Cortázar, planned a somewhat class-conscious division of his *ensanche*: the richest would live in the middle, he declared, the floating summer population would fringe the bay in buildings shielding the centre from the north-west wind, and the artisan and working classes would inhabit the southern areas 'protected from the wind but less favoured by good views'. The centre of the *ensanche* was to be the arcaded Plaza de Guipúzcoa, a delightful square in which on a marble table one can read the time differences between San Sebastián and the rest of the world.

The city became a fashionable resort in the last quarter of the nineteenth century largely because the royal family decided to go there for its summer holidays. San Sebastián had a long tradition of royalism. In 1699 the last Habsburg king awarded the town the title *'muy noble y muy leal'* ('very noble and very loyal') and by the coat of arms on the old town hall an inscription announces, *'ganadas por fidelidad, nobleza y lealtad'* ('won for fidelity, nobility and loyalty'). It was the first city to proclaim the infant Isabel II queen of Spain in 1833 and afterwards it defended her cause against a fervently Carlist countryside. In 1845 the young queen stayed in the town to try a hydrotherapeutic cure for a skin infection, and in subsequent years other European monarchs, including Napoleon III and Queen Victoria, were among the visitors. But the crucial visit was that of María Cristina, the queen mother and regent, who arrived with her children in 1887 and returned each summer for the next forty years. San Sebastián was suitably grateful for her choice and in 1905 named its grand new bridge over the Urumea the Puente de María Cristina. Some years later the queen mother was named honorary mayoress of the city.

María Cristina built herself a summer palace on the other side of the bay, and the authorities obligingly diverted the existing coast road through a tunnel so as not to spoil the view. Called the Miramar, it was designed by an English architect to resemble an

English country house; its blend of mock Tudor, mock Gothic and mock Queen Anne, however, made it look more like a villa in suburban Surrey. It was from the Miramar that the young king, Alfonso XIII, drove over to Biarritz in the winter of 1906 to court Queen Victoria's granddaughter, Princess Ena of Battenberg. And it was at the Miramar's chapel that Ena had to be 're-baptized' into the Catholic faith. The event 'was made as unpleasant for me as possible,' she recalled when describing a ceremony in which she had 'to deeply regret having transgressed' and 'renounce and abjure every error, heresy and sect' which opposed the Roman Church.

In the years after their marriage the king and queen spent the late summer and early autumn in San Sebastián. Alfonso liked to arrive there before his mother's birthday on 20 July, which annoyed Ena who would have preferred to extend her annual visit to England until Cowes week. But at San Sebastián she could play tennis and golf or go riding, and court life there was less pompous and suffocating than in Madrid. She resented the rigid protocol demanded by her mother-in-law (who had decorated the Miramar with 'endless little Austrian atrocities') and insisted on less formality for herself. As Marie, the exiled Grand Duchess of Russia, remembered, Ena was 'by far the most human representative of her kind in spite of the long period spent at the stiffest court in Europe'. She smoked cigarettes, wore a tight bathing-dress and liked to wander around the tea-shops of the town. The Duke of Sutherland once saw the queen swimming from the beach, escorted by two armed and fully clad soldiers, who entered the water on either side of her and kept advancing until the water reached their necks. Ena's pastimes were not always appreciated by the courtiers. She was particularly fond of San Sebastián's *thés dansants* which, according to a British diplomat, 'were not to the taste of Spain's aristocracy which was strictly "stay-at-home" and stingy'.

Alfonso and Ena used to drive over to Biarritz for polo and give a tea-party after matches. The French town also attracted Spain's aristocratic youths, especially in the 1920s after gambling had been made illegal in their own country. As the Russian grand duchess recalled, 'the majority of the San Sebastián colony spent their days, and especially their nights, in their automobiles, tearing madly backwards and forwards between San Sebastián and Biarritz, making the roads a menace to the rest of humanity'.

But San Sebastián was not simply a resort for the smart and wealthy. For two or three months every year it became the Simla of Spain, the place not only of the court but also of the government. Ministers who were obliged to move there with their secretaries usually found the town agreeable. The liberal prime minister Sagasta, however, loathed the place and refused to leave his beloved Avila unless there was a government crisis. A prolonged crisis in 1894 did in fact force him to spend the summer in San Sebastián, a sojourn he resented so much that his first words on resigning the following year were, 'Thank God! What I have done today I should have done at the beginning of last June, and then I would have been able to go, as is my custom, to Avila.'

In 1902 a Madrid journalist described the almost obligatory routine of smart society in San Sebastián: visits to the beach in the morning and the Alameda at midday, a promenade along the Paseo de la Concha in the early evening, and an appearance at the Gran Casino at night. Certain excursions were also permissible, to Biarritz, for example, or to the racecourse at Lasarte which was supposed to resemble Epsom. San Sebastián was adopted by the Spanish aristocracy to such an extent that more Andalusian grandees were born there than in Seville. Perhaps inevitably the noblemen brought some rather antiquated notions of honour with them. In 1919, when King Alfonso's elderly polo tutor, the Marquis of Villavieja, received 'an incredibly insulting letter' from a young *señorito*, he insisted on challenging him to a duel in San Sebastián. With the Duke of Alba ('Jimmy') as his second, he made a rendezvous at the racing stables at Lasarte and, fencing with an Italian sword ('model of San Donato'), quickly wounded his opponent. 'It had all been settled in the very first "chukka"!' declared the old polo player, adding that 'a man should be ready to fight for his honour, and I don't see why this should cause more criticism or win less respect than when a nation declares itself ready to do the same'.

The town's chief scenic attraction was and remains the bay of the Concha ('shell') with the *paseo* or promenade that fringes part of it. A century ago the French writer René Bazin watched the pairs of red oxen dragging bathing cabins on to the sand. By the time they had been erected, he observed, 'the elegant society swimmers have arrived. The men swim on the left, the women in the middle of the beach. All on entering the water wet the ends of their fingers and make the sign of the cross.' At one time a different division existed, the single-sex areas separated by a mixed bathing zone. Few similarities exist between the bathers of then and now. At the beginning of the century most people wore hats and went to great lengths to avoid getting sunburnt: bronzed skins were associated with peasants and mariners. Nowadays, according to a proud local journalist, there is more topless bathing at San Sebastián than at any other resort on the northern coast. Perhaps only the children, paddling and building sandcastles, have not changed.

In 1876 a Catalan writer, Mañé y Flaquer, travelled to the Basque province of Guipúzcoa and compiled a list of the promenades at San Sebastián with advice about the best times to visit them. For summer nights he recommended the Alameda, where the town hall's brass bands gave concerts, or the Paseo de Oquendo where one could hear military music on Sundays. The Paseo de Atocha had been one of the most fashionable walks, especially on winter afternoons, but by 1876 it was going rapidly downhill and was almost as sad as the Paseo de Cañería which was suitable for those of a 'melancholic inclination'. People who wanted good views of the sea, advised Mañé y Flaquer, should go to the Paseo de los Curas, while those wishing to watch a really good sunset should direct themselves to the Paseo de Puertas Coloradas. But the best of the promenades, curving with the bay, was the Paseo de la Concha which stretches from the Casino to the Miramar. One of its most well-known features remains the large group of tamerisk trees in the Alderdi Eder park. A town councillor apparently saw these trees in Nice at the end of the last century and thought they would look good in San Sebastián. Its citizens still think so although it is difficult for an outsider to appreciate their charm. Their shapes are dwarf and graceless, their colour a drab green, their branches stick out in all directions, and their ugly bark is so badly split it has to be held together with bits of iron. But no one would dream of cutting them down.

The population increased so rapidly, from 14,600 in 1860 to 52,500 by 1914, that Cortázar's *ensanche* had to be followed by several others to the south and also to the east, on the right bank of the River Urumea. These new housing schemes were accompanied by a profusion of theatres, schools, hospitals, bridges, markets and above all hotels. Some of these, such as the Mercado de la Brecha (created on the site of the breach made by British troops in 1813), were built in the town's traditional neo-classical manner, but the architecture of most was eclectic, a mixture of modern European and traditional Spanish styles. The Victoria Eugenia theatre and the Hotel María Cristina, neighbouring buildings overlooking the Urumea, were opened in 1912. Built by the same company, they could hardly look more different. The theatre is perhaps best described as 'neo-Plateresque' with some classical pillars and a couple of towers which look as if they have been reflected from Salamanca in a convex mirror. The hotel, designed by a French architect, is an enormous building in the international Ritz style. Like its rival, the Hotel Londres, it is so sumptuous and enticing that a local writer, Fernando Savater, sometimes wishes he did not live in the same town as them. 'If occasionally in my life I have wished I was not a native of San Sebastián, it has been on those occasions when I have imagined myself arriving as a foreigner and putting up at the María Cristina, opposite the turbid and nostalgic bridges of the Urumea, or breakfasting in a bed at the Londres with the balcony of my room wide open to the perpetual miracle of La Concha.' Coco Chanel, forced to eat in her room at the María Cristina because society ladies objected to the presence of a dress designer in the same dining-room as themselves, would probably have taken a less indulgent view.

The most fantastic and eclectic building of all is the Gran Casino, built in the 1880s in an amalgam of modern French and Italian Renaissance styles. Its position is striking, one flank on the bay, the other on the Alameda, with the southern front facing the tamerisks of the Alderdi Eder park. The construction of the building had aroused much opposition on moral grounds. One newspaper scoffed at the argument that the casino had to be built in order to prevent summer visitors from moving to Biarritz. Let them go, it demanded, for it was better to be poor and honest than to live off a vice that would ruin many innocent families. The building went up regardless and was followed in the next century by another elegant casino, the Gran Kursaal. But the puritans won in the end. General Primo de Rivera, the dictator in whose 1923 coup Alfonso XIII acquiesced, decreed the abolition of gambling a year later. The Gran Casino briefly became a hospital of the Red Cross before being transformed into the town hall in Franco's time. The Gran Kursaal fared even less well, enjoying only two years as a casino before becoming a theatre and then a cinema. It was demolished in 1973.

Spain's neutrality in the First World War prolonged San Sebastián's Belle Epoque beyond that of other European countries. The baccarat continued, with the concerts and the dancing and the saunters along the Paseo de la Concha. And after the armistice the Parisian couturiers returned and Diaghilev's ballets were put on at the theatre. For a few weeks in the summer of 1920 the city even hosted sessions of the Council of the League of Nations. But the town's fortunes turned sharply soon afterwards. Two disastrous events, robbing the city of many of its wealthy and aristocratic visitors, were the abolition of gambling and the royal family's decision to go to Santander instead of San Sebastián for its summer holidays. Reversals in the Moroccan war, the political crises of the 1920s, and the coming of the Second Republic further dampened the spirit of a resort which belonged so much to the turn of the century. San Sebastián enjoyed a limited revival during the Franco regime but before long it had been overtaken by newer and more fashionable developments on Spain's Mediterranean coast.

Most people associate the Basque country with heavy industry and violent nationalism. Both phenomena, which are closely linked, surfaced in the province of Vizcaya in the nineteenth century. San Sebastián and its province of Guipúzcoa were scarcely touched by either until after the First World War, but then, as in neighbouring Vizcaya, they came together. The imposition of massive industrial projects on a society which was rural, religious and conservative, and the arrival of a large immigrant population to work in the new factories, were the chief factors behind the emergence of Basque nationalism. Anyone who travels today in the valleys behind San Sebastián and sees the vast paper mills and other factories planted by insensitive capitalism in the middle of primitive villages, will understand the origins of the nationalist movement. The terrorist organization ETA may have had a series of Marxist and Maoist leaders, but its recruits still come from hilly backward areas like Goierri which have been barbarously mistreated by remote industrialists.

In spite of its Catholic and conservative following, the Basque Nationalist Party supported the republic in 1936 in the justified hope that it would be rewarded with a statute of autonomy for its loyalty. To Franco's supporters this was unexpected treason and Vizcaya and Guipúzcoa were termed the 'traitor provinces' after their capture by the rebels. During the years of the dictatorship Basque nationalism revived, stimulated by the regime's repression and its refusal to allow the Basque language to be taught in schools or used in publications. ETA's campaign of violence began in 1967 and increased rapidly in the last years of Franco's life. After the dictator's death it became even more intensive, in spite of the new government's concessions to Basque sentiment and the grant of another statute of autonomy. ETA and its political wing Herri Batasuna refused to accept that the country had changed or that democracy had been established. As late as 1982, the year of the first socialist election victory, the Herri Batasuna senator for Guipúzcoa, Miguel Castells, talked about 'the fascist regime in Madrid' and told me that ETA was doing the country a favour by carrying on the struggle!

I met Castells one late afternoon in San Sebastián. He was nervous and fidgety, squinting down each side street we walked past as if he feared innumerable assassins were lying in wait for him. The police were all fascists and torturers, he told me, and there could be no compromise with them or with their masters in Madrid. As we walked around the town, however, I could not help feeling that it was safer to be walking with him than with a policeman, a retired colonel or a centre party politician – the people usually targeted by the terrorists Castells supported. (In 1978 ETA had murdered sixty-eight people, in 1979 seventy-eight, in 1980 more than ninety.) And it was certainly safer to be with Castells than with the courageous civil governor, Pedro Arístegui, whom I saw during the same visit. Arístegui had survived four assassination attempts by ETA since taking office eighteen months earlier and talked nonchalantly about the chances of fresh efforts to kill him. In fact he did survive his years in San

174

Sebastián as well as a subsequent mission to Central America only to die from a stray shell when he was ambassador in Beirut.

Revisiting San Sebastián in 1990 after an absence of some years, I was struck by the increase in ETA's visible propaganda. The city was covered with daubed slogans and colourful, naïve murals exalting the merits of the armed struggle. Paintbrushes were being regularly applied also to the bilingual signposts, erasing the Spanish name and thus perplexing the foreigner who wants to go to Vitoria but doesn't know that its Basque name is Gasteiz. This was the work of the *borrokas*, young militants of Herri Batasuna who demonstrate their valour by marching and shouting and painting slogans. They are also fond of correcting people who refer to their city as San Sebastián instead of using the Basque name Donostia. The Calle de Juan de Bilbao in the old town, of considerable anthropological interest, is full of bars frequented by noisy *borrokas*.

The ETA/Herri Batasuna presence is even more intrusive in the Plaza de la Constitución. 'La Consti', as its inhabitants sometimes call it, is the heart of the old city, the site of the former town hall and a place for bull-running before 1902. It was long famous for the delightful small shops of herbalists, bakers, cabinet-makers and booksellers; it still has a bookshop which must be a good one because it has been the target both of Francoist ultras and gangs of *borrokas*. But by 1990 the square had been defaced by 192 white posters each bearing the name of a different ETA terrorist (or as the posters imply a martyr for the homeland) and by a plaque condemning the French government for handing over these 'refugees' to Spanish justice.

Yet San Sebastián is not Beirut nor even Belfast. One voter in seven supports ETA via Herri Batasuna, enough to prevent a peaceful solution to the Basque problem but not enough to dominate or permanently disrupt everybody else's lives. San Sebastián is faded and somewhat shabby, but it is still a fine resort with elegant hotels and beautiful scenery. It still has its international festivals, jazz in July and cinema in September, when the city briefly recaptures its cosmopolitan past and American film directors crowd the terrace of the Café Guría. And it retains its reputation for the best food in Spain, a tradition nurtured over the century by the city's Academia de Cocina and the later Cofradía

Vasca de Gastronomía. San Sebastián's restaurants have the highest proportion of Michelin stars in Spain.

The most notorious Basque eating tradition is the 'gastronomic society', a dining club which excludes women. The dinners of these numerous societies are noisy and rather boorish affairs with a good deal of singing to accompany the eating and drinking. Yet they have a social function as well, the members meeting on terms of complete equality and calling each other *tu*. An important businessman or politician will have to roll up his sleeves and do his share of serving and pouring drinks. Only on the Eve of St Sebastián, 20 January, do the gastronomic societies open their doors to women so that they too can drink champagne and eat baby eels in garlic. When asked about their exclusion for the rest of the year, Basque men reply rather sheepishly that theirs is a matriarchal society from which they need occasionally to take refuge with their fellows.

Another exclusively male activity is the *txikiteo* or bar crawl, which the local writer, Fernando Savater, describes as 'not only a pastime but almost a lifestyle'. This is not a haphazard affair like an Edinburgh pub crawl with the men rolling up and down Rose Street sampling the taverns at random. A group is formed, an itinerary planned and the timing arranged. The men then move off in a bunch towards the old city, which must have one of the highest concentrations of bars in Europe; indeed they are so close to each other in the streets around the Plaza de la Constitución that very little 'crawling' has to be done. As they are almost invariably excellent, it would obviously be unfair to concentrate on only a few. A large number must therefore be visited in the course of the evening, an obligation facilitated by helpful barmen who offer half-gins and tonic or small quantities of cider or the local wine *txakoli* which they pour from a great height into squat glasses. The routine is always the same. One man buys all the drinks, he stands with his friends in a circle to drink them, and then the group moves off to the next bar where someone else will pay. Many women go to San Sebastián's bars as well, though not usually in large groups, and so do teetotallers, for the snacks or *pinchos* are delicious and tend to leave one with little appetite for lunch. Indeed, the visitor who has sampled these bars will surely understand the epitaph Savater has composed for himself: 'He walked, he lived and he drank in the old city.' San Sebastián may be decadent, its role reduced and its atmosphere stained by political violence, but it remains one of the most delightful and hedonistic of Spanish towns.

La Plaza Mayor, Madrid

NINE

Madrid

European capitals have traditionally fallen into two categories, romantic cities and cities to be taken seriously. Paris, Rome and Vienna were leading members of the first group; London, Berlin and Moscow among others represented the second. Madrid never belonged to either list. The sort of traveller who wrote *Walks in Rome* or *A Wanderer in Paris* was not tempted to write a companion volume about Madrid. Moonlit strolls by the Tiber were more attractive to describe – and no doubt easier to sell – than a tramp along the banks of the unlovely Manzanares. 'The least interesting of all Spanish places' is a typical nineteenth-century traveller's view of Madrid, a city which was often said to contain nothing worth seeing except the Prado museum. Even Sacheverell Sitwell in 1931 could announce that Madrid had 'never had fine churches or palaces; indeed it is a disappointment in nearly all things except the Prado'.

Travellers who wanted to swoon over romantic Spain went to Granada or Seville, but they usually stayed in Madrid long enough to sneer at it. According to the Anglo-Italian visitor Gallenga, the city had 'hardly a building' that was 'not commonplace and insignificant, if not positively hideous'. He found his 'eye saddened by the squalor and decay of old Madrid, sick of the dwarfish turrets, clumsy domes, and unsightly pinnacles which disfigure the fronts of many public buildings'. Even worse was the 'shocking bad taste' of the churches – 'edifices in wigs and curl-papers one might say'; disgraceful as Baroque edifices might be in Italy, they could 'nowhere rouse such feelings of wrath and destructiveness as in this city of unredeemed architectural ugliness'. But that was not all. Madrid may have been 'the ugliest of

179

cities; but there is something uglier than the town itself, and that is the country around it'. It was 'worse than a blank – a great undulating wilderness'; 'anything looking more bald and dreary' could not be imagined. Nowadays this landscape is pretty hideous, littered with unplanned development and chalets creeping up the slopes of the Guadarrama foothills. But a century ago it had a wild, impoverished beauty invisible to Gallenga, a tawny, austere appearance under the grey sierra evoked in the poems of Antonio Machado. Perhaps Gallenga fitted Santiago Ramón y Cajal's description of 'someone with as biased a sense of colour as a caterpillar to be forever missing the damp and uniform green of the countries of the north, and to despise the penetrating poetry of the grey, the yellow, the dun-coloured and the blue'.

A favourite target, for Spaniards as well as foreigners, was the River Manzanares. The Seine inspired poetry and romantic dreams, the Thames served the largest city in the world, but Madrid's river was no use for anything. It was unattractive, unnavigable and practically dry. A French soldier in an army which invaded the country without encountering opposition is alleged to have seen the Manzanares and remarked, 'In this country even the rivers run away'. Alexandre Dumas, a Frenchman who appreciated Madrid and said he would like to live there, bought a glass of water, drank half of it and told the water-seller he should throw the other half into the Manzanares, which probably needed it more. On his return to Paris Dumas declared that he would not write about the river because, in spite of many searches, he had been unable to find it.

Dumas was following a long literary tradition of Spanish writers who had made jokes and composed verses about the inadequacies of the Manzanares. Quevedo called it an 'apprentice stream' where even the frogs and mosquitoes were dying of thirst; in summer one could not even wash one's feet in it. The land was moistened by the Manzanares, said Zabaleta, as if by a finger tracing saliva. When Lope de Vega was asked his opinion about an impressive new bridge, he replied that the town should either buy a river or sell the bridge. The Toledo and Segovia bridges are indeed disproportionate to the size of the river and provoked a later poet, Ventura de la Vega, to refer to them as 'two sarcasms of stone'. At the beginning of this century a town

180

councillor, perhaps irritated that people did not take the river seriously, decided to do some statistical research. Over the previous three years, he announced afterwards, twenty-nine people had died in the Manzanares, a higher total than the number of deaths in the Seine during the same period. Later he had to admit that the twenty-nine had not actually died from drowning, which would have been almost impossible, but from diving off the bridges and hitting their heads on the river bed.

At the beginning of this century Edward Hutton declared that in Madrid 'you will search in vain for any building, cathedral, palace or *ayuntamiento* [town hall], that is not modern, debased and feeble. Her streets are ill-paved and filthy, her people noisy, miserable and rapacious, her climate the worst in Spain.' Unjust in every respect except for the remarks about the cathedral and the noisiness of the inhabitants, the view was strikingly similar to the verdict of Charles III who in 1759 succeeded to the Spanish throne after twenty-five years as King of Naples. Madrid was badly designed, he wrote, dirty, ill-lit and without distinguished buildings; the place immediately made him feel homesick for Naples and Caserta. The city's growth had indeed been badly managed, its houses and religious institutions multiplying at chaotic speed after Madrid became the Spanish capital in 1561. Within three generations the population expanded from about 20,000 to 175,000, and the increase in the ecclesiastical population was proportionately even higher: by 1620 convents and monasteries occupied a third of the city's area.

King Charles and Mr Hutton decided to overlook such fine buildings as the Ayuntamiento and the Cárcel de Corte ('Court Prison') which is now the foreign ministry. There is nothing vulgar or debased about these dignified façades of red brick and granite framed by their low square towers. Nor is there anything feeble about the royal palace built by Charles's father Philip V. Based on rejected plans for the Louvre and built for a French monarch whose tastes owed much to his Italian wives, it might have been expected to win favour with those who jeered at Madrid's indigenous styles. Hutton, however, appeared as impervious to this as he was to the efforts of Charles III himself to improve the city. Madrid owes many of its finest buildings to this king, the only member of his dynasty before our time to have ruled Spain even adequately. Those which survive include the Prado, the Customs House (now the Treasury), the post office in the Puerta del Sol (now the seat of the Autonomous Community of Madrid) and the Royal Academy of Fine Arts.

The long and widespread disparagement of Madrid probably owes much to a feeling of disappointment with a city which failed to achieve the ambitions invested in it. Elevated suddenly to the position of imperial capital, the expected glory did not material-ize. In the words of the statesman Manuel Azaña, 'Madrid is a frustrated capital like the political idea to which it owes its position. It was destined to be the federal capital of Spain and its dominions, and instead of presiding over the integration of an empire it has had to witness the sinking of fleets and the loss of kingdoms.' The titles conceded by various kings – 'very noble and very loyal', 'imperial and crowned', 'very heroic' – came to sound like sarcastic jokes about a city which knew that it was neither imperial nor heroic. In the seventeenth century, as the country floundered and seemed on the verge of collapse, Madrid was widely seen as a parasitic city with a society that was corrupt and frivolous. It was evidently a highly dangerous place as well, for a guide-book had been published advising foreigners how to avoid being robbed or roughed up.

Yet in spite of its reputation and reduced role, Madrid retained its innate vanity. A French traveller in the eighteenth century was astonished to hear a sermon in which the priest remarked that Christ had been fortunate to be tempted by the devil in Palestine because from their mountain Madrid had been hidden by the Pyrenees. Had he been able to catch a glimpse of the Spanish capital, the priest suggested, Christ might have succumbed to the devil's offer. In the nineteenth century Madrid's prestige in Europe was lower than ever before, but the pretensions survived. Nevertheless, 'for all its ridiculous vanity,' wrote Galdós in his great novel *Fortunata y Jacinta*, 'Madrid was a metropolis in name only. It was a bumpkin in a gentleman's coat buttoned over a torn, dirty shirt.'

Although there is nothing rustic about contemporary Madrid, elderly people today can remember when it was still a bumpkin. The city has changed more in the last thirty years than it did between the building of the *ensanche* (begun in the 1860s) and the

1950s. By the time *Fortunata y Jacinta* appeared in 1876, the modern geography of old Madrid had been defined: the condemned convents and monasteries (forty-five from a total of sixty) had been demolished or converted to other uses; the main railways were in place, entering the capital from the south, the west and the north-east; and the Salamanca district was already fashionable. Apart from the major upheaval caused by cutting the Gran Vía through the old city, the ground plan of the central districts has changed little since. Galdós's Madrid thus survived for a further three or four generations, the Madrid of bureaucrats and coffee slurpers, of *serenos* (night-watchmen) and café philosophers, the city of the spittoon and the fan (Gautier could not find a woman without one, but they went out of fashion, apparently, when women needed their hands for cigarettes), the home of *La Chulapona* and other *zarzuelas* whose choruses look as if they have been just brought in from the Puerta del Sol.

Madrid's population growth in the late nineteenth and early twentieth centuries was much slower than that of Barcelona or Bilbao. Galdós's Madrid, its frontiers as well as its streets, was thus recognizable to anyone brought up in the city before the Civil War. Jorge Semprún, the former communist writer who resigned as the socialist minister of culture in 1991, has recalled the geography of his boyhood, the geography of a city which could then be walked with less difficulty than it takes to cross the modern metropolis by motor car. Semprún became aware of the literary city of earlier generations from his father who frequented the Ateneo, the spiritual home of Madrid's intellectuals, and various *cafés de tertulias*. But from personal exploration he could locate the physical limits of a city whose population since his childhood has multiplied by six. It was a Madrid bounded to the south by Atocha, the station of the southern immigrant, and to the north by that point in the Calle Serrano where the traffic now charges around the Plaza de la República Argentina. To the east the frontier was the Retiro, the only real park in Madrid and therefore the only place where people from all classes could meet. Pío Baroja found there the aristocracy, the plutocracy, various grades of bourgeoisie and courtesans with names like 'the Venus of the Necropolis'. A later chronicler, the entertaining Fernando Díaz-Plaja, recalls the smart sailor-suited children from the Salamanca district escaping from their nannies and playing with working-class children from Atocha. All *madrileños* liked the Retiro, according to Baroja, but 'foreigners simply did not see the point of the gardens ... Frenchmen found very little licence to talk to women and Germans asked, surprised: "But where can one can get something to drink?"'

Although new working-class districts were being established to the north of the *ensanche*, in Cuatro Caminos and Tetuán de las Victorias, the traditional home of the Madrid poor was in districts like Lavapiés to the west of Atocha. This was the *barrio* of the Madrid 'Cockneys', the *manolos* and *chulapas* of Goya and Ramón de la Cruz, and its long sloping streets still retain the atmosphere of a Madrid 'East End'. Another traditional area is the Rastro, the enormous flea-market a little further west, which has not yet been entirely taken over by antique dealers. Baroja remembered the Rastro when he was a child as an 'almost medieval' place where one could buy anything from false teeth to coach wheels: 'there were also artful players of the three-card trick and small-time swindlers and tricksters'. He found it had been smartened up a bit at the beginning of the century before reverting during the period of shortage and the black market after the Civil War. Fernando Chueca recalls such characters of the time as the rag-dealers and the gypsies who tried to sell fake Parker pens.

To the north of Lavapiés and the Rastro is the traditional centre of the city, the Puerta del Sol. This fan-shaped square is architecturally undistinguished except for the old post office, and even that has seemed a sinister building since it was used as Franco's directorate-general of security. Yet it is the quintessential place of Madrid, the square which typifies the city and its people. Borrow described it somewhat churlishly as 'the great place of assemblage for the idlers of the capital, poor or rich', but many of its pedestrians are now people rushing to appointments. Ramón Gómez de la Serna, the most prolific of many chroniclers of Madrid, wrote two books about the Puerta del Sol. In one he drew a portrait of the city through observing the people who crossed the square at different hours. In the other he illustrated the place's importance with the remark that 'if a wedding or a baptism did not pass through the Puerta del Sol, it was neither the wedding nor the baptism which God had ordered'. For a long time it was the centre of the city, but since the beginning of this century the centre has moved east (city centres usually move west) towards the wide boulevard of the Castellana, near the Cortes, the grand hotels and the Banco de España.

The Calle Alcalá leaves the Puerta del Sol and meets the Gran Vía shortly before the combined artery crosses the Castellana. It was once Madrid's only important street and it still has several fine buildings; the view to the Alcalá gate, however, is ruined by the city's worst excrescence, the Torre de Valencia, which looms gigantically beyond. The Gran Vía is a much newer street, begun in 1910 as a thoroughfare linking the old city with the *ensanche*. Descriptions of it normally contain references to Haussmann, the destroyer of much of Paris, and contemptuous dismissals, such as V. S. Pritchett's, of 'that preposterous South American street'. It did cause a fair amount of destruction (fourteen streets went completely and fourteen others were mutilated) but it is difficult now to imagine – or even to want – Madrid without it. The cluster of buildings that rears up on the curve before plunging down to the Calle Alcalá is haphazardly planned and yet, despite differences of height and architectural style, forms a harmonious group. Even the disparate colours do not matter, for the pale browns, reds and greys are all colours of the *meseta*.

Until the second half of the nineteenth century Madrid's social classes had generally lived together in the same *barrios*, often in the same building. As the rich did not like climbing stairs, the top floors of their buildings were inhabited by poorer people. After 1860, however, the aristocrats and middle classes began moving out to the new streets of the *ensanche*, particularly in the Salamanca district which was the first in Madrid to have water closets and running water. Some did not go, from habit or because they thought it was too far away from the centre. Galdós describes a wealthy lady who would never 'have exchanged her neighbourhood, that "corner of Madrid" where she had been born, for any of the flamboyant sections of town that enjoyed the reputation of being airier and cheerier. No matter what they said, the Salamanca neighbourhood was *country*.' But she was exceptional. Most bourgeois ladies did not hesitate to move to an exclusively middle-class district like Salamanca. There they had no problems with increasingly radical workers or, after the invention of lifts,

185

with poor people of any sort other than domestic servants. Elevators, those underrated agents of social change, meant that even the most sluggish of sybarites could live on the top floor.

In the Salamanca quarter aristocrats and bourgeois could insulate themselves not only from the dangers of riots and revolutionary agitation; they could also avoid contamination from Madrid's notorious intellectuals. In contrast with Barcelona, the capital's high society at the turn of the century had few artistic interests. A man as stuffy as the Marquis of Villavieja, King Alfonso's polo tutor, could complain of a 'dense wall of reserve' and a 'rigorous maintaining of etiquette and old ceremonial' in that society. Even in Madrid in the 1920s, he said, 'it was a rare thing for a lady to keep a real *salon* where scientists, writers and artists could find good listeners and encouragement. This delightful French form of social intercourse did not seem to appeal very greatly to the Spaniards who ruled the Madrid society.' Not that the marquis regretted this from his personal point of view. If his wife, who was one of the few aristocrats who did enjoy intelligent conversation, invited intellectuals to dinner, she suggested that Villavieja might like to stay with his sister at the Montellano Palace. 'She knew', wrote her husand, 'that unless people were interested in sport, it was difficult to tempt me.'

In the early 1950s the young historian Raymond Carr attempted to persuade Gerald Brenan to write the Spanish volume of the *Oxford History of Modern Europe*. Brenan, who had already written *The Spanish Labyrinth*, a brilliant book on the origins of the Civil War, declined with the unusual explanation that the truth could only be reached through literature not history. One happy result of these failed negotiations was that Carr, who had planned to study brigands in southern Italy, wrote the Oxford volume himself, his magisterial *Spain 1808–1939* duly appearing in 1966. Whoever was right about the respective merits of a literary or political explanation of Spanish history, it would be difficult to deny that Madrid lends itself more easily to a literary approach. For the capital has always been a city of writers. Seville or Barcelona may win any competition for painters, sculptors or architects, but Madrid would defeat both of them together in a contest over poets and novelists.

'To write in Madrid is to weep,' proclaimed Mariano José de

Larra, and it is true that the city has produced a prodigious number of impoverished writers attracted by illustrious predecessors and contemporaries. They were drawn too by the special character of a city which seemed as if it had been designed as a fictional setting, a place 'so novelistic', in the words of Gómez de la Serna, 'that its perfect novel would be that which has really happened'. Madrid has also given birth to a high proportion of the country's most successful authors: Lope de Vega, Quevedo, Tirso de Molina and Calderón were all born there in the last forty years of the sixteenth century. Later writers tended to be identified with their own versions of Madrid, the nineteenth-century world of Galdós, the Bohemian city of Valle-Inclán, the tragic town of the romantics or the decadent metropolis of the naturalists, the Madrid of Hemingway, of Cela, of Francisco Umbral, the place observed and described interminably by Gómez de la Serna. Madrid has entertained its writers and provided them with inspiration, but it has not fed them well or even commemorated them adequately. Lope de Vega lived in what is now the Calle Cervantes, Cervantes was buried in the Calle Lope de Vega, and Góngora lived in the Calle Quevedo. How typical this is of a city which specializes in contradictory names: the Plaza de Oriente is on the western extremity, Villaverde is the least green part of Madrid, the Ciudad de los Poetas has not a single street named after a poet. No place, however, has had as confusing a past as the Plaza Mayor which has had its name changed nine times in its history.

An excellent social history of Madrid could be written after studying its cafés and observing the hours and routines of their customers. Josep Pla's remark that 'man is partly a son of the cafés of his age' is particularly true of Madrid, at any rate since the middle of the last century. Before that the few cafés in the city were very bad. Théophile Gautier, who admitted that he was accustomed 'to the dazzling and enchanting luxury of the Parisian cafés', found them 'fifth-rate suburban places' whose decoration recalled 'the booths at fairs in which the bearded women and the living sirens are exhibited'; he conceded, however, that the lemonade was better than in Paris. The improvements in the cafés and the growth in their number, particularly in the Puerta del Sol and the surrounding streets, coincided with the growing popular-

187

ity of *tertulias*, those regular meetings of friends and colleagues chatting for hours over a cup of coffee. The *café-tertulia* was the most important institution in male social life in Madrid from the 1860s to the Civil War.

Poverty and loneliness were no doubt responsible for many people's participation in the *tertulias*. An unsuccessful writer living in a cold and uncomfortable room in a *pension* could at least find warmth and companionship in a café. His spirits would rise with the witty conversation and the warm coffee, and the *tertulias*, which could take place at almost any time of the day or night, would become the high point of an otherwise dreary day. As Galdós writes of one of his characters, Juan Pablo Rubín, 'the only delight in his sad existence was the café'. A fight, however, led to Rubín's expulsion from his usual place and he and his friends had to find a new café for their *tertulias*. One was suggested because it provided more sugar than the others, but a member of the group argued that the matter should not be viewed 'through the exclusive prism' of the sugar because the important thing was the quality of the coffee. However, the Café Imperial 'was eliminated because of the bullfighters ... another because of its vulgar, pretentious patrons' and a third 'because they didn't want to be surrounded by Frenchmen all the time'.

One of the most famous *cafés de tertulias* around 1920 was the Pombo near the Puerta del Sol, where Gómez de la Serna held forth in front of a large following of avant-garde writers and artists. He delighted his companions with his *greguerías*, epigrams which he defined as a combination of humour and metaphor, and in a passage which could stand as the epitaph of the true *madrileño* he described himself as 'a passer-by, an actor, an optimistic and impudent life, ambling towards death with the naïve happiness of one not going in that direction'. The most celebrated *café-tertulia* of all was the Café Gijón, which still stands in the Paseo de Recoletos opposite the National Library. Its supporters compare it enthusiastically with Florian's in Venice, the Greco in Rome and the Deux Magots in Paris, comparisons which would surprise anyone familiar with these three elegant establishments who enters the Spanish café for the first time. Like its city, the Gijón has much character but little charm. Despite its unglamorous interior, however, the café has consistently been a centre of Madrid's intellectual life since its foundation in 1888. It has also been the subject of various histories and novels.

Some customers, like Galdós or the liberal politician Canalejas, went to the Gijón to seek peace, to sit in a corner and read the newspapers. But most went to participate in the numerous *tertulias*, that of Lorca, Alberti and other poets, that of the magazine *Garcilaso*, those of groups of painters, novelists or actors who, for some reason, invariably talked standing up. The café was always full of 'the best Bohemia', said the writer Mercedes Formica, 'that is to say, the Bohemia which creates'. By the 1960s the *tertulias* had changed so much that they were almost unrecognizable. Only the poets still drank coffee or infusions of manzanilla; the other groups had discovered gin and whisky. But by then the institution of the *tertulia* was fast disappearing, partly because of modern pressures of time but also because the country was becoming richer. Declaiming for hours over a cup of coffee rather loses its appeal when Madrid's intellectuals can now afford to chat in the capital's excellent restaurants.

From time to time Madrid harboured a maverick who did not enter into the spirit of the *tertulias*. Pío Baroja refused to enter the Gijón, where he was horrified to hear that some writers drank chocolate with fried bread or consommé, and insisted that it must be a very boring place. Azorín never entered either, though he sometimes glanced in from the door, and Ortega apparently came in once, sat down, was subjected to a toast and fled as soon as he could. One day, when Hemingway was walking along the Paseo de Recoletos, a friend tried to persuade him to enter the café and meet various people who admired him and his work. 'I am an enemy of literary *tertulias*,' the American told him, 'and above all of the Gijón's. All those people, I assure you, are windbags. I advise you as a friend not to waste your time with them.'

Hemingway and his fellow mavericks had a point. The *tertulias* did consume a great deal of time that could have been spent in reading or writing. They did tend to become mutual admiration societies encouraging people to make facetious rejoinders rather than slower, more profound remarks. And they flattered the leading members excessively. The Aragonese novelist Ramón J. Sender refused to go to the *tertulias* in the Pombo partly because the café was 'airless, full of evil-smelling people sandwiched together', but also because Gómez de la Serna became so garrulous in this company that 'in the end he became boring, although basically he was not a boring man. There he became puffed up and conceited among idiots, mediocrities, the odd man of talent and a few queers.'

Early in the nineteenth century the writer Mesonero Romanos had criticized the tendency of *madrileños* to 'talk on all subjects with a dishonest superficiality which they learn in society'. This trait, encouraged by the *tertulia* institution, is still alive today. Every intellectual or café philosopher in Madrid feels he must be able to discuss any subject that comes up. His opinion, usually delivered with much frowning, brow-clutching and a seriousness worthy of Rodin's *Penseur*, often sounds lucid and learned even when its author has little idea what he's talking about. But sometimes, inevitably, it flops badly. The late Enrique Tierno Galván was a fine academic, a courageous opponent of Franco and at the end of his life a good socialist mayor of Madrid. But 'the old professor', as he was universally known, shared his fellow intellectuals' weakness for wishing to appear omniscient and trendy and in tune with the young. After John Lennon's murder in New York, he mistakenly agreed to go on television and discuss the former Beatle. It has been suggested that in front of the camera he suddenly became confused by the name and began thinking about the Calvinist preacher John Knox. At any rate he conflated the two names repeatedly throughout the interview, saying, 'I am very sorry about John Lennox ... His music was very good, very interesting ... I have always liked John Lennox very much.'

At a Madrid dinner party one might hear Proust being discussed by someone who works all day, except for a long lunch with other people, who goes out with friends almost every evening and spends his holidays in Marbella or Sotogrande, where the social life is even more exhausting than in Madrid. When, one wonders, has he sat down and read the ten complex volumes of Proust or any of the other writers whose names fly around his conversations? A possible answer was given, before Proust wrote a word, by Galdós, an author who modelled himself on Dickens and did for Madrid what his hero did for London. In his great epic *Fortunata y Jacinta* he observes that 'in a café one hears the stupidest and also the most sublime things. There are people who have learned everything they know about philosophy at a café table ... There are famous figures from parliament or the press who have learned all they know in cafés. Men with great assimilatory powers can reveal a considerable wealth of knowledge without ever having opened a book, and it is because they have appropriated ideas poured into these nocturnal circles by studious men who allow themselves an idle hour to scatter their knowledge in these pleasant and fraternal *tertulias*.' Galdós pointed out that café conversations were not all 'frivolity, stale anecdotes, and lies'; one could hear 'eloquent observations and pithy expositions of complex doctrines'. But naturally there were more 'trinkets' than 'priceless gems'.

Madrid's pretensions were ridiculed by Manuel Azaña in the days before he became a politician. Azaña was a genuine intellectual and the least *madrileño* of men, although he spent most of his life in the city and was born nearby in Alcalá de Henares. In his view 'the entire history of Madrid consists of handkissing and private or royal intrigues'. The people had 'always been absent from the history of the city except to cry of hunger', apart from that unique occasion when they rose against Napoleon. Madrid, said Azaña, 'grabs what people give it; it gobbles up but it does not assimilate or purify itself. Our city is not normal in anything; it provokes but does not satisfy; it neither speaks nor hears; it traps but does not retain.' One might attribute some of Azaña's bitterness to his rather modest success as a writer. As Unamuno said with unkind exaggeration, 'Beware of Azaña. He is an author without readers. He would be capable of starting a revolution in order to be read.' Yet Azaña was justified in mocking the pretensions of the know-all, non-reading intellectuals, and there was some truth in his observation that 'the best way to keep a secret in Spain is to write it in a book'. Even today over a third of Spanish households do not possess a book of any kind.

Much of Galdós's Madrid died in 1936 when the capital entered its second phase of heroism, echoing to shouts of '¡no pasarán!' as the International Brigades marched through the city to hold Franco on the western outskirts. After the war it reverted to the sub-Galdosian world of José Camilo Cela's *La Colmena*, an aimless, impoverished world of the hopeless and the defeated. Madrid was a city dominated by hunger, the black markets and the language of victorious fascism; even football teams in the Cup Final were required to stand in a line and give the fascist salute. As with Galdós, Cela's café, in spite of its tyrannical *patrona* and cringing staff, is a refuge from the misery outside where war widows struggle to survive, plain-clothes policemen bully suspects and desperate smokers join cigarette butts together.

By the 1950s Madrid was a more hopeful place, for Spain was benefiting from American aid and mass tourism was beginning. These were years characterized by sporting achievement and the Seat motor car, whose '600' soon became the most familiar sight on Spanish roads. Franco's regime took sport almost as seriously as the countries of Eastern Europe and its champions were hailed as national heroes. In 1955 Guillermo Timoner became the world motor-cycle champion, in 1959 a Spanish cyclist won the Tour de France for the first time, in 1965 the Real Madrid basketball team won the European Cup and the following year Santana won Wimbledon. But the greatest success was in football. Real Madrid proved itself to be the greatest team in Europe by winning the European Cup Final in 1956, the first of five successive victories. This was perhaps not quite the national achievement it was hailed as – of the seven goals scored against Eintracht Frankfurt in the 1960 Final, four were scored by the Hungarian Puskas and the other three by the Argentinian Di Stefano – but it helped the regime's aim of focusing the population's attention on sport instead of politics. During this era the sporting papers *Gol* and *Marca* sold more daily copies than any of the serious political papers such as *ABC* and *La Vanguardia*.

Madrid in the post-Civil War epoch was undoubtedly a boring and provincial place. It had lost its intellectuals and many of its most talented people and had retreated into one of its hermetic periods – what Ortega called Spain's 'Tibetanization' – a recurring condition when Spaniards go around saying their country is different and no foreigners understand them. By the early 1960s they were trying to break out again, only to find that the world had travelled a fair distance since they had last belonged to it. James Morris visited Madrid in these years and found it was 'the only city in Spain that feels provincial ... because the young *madrileños* want to be cosmopolitan, and look like small-town

Romans'. Cosmopolitanism was discouraged, however, by the capital's Ritz Hotel which refused to allow actors or actresses to stay, not apparently because they were inherently immoral but because they attracted fans. James Stewart managed to avoid the ban by using his wartime air force rank to reserve a room.

Franco, who more than anyone else was responsible for Madrid's provincialism and irrelevance in international affairs, was nevertheless obsessed by the idea of making the city bigger and grander, as if its prestige depended simply on the number of inhabitants. The dictator had once dreamed of an imperial future for Spain, signing his name in the golden book of Seville's Archivo de Indias and adding the words, 'before the relics of one empire, with the promise of another'. Presumably he had given up the idea by 1956, when Spain recognized Moroccan independence, but he was still intent on enlarging the imperial capital, encouraging the growth of banking and industry in an attempt to diminish the importance of Barcelona and Bilbao. During his dictatorship the city certainly became a much wealthier place and the population increased from barely a million at the end of the Civil War to nearly four million by the time of his death. Industrialization, however, was a mixed success. The 'dark beret' of pollution which hangs over the city, as Díaz-Plaja observes, comes less from factories than from inefficient boilers, bad quality coal and the exhaust pipes of cars stuck in Madrid's notorious traffic jams.

Unlike the *ensanche* of the nineteenth century, the modern expansion of Madrid has been chaotic and thoughtless, justly described by Semprún as 'ridiculous, disorganized and savage'. In 1950 Brenan could describe the outskirts as 'not scarring and antagonizing the landscape ... but blending with it in colour because [they are] made of materials that first came out of it and have then been reduced by the devouring heat and light to the same tonality'. Nowadays the word 'blending' could hardly be less appropriate; from any direction the hunched masses of apartment blocks can be starkly seen at a distance of twenty miles. Nearer in, the horrors of Getafe, Vallecas, Barajas and Villaverde announce the new Madrid. So do the motorways running along the banks of the Manzanares, cutting through the poplars and meadows that once bordered the river. And so, from a different angle, do places like Somosaguas, Puerta de Hierro and La Moraleja, luxurious modern oases for the very rich. La Moraleja is like one of the greenest and most prosperous areas of the Home Counties transported to the *meseta*, assured of a good water supply to keep it green, and then fenced and patrolled to prevent the real Castile from intruding. Living in a suburb, quiet and agreeable though it may be, is so alien to the *madrileño* temperament, however, that some families like to spend the week in the Salamanca district, in a flat in Serrano or the Castellana, and the weekend in a 'cottage' beside a golf course in the outskirts.

In the centre of the city the ugliest new building took place in the Castellana, the Plaza de Colón and various adjacent streets. As usual the worst vandals were banks, insurance companies and department stores; a number of Madrid's oldest cafés fell victim to one or other of them. Some things have improved. In spite of the pollution, for instance, Madrid has become a greener place, the number of trees in its streets and squares growing from about 50,000 at the outbreak of the Civil War to over 200,000 by 1989. It also has more tulips. On completing seventy-five years of working for the municipality in 1950, a gardener was given 30,000 tulip bulbs which were planted in the Retiro and the Puerta de Alcalá. Tierno Galván was also a tulip enthusiast, planting so many of them that finally the Dutch created a new dark red variety which they named after 'the old professor'.

In traditional Madrid, away from the Castellana, the speculation has fortunately been limited. There are few tall buildings either in the centre or in the Jerónimos district on the west side of the Retiro. The streets and squares of the old city reveal a contradictory combination of preservation, destruction and neglect. A *plaza* in which Galdós would recognize every window on three sides will be desecrated by a concrete cinema on the fourth. One representative Madrid square contains the beautiful convent of the Descalzas Reales, which belongs to the state and is very badly preserved, its pictures full of holes; the best antiquarian bookshop in Spain, Luis Bardón's; a car park in the middle; and the vast Caja de Ahorros y Monte de Piedad, a typical glass and concrete building of the 1960s except that it preserves, absurdly, the old Churrigueresque doorway. A good example of neglect without demolition is the old palace at Number 9 Calle del Arenal, the street which stretches from the Puerta del Sol to the old opera-house. The ground floor looking outwards contains various establishments such as a jeweller, a jeans shop and a branch of the Banco Exterior de España; inside on the same floor there are more than twenty low-quality shops. At the bottom of the massive marble staircase a stall sells car radios; coats of arms and ancestral faces in the entrance ceiling look down on glass cases of tennis shoes in the hall; the gilt on the frescos of nymphs and fruit is lit up by neon signs and in the covered patio slender, pseudo-Corinthian pillars disappear in the shop front of a clock mender.

According to the novelist Francisco Umbral, Madrid was once the domicile of dress designers and bureaucrats and is now the home of executives and transvestites. Regrettable or not, the change suggests that the city has become more modern and international and has inverted its original character: instead of being a provincial city aspiring to be imperial, it is now a cosmopolitan city preserving the provincial characteristics which it values. Madrid's economic weight inside Spain and in Europe has steadily increased over the last twenty years. In 1970 the capital had barely a quarter of the head offices of Spain's banks; by 1975 it had a third and by 1985 a half. Ninety per cent of the offices of foreign banks were also in Madrid. The stock exchange too expanded, handling just over half the country's transactions in 1975 but nearly 80 per cent ten years later. This growth has been mainly at the expense of Barcelona. Madrid is now the third largest capital in Europe and has the fifth largest stock market on the Continent.

In 1964 the interior ministry tried to change Spanish working hours in an attempt to bring them into line with the rest of Europe's. Spanish television co-operated, altering the time of the News to 8.30 p.m. in the belief that this would persuade people to leave their bars and offices earlier and go home to watch it. The only consequence was that far fewer people turned on the News than previously. Since then the capital's hours have changed, but only at the other end of the day. Twenty-five years ago it would have been difficult to find a cup of coffee on the Gran Vía before half past nine in the morning. Nowadays people get up and go to

195

work only slightly later than other Europeans. There has been no alteration, however, in the evening hours. Cinemas and theatres still end after midnight and they are still followed by the obligatory drink or cup of coffee in a bar. One consequence of this, according to Díaz-Plaja, is that *madrileños* sleep less than other people and are correspondingly more intolerant of their compatriots' driving the next morning.

A hundred and fifty years ago Borrow described the Madrid population as 'the most extraordinary vital mass to be found in the entire world'. Perhaps it is still the case. Madrid must be the most lonely city in the world for lonely people, because everyone else seems to be rushing to an appointment or to meet someone. *La movida* gets going in Madrid when other European capitals are going to bed. The cafés in the Via Veneto, Rome's most fashionable street, are empty by midnight when Madrid dinner parties are still at the first course and no one has decided which of the 'in' nightclubs they are going to visit later. It is not surprising that the central district of Madrid should have more bars than the whole of Holland. And yet the object is not to stay up to get drunk. Spaniards drink more than the British but get less drunk, because they pace themselves during the day and don't have to try to down as many pints as possible before the pubs close at eleven o'clock. *Madrileños* stay up late like children, for the sake of staying up. 'Few cities', noted a British journalist in the 1920s, 'have a more energetic idleness' than Madrid. The remark remains true today. *Madrileños* have made a science of idleness; they like staying up talking until three in the morning without getting drunk.

In spite of *la movida* and the four million inhabitants, Madrid preserves much of its 'small-town' character: the crowd in the Puerta del Sol, the small shops, the stamp collectors' market on Sundays in the Plaza Mayor. It also retains much of the social hypocrisy portrayed by Galdós. 'Everyone in Madrid knows about it,' a busybody explains in *Fortunata y Jacinta*, 'and it's high time you knew too.' The listener's husband had sinned by failing to keep his mistress a secret. 'Keeping ... up ... appearances: following ... the rules' is another character's advice to Fortunata, an exhortation which will sound familiar to anyone who has lived in contemporary Madrid. Its society is very different from that in

Galdós's day, a fast-moving world of compulsory infidelity and (when caught) compulsory divorce (which only became legal in 1981). But the compulsory hypocrisy remains the same. 'At all events,' declares Galdós's Don Evaristo, 'you must keep up appearances and pay society the external worship without which we'd regress to our primitive state.'

A kinder observation of Galdós, that Madrid society is 'the most pleasant in the world because it knows how to blend courtesy with informality' has also survived the intervening century. In Madrid people don't ask you where you come from or what you do. It is an open and receptive city which does not welcome foreigners extravagantly but treats them properly, judges them on their merits and accepts or rejects them accordingly. People who say they *adore* Spain but dislike Madrid cannot really understand the country. The capital may not seduce but it does attract, slowly, those who genuinely like Spain. It is an elusive city which requires time and patience to understand it, but those who make the effort are usually captivated in the end.

Bibliography

Aguilar Piñal, Francisco, *Historia de Sevilla: Siglo XVIII*, Universidad de Sevilla, 1989.

Alcalá Galiano, Antonio, *Recuerdos de un anciano*, Madrid, 1907.

Aliberch, Ramón, *Un siglo de Barcelona*, Freixenet, Barcelona, n.d.

Allison Peers, E., *Royal Seville*, Harper and Brothers, London, 1926.

Alonso de la Sierra Fernández, Lorenzo and Juan, *Guía artística de Cádiz*, Fundación Municipal de Cultura, Cádiz, 1987.

Alonso Montero, Xesus, *Galicia vista por los no gallegos*, Jucar, Madrid, 1974.

Altamira, Rafael, *Historia de España y de la civilización española*, Vol. 4, Herederos de Juan Gili, Barcelona, 1914.

Aranda Doncel, Juan, *Historia de Córdoba: La época moderna*, Monte de Piedad y Caja de Ahorros de Córdoba, 1984.

Azaña, Ministerio de Cultura, Madrid, 1990.

Azcue, D.de, *Mi pueblo, ayer*, Librería Internacional, San Sebastián, 1975.

Azorín, *España: Hombres y Paisajes*, Francisco Beltrán, Madrid, 1909.

Azorín, *Madrid*, Avapiés, Madrid, 1988.

Bazin, René, *Terre d'Espagne*, Paris, 1905.

Bell, Aubrey, *The Magic of Spain*, Bodley Head, London, 1912.

—— *A Pilgrim in Spain*, Methuen, London, 1924.

Beltrán de Heredia, Vicente, *Los orígenes de la Universidad de Salamanca*, Universidad de Salamanca, 1983.

Bergamín, José, *La claridad del torero*, Turner, Madrid, 1985.

Bermejo, J.C., *et al.*, *Historia de Galicia*, Alhambra, Madrid, 1981.

Bernardo Ares, José Manuel de, *Textos histórico-geográficos de Córdoba y su provincia*, Diputación provincial, Córdoba, 1988.

Bevan, Bernard, *History of Spanish Architecture*, Batsford, London, 1938.

Blunt, Anthony (ed.), *Baroque and Rococo*, Paul Elek, London, 1978.

Bohigas, Oriol, *Reseña y catálago de la arquitectura modernista*, Lumen, Barcelona, 1973.

Borrow, George, *The Bible in Spain*, Collins, London, 1843.

Boyd, Alastair, *Companion Guide to Madrid and Central Spain*, Collins, London, 1974.

Braudel, Fernand, *The Mediterranean* (2 vols.), Collins, London, 1972–3.

Brenan, Gerald, *The Face of Spain*, Penguin, London, 1987.

—— *The Literature of the Spanish People*, Cambridge University Press, 1951.

—— *Personal Record*, Cambridge University Press, 1979.

—— *The Spanish Labyrinth*, Cambridge University Press, 1974.

Brown, Rica, *Bécquer*, Aedos, Barcelona, 1963.

Buñuel, Luis, *My Last Breath*, Flamingo, London, 1985.

Cabezas, Juan Antonio, *Diccionario de Madrid*, Avapiés, Madrid, 1989.

Cabo Alonso, Angel, and Ortega Carmona, Alfonso, *Salamanca*, Ayuntamiento de Salamanca, 1986.

Cabra Loredo, María Dolores, *Iconografía de Sevilla 1400–1650*, El Viso, Madrid, 1988.

Capel, Horacio, *Capitalismo y morfología urbana en España*, Libros de la frontera, Barcelona, 1983.

Carlé, María del Carmen, *et al.*, *La Sociedad Hispano Medieval: La Ciudad*, Gedisa, Barcelona, 1985.

Caro Baroja, Julio, *Toledo*, Destino, Barcelona, 1988.

Carr, Raymond, *Spain 1808–1939*, Clarendon Press, Oxford, 1966.

Casals, Pablo, *Joy and Sorrows*, Eel Pie, London, 1981.

Casos notables de la ciudad de Córdoba (¿1618?), Montilla, Córdoba, 1982.

Castro, Americo, *The Spaniards*, University of California Press, Berkeley, 1971.

Cela, Camilo José, *La colmena*, Noguer, Barcelona, 1980.

Cervantes, Miguel de, *Don Quixote*, Penguin, London, 1950.

—— *Exemplary Novels*, Bohn's Standard Library, London, 1881.

Chanes, Rafael, and Vicente, Ximena, *Descubrir el Madrid antiguo*, Ximena Vicente, Madrid, 1988.

Chueca Goitia, Fernando, *La destrucción del legado urbanístico español*, Espasa-Calpe, Madrid, 1977.

Cirici, Alexandre, *Barcelona paso a paso*, Teide, Barcelona, 1975.

Collins, Roger, *Early Medieval Spain*, Macmillan, London, 1983.

Conrad, Barnaby, *Gates of Fear*, Michael Joseph, London, 1958.

Cornford, John, *Collected Writings*, Carcanet, Manchester, 1986.

Cortés Vázquez, Luis, *La vida estudiantil en la Salamanca clásica*, Universidad de Salamanca, 1989.

Cossío, M.B., *El arte en Toledo*, Blass, Madrid, 1913.

Crow, John A., *Spain: The Root and the Flower*, University of California Press, Berkeley, 1985.

Dalrymple, William, *Travels through Spain and Portugal in 1774*, London, 1777.

Díaz-Plaja, Fernando, *Madrid desde (casi) el cielo*, Maeva, Madrid, 1987.

Domínguez Ortiz, Antonio, *et al.*, *Córdoba: Apuntes para su historia*, Monte de Piedad y Caja de Ahorros de Córdoba, 1989.

Domínguez Ortiz, Antonio, *The Golden Age of Spain 1516–1659*, Weidenfeld & Nicolson, London, 1971.

—— *Orto y ocaso de Sevilla*, Universidad de Sevilla, 1981.

—— *La Sevilla del siglo XVII*, Universidad de Sevilla, 1984.

Dumas, Alexandre, *From Paris to Córdoba*, Peter Owen, London, 1958.

Durand-Viel, Ana María, *La Sevillana*, Ayuntamiento de Sevilla, 1983.

El Greco of Toledo, Little, Brown and Co, Boston, 1982; Caja de Ahorros de Córdoba, 1981.

Elliott, J.H., *The Count-Duke of Olivares*, Yale University Press, Newhaven, 1986.

—— *Imperial Spain 1469–1716*, Penguin, London, 1978.

—— *Spain and its World 1500–1700*, Yale University Press, Newhaven, 1989.

Epton, Nina, *Love and the Spanish*, Cassell, London, 1961.

Escobar Camacho, José Manuel, *Córdoba en la baja edad media*, Caja

Provincial de Ahorros de Córdoba, 1989.

Estébanez Alvarez, José, *Las ciudades: morfología y estructura*, Sintesis, Madrid, 1989.

Fernández-Armesto, Felipe, *Barcelona*, Sinclair-Stevenson, London, 1991.

Filgueira Valverde, J., *Historias de Compostela*, Xerais de Galicia, Vigo, 1982.

Fletcher, R.A., *Saint James's Catapult: The Life and Times of Diego Gelmírez of Santiago de Compostela*, Clarendon Press, Oxford, 1984.

Folguera, Pilar, *Vida cotidiana en Madrid*, Comunidad de Madrid, 1987.

Ford, Richard, *Handbook for Travellers in Spain*, John Murray, London, 1845.

Formica, Mercedes, *Visto y vivido*, Planeta, Barcelona, 1982.

Franco Taboada, Arturo, *Los orígenes de Compostela*, La Coruña, 1986.

Gallenga, A., *Iberian Reminiscences* (2 vols.), Chapman and Hall, London, 1883.

García-Baquero González, Antonio, *Cádiz y el Atlántico 1717–1778* (2 vols.), Diputación Provincial de Cádiz, 1976.

García y Bellido, Antonio, *et al.*, *Resumen histórico del urbanismo en España*, Instituto de Estudios de Administración Local, Madrid, 1987.

García Espuche, Albert, *El Quadrat d'Or*, Lunwerg, Barcelona, 1990.

García de Valdeavellano, Luis, *Sobre los burgos y los burgueses de la España medieval*, Madrid, 1960.

Gates, David, *The Spanish Ulcer*, Allen & Unwin, London, 1986.

Gautier, Théophile, *A Romantic in Spain*, Alfred Knopf, London, 1926.

Gea Ortigas, María Isabel, *Casas, Cosas, Casos de Madrid*, Kaydeda, Madrid, 1989.

Gibson, Ian, *Federico García Lorca*, Faber, London, 1989.

Gómez de la Serna, Ramón, *Elucidario de Madrid*, Ayuso, Madrid, 1988.

—— *Madrid*, Almarabu, Madrid, 1987.

Gómez Rufo, A. (ed.), *Así es Madrid*, Temas de Hoy, Madrid, 1988.

González Cordón, Antonio, *Vivienda y Ciudad: Sevilla 1849–1929*, Ayuntamiento de Sevilla, 1985.

González Egido, Luciano, *Salamanca, la gran metáfora de Unamuno*, Universidad de Salamanca, 1983.

Gudiol, José, *The Arts of Spain*, Thames & Hudson, London, 1964.

Guzmán, Eduardo de, et al., *Historias de Madrid*, Penthalon, Madrid, 1987.

Hare, Augustus, *Wanderings in Spain*, London, 1873.

Harrison, Joseph, *An Economic History of Modern Spain*, Manchester University Press, 1978.

Harvey, John, *The Cathedrals of Spain*, Batsford, London, 1957.

Hemingway, Ernest, *Death in the Afternoon*, Jonathan Cape, London, 1932.

Hitti, Philip, *History of the Arabs*, Macmillan, London, 1979.

Homage to Barcelona, Arts Council of Great Britain, London, 1986.

Hutton, Edward, *The Cities of Spain*, Methuen, London, 1906.

Jackson, Gabriel, *The Spanish Republic and the Civil War*, Princeton University Press, 1965.

Jiménez de Gregorio, Fernando, *Los pueblos de la provincia de Toledo hasta finalizar el siglo XVIII*, Diputación Provincial, Toledo, 1986.

Kamen, Henry, *Spain 1469–1714*, Longman, London, 1983.

—— *Spain in the later Seventeenth Century 1665–1700*, Longman, London, 1980.

Kazantzakis, Nikos, *Spain*, Creative Arts Book Company, Berkeley, 1983.

Kubler, George, and Soria, Martin, *Art and Architecture in Spain and Portugal and their American dominions 1500–1800*, Penguin, London, 1959.

Laiglesia, Beatriz, *Efemerides 1939–1989*, EFE, Madrid, 1989.

Lee, Laurie, *As I walked out one midsummer morning*, Penguin, London, 1971.

—— *A Rose for Winter*, Penguin, London, 1971.

Levi-Provençal, E., *España musulmana* (2 vols.), Madrid, 1950–7.

Longford, Elizabeth, *Wellington: The Years of the Sword*, Weidenfeld & Nicolson, London, 1969.

López Alsina, Fernando, *La ciudad de Santiago de Compostela en la alta edad media*, Ayuntamiento de Santiago, 1988.

López-Cuervo, Serafín, *Medina Az-Zahra*, Ministerio de Obras Publicas y Urbanismo, Madrid, 1985.

López Ferreiro, Antonio, *Historia de la Santa A.M. Iglesia de Santiago de Compostela*, Vol. 9, Santiago, 1907.

Luján, Nestor, *Madrid de los últimos Austrias*, Planeta, Barcelona, 1989.

Machado, Antonio, *Poesías completas*, Espasa-Calpe, Madrid, 1981.

Mackay, Angus, *Spain in the later Middle Ages*, Macmillan, London, 1977.

Mckendrick, Melveena, *Cervantes*, Little, Brown & Co, Boston, 1980.

Majada, Jesús, and Martín, Juan, *Viajeros extranjeros en Salamanca (1300–1936)*, Centro de Estudios Salmantinos, Salamanca, 1988.

Malefakis, Edward, *Agrarian Reform and Peasant Revolution in Spain*, Yale University Press, Newhaven, 1970.

Mañé y Flaquer, Juan, *Viaje por Guipúzcoa*, Villar, Bilbao, 1969.

Marañón, Gregorio, *Elogio y nostalgia de Toledo*, Espasa-Calpe, Madrid, 1983.

Marchand, Leslie A., *Byron's Letters and Journals*, Vol. 1, John Murray, London, 1973.

Marías, Fernando, *La Arquitectura del Renacimiento en Toledo (1541–1631* (4 vols.), Instituto Provincial de Investigaciones y Estudios Toledanos, Toledo, 1983.

Marie, Grand Duchess of Russia, *A Princess in Exile*, Cassell, London, 1932.

Martínez Alcalde, Juan, *Hermandades de gloria de Sevilla*, Boletín de las Cofradías de Sevilla, 1988.

Mena, José María de, *Historia de Sevilla*, Plaza y Janés, Barcelona, 1988.

—— *Personajes sevillanos celebres en la historia*, Seville, 1983.

Mendoza, Cristina and Eduardo, *Barcelona modernista*, Planeta, Barcelona, 1989.

Mendoza, Eduardo, *City of Marvels*, Collins Harvill, London, 1990.

Mesonero Romanos, Ramón de, *Manuel histórico-topográfico de Madrid*, Abaco, Madrid, 1977.

Mitchener, James A., *Iberia* (2 vols.), Corgi, London, 1971.

Molina, Ricardo, *Córdoba en sus plazas*, Posada, Córdoba, 1987.

Montoto, Santiago, *Biografía de Sevilla*, J. Rodríguez Castillejo, Seville, 1980.

Morales Padrón, Francisco, *La ciudad del Quinientos*, Universidad de Sevilla, 1977.

—— *Sevilla insolita*, Universidad de Sevilla, 1987.

—— *Sevilla: La ciudad de los cinco nombres*, Turner, Madrid, 1987.

Morris, James, *Spain*, Faber, London, 1964.

Morton, H.V., *A Stranger in Spain*, Methuen, London, 1955.

Muñoz Molina, Antonio, *Córdoba de los omeyas*, Planeta, Barcelona, 1991.

Nieto Cumplido, Manuel, *Historia de Córdoba: Islam y Cristianismo*, Monte de Piedad y Caja de Ahorros de Córdoba, 1984.

Noel, Gerard, *Ena: Spain's English Queen*, Constable, London, 1984.

Onís, Federico de, *Unamuno en su Salamanca*, Universidad de Salamanca, 1988.

Ortiz de Zuñiga, Diego, *Anales eclesiásticas y seculares . . . de Sevilla* (6 vols.), Guadalquivir, Seville, 1988.

Orwell, George, *Homage to Catalonia*, Secker and Warburg, London, 1938.

Otero Pedrayo, R., *Guía de Galicia*, Galaxia, Vigo, 1980.

Parry, J.H., *The Spanish Seaborne Empire*, Hutchinson, London, 1966.

Peláez del Rosal, Jesús (ed.), *Los Judíos en Córdoba*, El Almendro, Córdoba, 1988.

Pemán, J.M., *Andalucía*, Destino, Barcelona, 1958.

Pérez-Arregui Fort, Ignacio, *Perfiles de San Sebastián*, Zarauz, 1963.

Pérez Galdós, Benito, *Fortunata and Jacinta*, Penguin, London, 1988.

Pérez Higuera, Teresa, *Paseos por el Toledo del siglo XIII*, Ministerio de Cultura, Madrid, 1980.

Pérez Varas, Feliciano, *Salamanca y su universidad en la cultura española*, Universidad de Salamanca, 1985.

Perona Villareal, Diego, *Geografía cervantina*, Albia, Madrid, 1988.

Peyré, Joseph, *La pasión según Sevilla*, J.Rodríguez Castillejo, Seville, 1989.

Pike, Ruth, *Aristocrats and Traders: Sevillian Society in the Sixteenth Century*, Cornell University Press, Ithaca, 1972.

Porres Martín-Cleto, J., *Historia de Tulaytula (711–1085)*, Instituto Provincial de Investigaciones y Estudios Toledanos, Toledo, 1985.

Pritchett, V.S., *The Spanish Temper*, Chatto & Windus, London, 1954.

Ridruejo, Dionisio, *Escrito en España*, Losada, Buenos Aires, 1964.

Rodríguez Sorondo, María del Carmen, *Arquitectura pública en la ciudad de San Sebastián (1831–1922)*, Sociedad Guipuzcoana de Ediciones y Publicaciones, San Sebastián, 1985.

Romero, Luis, *Barcelona*, Barna, Barcelona, 1954.

Rossinyol, Jaume, *Le problème national catalan*, Mouton, Paris, 1974.

Saint-Simon, Duke of, *Mémoires*, Gallimard, Paris, 1961.

Salvador y Conde, José, *El libro de la peregrinación a Santiago de Compostela*, Guadarrama, Madrid, 1971.

San Sebastián: Curso breve sobre la vida y milagros de una ciudad, Comité Ejecutivo de las Conmemoraciones Centenarias de la Reconstrucción y Expansión de la Ciudad, San Sebastián, 1964.

Sánchez Mantero, Rafael, *et al.*, *Las cofradías de Sevilla en la modernidad*, Universidad de Sevilla, 1988.

Sánchez Mármol, Fernando, *Andalucía monumental*, Biblioteca de la cultura andaluza, Granada, 1985.

Savater, Fernando, *San Sebastián*, Destino, Barcelona, 1987.

Sevilla en el siglo XVII, Ministerio de Cultura, Madrid, 1983.

Sevilla: Imagenes de hace cien años, Equipo 28, Seville, 1988.

Sitwell, Sacheverell, *Spanish Baroque Art*, Duckworth, London, 1931.

Solís, Ramón, *El Cádiz de las Cortes*, Silex, 1987.

Sordo, Enrique, *Moorish Spain*, Elek, London, 1963.

Suárez, Federico, *Las Cortes de Cádiz*, Rialp, Madrid, 1982.

Suárez Garmendia, José M., *Arquitectura y Urbanismo en la Sevilla del siglo XIX*, Diputación Provincial de Sevilla, 1987.

Swinburne, Henry, *Travels through Spain in the years 1775 and 1776*, P.Elmsly, London, 1787.

Teba, Juan, *La Sevilla de Rojas Marcos*, Planeta, Barcelona, 1981.

Terán, Fernando de, *Planeamiento urbano en la España contemporánea (1900–1980)*, Alianza, Madrid, 1982.

Terán, Manuel de, *et al.*, *Geografía regional de España*, Ariel, Barcelona, 1988.

Thomas, Hugh, *Madrid: A travellers' companion*, Constable, London, 1988.

—— *The Spanish Civil War*, Hamish Hamilton, London, 1977.

Toledo: ¿ciudad viva? ¿ciudad muerta?, Colegio Universitario de Toledo, 1988.

Torrente Ballester, Gonzalo, *Santiago de Rosalía de Castro*, Planeta, Barcelona, 1989.

Torres Balbás, Leopoldo, *Ciudades Hispanomusulmanas*, Instituto Hispano-Arabe de Cultura, Madrid, 1985.

Townsend, Joseph, *A Journey through Spain in the years 1786 and 1787*, C.Dilly, London, 1972.

Tudela, Mariano, *et al.*, *Café Gijón: 100 años de historia*, Kaydeda, Madrid, 1988.

Twiss, Richard, *Travels through Portugal and Spain in 1772 and 1773*, London, 1775.

Urabayen, Félix, *Por los senderos del mundo creyente*, Espasa-Calpe, Madrid, 1928.

Vázquez Montalbán, Manuel, *Barcelonas*, Empúries, Barcelona, 1990.

Vicens Vives, Jaime, *Approaches to the History of Spain*, University of California Press, Berkeley, 1970.

—— *An Economic History of Spain*, Princeton University Press, 1969.

—— *Los catalanes en el siglo XIX*, Alianza, Madrid, 1986.

Vilar, Pierre, *Spain: A brief history*, Pergamon Press, Oxford, 1980.

Villares, Ramón, *Historia de Galicia*, Alianza, Madrid, 1986.

Villavieja, Marquis of, *Life has been Good*, Chatto & Windus, London, 1938.

Vivienda y Urbanismo en España, Banco Hipotecario de España, Barcelona, 1982.

Ward, Philip (ed.), *The Oxford Companion to Spanish Literature*, Clarendon Press, Oxford, 1978.

Zorrilla, José, *Recuerdos del tiempo viejo*, Publicaciones Españolas, Madrid, 1961.

Zueras Torrens, Francisco, *Julio Romero de Torres y su mundo*, Cajasur, Córdoba, 1987.

Index

A NOTE ON THE AUTHOR

David Gilmour was born in 1952 and studied at Eton
and Balliol College, Oxford, with an emphasis in
modern history. His book *The Transformation of Spain*
has been highly praised as "by far the best general
account" of the period from Franco to the advent of the
constitutional monarchy. Mr. Gilmour has also written
Lebanon: The Fractured Country, The Hungry Generations,
and *The Last Leopard,* a biography of Giuseppe di
Lampedusa which has been widely acclaimed. He
lives in Edinburgh with his wife and four children.

307.76   Gilmour, David
GIL
         Cities of Spain

$22.50   9/92

DATE			
Oct 30			

WITHDRAWN

© THE BAKER & TAYLOR CO.